Women and Children First

Women and Children First

The Life and Times of Elsie Wilcox of Kaua'i

Judith Dean Gething Hughes

University of Hawai'i Press
Honolulu

© 1996 University of Hawai'i Press
All rights reserved

01 00 99 98 97 96   5 4 3 2 1

Library of Congress Cataloging-in-Publication Data
Hughes, Judith Dean Gething, 1940–
    Women and children first : the life and times of Elsie Wilcox
of Kaua'i / Judith Dean Gething Hughes.
    p.   cm.
    Includes bibliographical references and index.
    ISBN 0-8248-1621-8 (alk. paper)
    1. Wilcox, Elsie, 1879–1954.   2. Hawaii—Politics and government—1900–1959.   3. Kauai (Hawaii)—Politics and government.
4. Hawaii—Social conditions.   5. Women politicians—Hawaii—
Biography.   I. Title.
DU627.7.W37H84   1996
996.9'03'092—dc20
[B]   95-30294
                                                                                                                         CIP

University of Hawai'i Press books are printed on acid-free paper and meet the guidelines for permanence and durability of the Council on Library Resources

Designed by Paula Newcomb

To my parents, Walter and Katherine Dean, and my husband, Robert Hughes, without whom nothing would have been possible or worthwhile.

Contents

	Acknowledgments	ix
	Introduction	xi
1	In the Beginning	1
2	The Early Years	17
3	The Good Years	57
4	The Plunge into Politics	96
5	Lady Politician	125
6	Defeat and Victory	143
7	Evaluations	157
	Appendix	161
	Notes	167
	Bibliography	183
	Index	189

Acknowledgments

I am pleased to acknowledge several people who contributed to this book. The person who first interested me in Elsie Wilcox as a possible subject for a biography was Barnes Riznik, Museum Director of Grove Farm Homestead and Waioli Mission House and adjunct professor of American Studies at the University of Hawai'i at Mānoa. His unfailing help and insights were a sustaining force behind this effort. Patricia Palama, secretary at Grove Farm Homestead, has been one of the best people to work with during this enterprise. She was always cheerful, even after enduring hurricane 'Iniki. Robert Schleck did a remarkable job of finding the photographs and having them reproduced.

Several other people read the manuscript or discussed it with me, including Franklin Odo, professor of Ethnic Studies, Linda Menton, associate professor of Education, and Paul Hooper, chairperson of the Department of American Studies, all at the University of Hawai'i at Mānoa, and Betty Ch'maj, professor emeritus, California State University at Sacramento. Special thanks go to Agnes Conrad, retired State of Hawaii Archivist, who is unfailingly helpful about anything having to do with the history of Hawai'i.

Two research assistants, Katherine Teheranian, now an assistant professor of American Studies, and Anita Hodges, a graduate student in the Department of American Studies, used their considerable expertise to assist in the gathering of data.

I was privileged to interview many people in the course of writing this book. Some are acknowledged where they are quoted directly. To them and the others who generously shared their time and knowledge, I extend my deep appreciation.

I am grateful for the help provided over many years by Sandra

Enoki, secretary in the Department of American Studies. In addition, the staff in the office of the dean of the College of Arts and Humanities, and particularly Janet Agena and Jack Katahira, made getting up and going to work something to look forward to with pleasure. Dean Robert Hines was generous in helping me find time among many other duties to complete this biography. Iris Wiley, retired executive editor, and Cheri Dunn, managing editor, of the University of Hawai'i Press provided both assistance and encouragement. Despite all this help, the errors in the text are mine alone.

Introduction

More than a decade ago, I became interested in Elsie Wilcox because she was a "first," the first woman in the territorial Senate of Hawai'i. As my research progressed, Wilcox came to represent many threads in the history of Hawai'i—the enormous impact of Christian missionaries in the early and middle-nineteenth century, the sugar plantations that dominated the economy of Hawai'i for one hundred years after the American Civil War, the influence of the American progressive movement in public education and social welfare, and the "peaceful revolution" of 1954, which replaced the Republican Caucasian oligarchy's political control with a Democratic party led by second-generation Asian Americans.

The past twenty years have seen an outpouring of research in several areas related to the life of Elsie Wilcox. Feminist scholarship has raised new issues, and two in particular have been helpful in shedding light on how to write about a complex person like Wilcox. The first, eloquently posed by Gerda Lerner, was a question: What would history be like if seen through the eyes of women?[1] Lerner was looking at the large scope of history, but the question has applicability to the individual biographer. The second was the debate, still continuing, between scholars such as Cynthia Fuchs Epstein, who focused on the similarity between men and women, and scholars such as Mary Daly, Shulamith Firestone, Jessie Bernard, and Naomi Black, who, in very different ways, focused on the differences.[2]

Elsie Wilcox was both autonomous and family centered. She was equally comfortable in the separate, private, female sphere common in the early twentieth century and in the public male sphere of politics and economics. She was a progressive in a predominantly conservative community, and her life shows some of the strengths and shortcomings of the progressive movement. She possessed an unusual combination of values, based on traditional Christianity and capitalism, and her behavior was both feminine and feminist. I have chosen to adapt Lerner's question and apply it to the biographical part of this book. I have tried to write about Elsie Wilcox and her times from her point of view, which was intensely female in some ways and remarkably androgynous in others.

This is also a generational study. Elsie Wilcox's grandparents were primarily concerned with salvation—theirs and the Hawaiians—and also with the many cares of everyday life. The second generation was more interested in development—of the economy, the political system, and technology—and in establishing various forms of personal security. That generation also had a strong sense of Christian obligation, responsibility, and charity. Elsie Wilcox represented a concentration of the same Christian values. In addition, another theme emerges—a strong sense of the need for reform, based on ideas of social justice and a sensitivity to institutionally created problems that were not as obvious to the preceding generations. In fact, much of her life was spent dealing with the issues raised by the two previous generations' solutions to the dilemmas they faced. In examining these issues, some readers may find I have included more background information about the territorial period of Hawai'i than they are interested in, but unfortunately, there is as yet no comprehensive history of the territory for the more serious scholar.

Frederick Jackson Turner said, "Each age writes the history of the past anew with reference to the conditions uppermost in its own time."[3] If I knew when I began this book what I know now, I probably would not have put finger to keyboard. Conducting the research has been a pleasure, but the conditions uppermost in our time have led to conflict and confusion. Elsie Wilcox's history is inextricably mixed with that of the missionaries, the plantations, and the politics of Hawai'i, including the overthrow of the Hawaiian monarchy, Americanization, mass education, and social work. All of these events or institutions are under severe attack from some contemporary scholars.

I have tried to be neither an apologist for the past, including Wilcox's part in that past, nor an ahistorical critic of the past, seeing it only through the eyes of the present. This approach will no doubt result in attacks from all sides, since, from today's perspective, there is blame and praise to go around several times over.

1 *In the Beginning*

The 1940 election returns were in, and Elsie Wilcox had lost. She did not feel particularly unhappy about the loss for herself, because she had not wanted to be in the territorial Senate again anyway. Nor did she share the anger of some of her supporters at what they viewed as the patent ingratitude of people whom she had spent much of her life helping. What she mainly felt was apprehension. The fear had become real in 1938, and it was palpable now. It was a fear that the way of life she knew and loved was changing, that Kaua'i, Hawai'i, and the world were changing, and that her best efforts to influence that change were not enough. The great irony was that her electoral loss was in many ways the triumph of her life's goals.

Genesis

Elsie Wilcox was born March 22, 1879, the second daughter and third child of Emma Lyman and Samuel Wilcox. Many biographers have observed how important family can be in shaping a person's values, goals, and behavior, and this was certainly the case with Elsie Wilcox. Had she not been the granddaughter of missionaries to Hawai'i and niece of a highly successful sugar plantation owner, her gender alone would have made it impossible for her to lead the life she led. Her assigned status, based on her class and race, and the status she achieved on her own, were largely the result of her family background.

Elsie Wilcox had a deep respect for her grandparents. Her mother's parents, David and Sarah Joiner Lyman, and her father's parents, Abner and Lucy Hart Wilcox, were all Congregational missionaries in Hawai'i. Elsie and her family were steeped in the missionary tradition. Thus, some background on the missionary experience in Hawai'i is important, particularly because it played a key role in Elsie Wilcox's adult career choices.

The Congregational missionaries were sent to Hawai'i by the American Board of Commissioners for Foreign Missions (ABCFM), an outgrowth of a major religious revival in the United States known as the Second Great Awakening. The first group arrived in Hawai'i in 1820. The mission began on a high note. The young men and women who gathered in Boston to sail for Hawai'i on October 23, 1819, were given a detailed charge:

> Aim at nothing short of covering these islands with fruitful fields, and pleasant dwellings and schools and churches, and of raising up the whole people to an elevated state of Christian civilization. You are to obtain an adequate knowledge of the language of the people to make them acquainted with letters; to give them the Bible, with skill to read it; . . . to introduce and get into extended operation and influence among them, the arts and institutions and usages of civilized life and society; and you are to abstain from all interference with local and political interests of the people and to inculcate the duties of justice, moderation, forbearance, truth and universal kindness. Do all in your power to make men of every class good, wise and happy.[1]

The first missionaries to Hawai'i had little idea of what to expect. What they found was a culture in the throes of major transition and in many ways ripe for the missionizing experience and Christianity. In 1778, an Englishman, Captain James Cook, and his crew had sailed into Hawaiian waters, introducing a new world that the Hawaiians, isolated from outsiders for generations, did not know existed. The Westerners were unfettered by the various restrictions placed on Hawaiians under the *kapu* system, which mandated or forbade behavior in important aspects of Hawaiian life. They broke even the most serious *kapu* with impunity. Hawaiians who later sailed with the Westerners found that they, too, did not suffer when they broke the *kapu*. Many explanations have been set forth by scholars for the reason why in 1819 the king, Liholiho, went against the *kapu* and abolished the national level of temple worship. Whatever the reason, or, more likely, the combination of reasons, leading to this momentous step, when the first missionaries arrived in the islands, fundamental changes were already taking place.[2]

It was not just that the *kapu* were undermined, although this was of great importance to the success of the missionaries, since they had no state-sanctioned religion to compete against, as was the case in most of the places missionaries went. Already, the worldview of Hawaiians and their relationships among themselves and to their own power structure had been called into question. In addition, Western diseases were making devastating inroads into a highly susceptible population.[3] Although perhaps not obvious to most people at the time, the changes that were to transform Hawai'i in the next eighty years were already under way.

In retrospect, the missionaries were remarkably successful in achieving some of the goals set forth in the charge to the first company. By 1822, they had established a printing press and were publishing books of the Bible and school lessons on various subjects, all in the Hawaiian language, which they had committed to written form. By 1830, they had founded nine hundred schools and were teaching reading and writing, as well as religious principles, to 44,895 pupils in Hawaiian.[4] The mission wives had brought together Hawaiian women in various communities to discuss maternal matters and child care. Until they became overburdened with the care of their own children, the women of the mission also ran schools for girls and women.[5] Thus, in terms of the more secular part of their charge, the missionaries were, by their terms, successful.

Their victories on the religious front came later and were more difficult. By 1830, although many Hawaiians professed Christianity, only 279 had been admitted to full church membership.[6] The tests for membership were stringent, much as they had been in the United States. Eventually, the missionaries' sponsors admonished them to face the reality that the Christian experience in Hawai'i did not need to have exactly the same components as in the United States to be genuine. They were directed to bend somewhat, so that more Hawaiians could experience the full benefits of church membership. Also, the home contingent was having difficulty raising money for the Hawai'i mission given its poor track record in producing converts—the main reason, after all, for the mission.[7]

In the 1830s, the ABCFM sent the Wilcoxes and the Lymans to Hawai'i to teach and preach. All four spent the remainder of their lives in Hawai'i. By the time they arrived, many changes had already taken place. Some of the *ali'i*, the chiefs, had converted to Christianity. In the larger towns, many people could read the Hawaiian language. Laws establishing the basic tenets of Christianity had been promulgated. Perhaps the most dramatic change was the high death rate among Hawaiians because of imported diseases and a changing economy.

The Lymans and Wilcoxes

From an early age, David Belden Lyman had been "set apart by his parents for the ministry of the gospel."[8] He had graduated from Williams College and Andover Seminary in Massachusetts, an accomplishment achieved at considerable sacrifice in a family of nine children. Sarah Joiner was a schoolteacher when she and David met. Upon their arrival in Hawai'i, they were assigned to Hilo and stayed there the remainder of their lives. David preached, and he founded and ran the Hilo Boarding School for Native Hawaiians. Sarah helped with the boarding school and also taught women and children for a few years. They had eight children: David Brainerd (the first, who died at age two), Henry Munson, Frederick Swartz, David Brainerd (the second), Rufus Anderson, Ellen Elizabeth, Francis Ogden, and Emma Washburn. David died in 1884 and Lucy in 1885.

Abner Wilcox had been a teacher and farmer in western Connecticut. He was educated in common schools and had spent two

Lyman House Memorial Museum, in Hilo, Hawai'i. Home of David Belden and Sarah Joiner Lyman, Elsie Wilcox's maternal grandparents.

years at an "academy." Lucy Hart was a twenty-two-year-old schoolteacher when she and Abner were married. Her parents were "in somewhat indigent circumstances," according to Abner Wilcox, who wrote the ABCFM for assistance in providing Lucy clothes and household goods for the trip to Hawai'i.[9]

The Wilcoxes were sent first to Hilo, then seven years later to Waialua on the island of O'ahu. Although they had been happy in Hilo with the other missionary families—Titus and Fidelia Church Coan and the Lymans—they were isolated in Waialua and did not like the rainy weather, even though Hilo had been much wetter. In 1846, after only two years in Waialua, they were transferred to Hanalei on the island of Kaua'i, where they lived until their deaths on a trip to America in 1869. Like the Lymans, they too had eight children: Charles Hart, George Norton, Edward Payson, Albert Spencer, Samuel Whitney, William Luther, Clarence Sheldon, and Henry Harrison. Clarence lived only a year.

Abner Wilcox was the kind of missionary from which the stereotype was drawn. The positives and negatives, the strengths and excesses appear not only in secondhand portrayals of him but in his

Waioli Mission House, in Hanalei, Kaua'i. Home of Abner and Lucy Hart Wilcox, Elsie Wilcox's paternal grandparents.

own writings. His description of his conversion to Christianity is typical:

> Seven years ago last summer I hope I found the Savior. . . . At this time my heart was harder than a nether millstone; I could not pray; every petition was the most impious mockery and so fully was it impressed upon my mind that I had committed the unpardonable Sin and that my eternal damnation was sealed that I was on the point of resolving if possible to get rid of all my seriousness and of making the most of this short life. . . . In this condition I remained about 4 hours when the overwhelming horrors I had endured seemed to be removed and I ventured to open my eyes and found that I was not yet in hell. [K]nowing that I was lost and that if ever I was saved my salvation must come from Christ alone, I groaned out a feeble prayer that if God through Christ could do any thing for me he would have compassion on me and help me. And then for a few moments I waited anxiously for an answer to my petition, when lo! a flood of light and glory burst upon my soul. It was as if the sun had been placed in the twinkling of an eye at the zenith at Midnight. Christ appeared the chiefest among the thousand and the one altogether lovely. I felt my heart drawn out towards Christians of whatever name and subsequently felt deep compassion and distress for perishing souls and was anxious to evince my gratitude to Christ by laboring in his vineyard.[10]

For Christians in the Congregational Church, a conversion experience was important. Philip Greven recorded his observations about the group he called "evangelicals" in *The Protestant Temperament*:

> [Evangelicals] shared the experience of the new birth, a transforming crisis which seemed to reshape their innermost selves into radically new and more acceptable forms, for they believed that regeneration could be accomplished only when the self had been conquered. . . . [They] took heart from the inner assurance that their personal wills had been broken so they could at last follow the will of God wherever it might lead, no matter what the cost might be in personal suffering. Once reborn, evangelicals often felt themselves freed from the burdens of their sinful past, and able finally to war with the sins of the unconverted, who seemed always to be so numerous. Evangelicals thus often became extremists and purists, eager to restore their inner and outer worlds to a primitive order of harmony, unity and self-lessness.[11]

The conversion experience left Wilcox convinced both of his salvation and his unworthiness. He was stern and critical, of himself and of others. Throughout his life, he strictly observed the Sabbath and demanded that those around him do likewise. He disapproved of frivolity and chastised those who seemed to lack the serious demeanor appropriate for their station. Sam Wilcox, Elsie Wilcox's father, recounted a story about his parents' differing attitudes toward merriment:

> Mother Rice [a missionary wife] used to tell of a visit once at Waioli. Father Rice and Mother Wilcox fell into chatting and laughing over things together, just kindred spirits in cheerful mood. But Father Wilcox was shocked at what seemed to him untimely mirth, and at family worship he prayed earnestly and long for their complete regeneration, for their conviction of frivolity and conversion to an earnest purposefulness in this dark vale here below. During the long exhortation to the Lord, Mother Rice knelt quivering and mortified that her husband should be so weak and frivolous a brother. And when she rose from her knees she scarce knew where to turn her tearful eyes.

Lucy's response to this scene gives some indication of her personality:

> At last, standing at the window, torn between humiliation and eager desire for conformance to Brother Wilcox's strict sense of worthiness, she [mother Rice] felt two strong hands on her shoulders. Turning she met the glance of Sister Wilcox, who burst into a loud "Ha! Ha!" of delicious amusement at the thought of praying for the erring brother and her own jolly self, over what Father Castle called "the sin of levity."[12]

Yet, Abner Wilcox was devoted to his wife and sons and to his family in the United States. His letters, which have been preserved, show consistent concern for his relatives' health and welfare. After long discussions between Abner and Lucy, Abner took their six-year-old son, Albert, to the United States for an operation on his club feet. Both parents were willing to endure hardship to get Albert's feet cured. While Abner was gone, Lucy was in charge of the family and his school. When he returned, he insisted that she take several months' vacation in Honolulu, by herself, for a much-needed rest.

Lucy Wilcox experienced ill health for years, a problem seemingly related to the fact that she bore many children close together. She had eight children in the space of twenty years, the first two born within a year of each other. Sarah Lyman had a similar experience. She was ill much of the time and exhausted most of the time. Her diary contains many passages such as this, written following the birth of their fourth child: "When my babe was three weeks old I bore my weight, and when 4 weeks and three days old I began to walk alone, but though he is now 5 weeks old I have by no means regained my strength. A little effort entirely exhausts me."[13] As Greven observed in his study, despite the fact that the evangelicals were at odds with their bodies, and particularly with their sexuality, as a group they had many children, higher than the norm for their generation.

The letters do not portray Lucy's personality as clearly as Abner's. She was devoted to her religion, her husband, and her family. Although the sons referred to her with great fondness, it was primarily respect that they displayed in their conversations about their father.

The Lymans and Wilcoxes did not expect their children to become missionaries or ministers, but they did hope they would become Christians. Abner Wilcox in particular adhered to rather extreme child-rearing theories in an effort to raise his sons as Christians. None of the sons seems to have had the all-important conversion experience, although all of them were nominal Christians. Sam articulated his recollections of his father:

> Oh, he believed in the Bible command, "Spare not the rod!" And to him the safest thing he could do was to "break the child's spirit." The little room where we hung our saddles next to my mother's room was where he whipped us. Then, if he had time, he would kneel down and pray for us.
>
> And Sundays? My! I should say he was strict. In the morning after prayer we all had to go to the long service at the Hawaiian Church, but in the afternoon my father kept us at home from the Hawaiian Church to have a service of his own.... It seemed endless, but perhaps it was only 2 or 3 hours.... And in the evening every one of us had to have his seven verses of scripture learned by heart to recite.[14]

Abner Wilcox could have been the model for Philip Greven's analysis of the evangelicals' child-raising practices:

> With remarkable consistency and persistence, evangelicals through the centuries insisted that parents must control and break the emerging will of children in the first few years of life. The central issue, as they per-

ceived it, was this: the autonomous will and self-assertiveness of the child must be reduced to impotency, be utterly suppressed and contained, or the child ultimately would be damned for eternity. "Break their wills," urged John Wesley, "that you may save their souls."[15]

Because the parents were all teachers who prized education, they attempted to provide their children with as much education as they could afford. They began by teaching them at home and then sent them to Punahou, a missionary-run school on Oʻahu. They were ambivalent about whether the children should stay in Hawaiʻi as they grew to adulthood. In 1853, Abner wrote his brother and sister about the matter:

> It is not merely to prepare them to get a living that we are anxious about them. Were that the case, we would keep them all at the islands. We are not anxious to make missionaries of any of them, but to fit them for usefulness in whatever station of life Providence shall call them to occupy. Should they all be farmers, we should wish them to be better educated than their parents.[16]

His brother offered to take one or two of the boys, but, in the end, the parents decided to keep them in Hawaiʻi until they graduated from Punahou.

The Wilcoxes and Lymans were the focus of an ongoing debate about what to do with the mission children. During the 1851 trip to Boston for Albert's operation, Abner had a conversation with Dr. Rufus Anderson, president of the ABCFM, that verged on a confrontation. The Wilcoxes wanted the option of sending the children to the United States for education. Anderson objected. Abner recorded his account of the exchange:

> [Dr. Anderson asked] why cannot your children receive such a training at the islands without being sent out of the country as shall make them all potent and successful as well as qualified in the great work of doing good? . . . The fact is that for the sake of saving money they want us to keep our children all at the Islands and mean to make me promise to do so if they can.[17]

Money, or the lack of it, increasingly troubled some of the missionaries. The Lymans, although not wealthy, seem to have had enough money from the ABCFM and the boarding school to enable them to live a comfortable life, but this was not so with the Wilcoxes. Abner and Lucy Wilcox went out to the Sandwich Islands with the expectation that they would live in poverty, "serving the Lord." As young adults in their early twenties, full of the effects of the Second Great Awakening, it had been easier to make such a decision than it was to live with it after they became parents of an increasingly large family. Many of Abner's letters—to family and friends, to the ABCFM, and to the missionary headquarters in Honolulu—express his concern about money and his growing anxiety to provide adequately for his family. In 1861, he wrote the ABCFM, almost pleading for help:

> I was sent out with a limited education as a teacher, and *advised* to remain so—to labor and die at the Islands. I have remained so, and I have so labored.... Perhaps I have followed the Board's instructions too literally to mind my own work and receive bread from the Board. Yet, as we have always been told that the Board never changes its policy, I supposed that I might do so with impunity. Have I then erred?
>
> Were I without a family, I would step quietly out of the way. But I have a family dependent on me. My youngest child is 3 years old. I have 5 children under age. They need to have the advantages of a school. Two or 3 we wish to send to Punahou School this year. One who is of age is at School in New Haven at our expense.... I shall soon die. Cannot the Prud. Com [Prudential Company, the ABCFM] have patience with one poor man and feed him a few days longer? In the mean time, that poor man will watch the heavens for manna and water, and if the Lord give them, will gladly look to him alone.
>
> I think it is a mistake that the Gov't have refused to assume the support of the school.... I should be pleased to have the Gov't adopt it and relieve the Board. Perhaps it will, tho' deeply in debt.... I do not, however, like the idea of dropping all work of a missionary character and going into worldly business. How much the Board cautioned us against it formerly.[18]

In 1863, the ABCFM declared the islands "Christianized" and began withdrawing support from the mission. Some missionaries went into business and became wealthy, but some of the teachers found themselves in a difficult situation. Unlike ministers, they could not rely on a local church in Hawai'i for their income. Abner Wilcox felt betrayed. Never a particularly happy person, he became more bitter about his circumstances as he grew older. The poverty he experienced, whether relative or absolute, left a deep impression on his sons. None of them chose to lead the kind of life their parents had led, and some of them accumulated great wealth.

The Lymans, in contrast, seemed to retire in contentment. Sarah's letters from her older years depict a couple with children and grandchildren nearby, and many friends.

Elsie Wilcox revered her grandparents. Their traits of hard work, simple living, seriousness of purpose, devotion to education, and support of charity became integral to her personality. However, unlike many other women in similar circumstances, she was able to put these values into effective practice to change the community where she lived because of the wealth provided by her uncle, George Norton Wilcox.

The Second Generation

During the time the ABCFM mission was in Hawai'i, the missionaries tried to bring about many changes in the values, beliefs, and behavior of the native Hawaiians. The second generation of the mission—the missionaries' children—was a significant part of a watershed generation that had a tremendous impact on the economic, political, and social life in Hawai'i. Already, as described by political scientist Noel Kent, Hawai'i was in the process of changing from a self-contained unit to part of a concentric circle dominated by the hub, the United States.[19] In about sixty years, Hawai'i shifted from having an economy based on Hawaiian farming and fishing units to one dominated by large sugar plantations owned by relatively few men, many of whom had been born in Hawai'i, but none of whom was native Hawaiian. It went from being a kingdom to a territory of the United States. English became the standard language. To provide workers for their plantations, the plantation owners imported thousands of laborers from Asia, permanently changing the racial composition of the islands. Changes such as these, coming as quickly as they did, had a profound effect on the islands and the people who lived there. Historian Elizabeth Buck summarized the situation: "During that period, fundamental social relationships, cultural frameworks, long-standing political and economic practices, and hence structures of power were radically altered."[20]

By the time Elsie Wilcox became an adult, the changes, for better or worse, were a fait accompli, and her family had played a part in bringing them about. Just as her grandparents were part of the missionary movement that sought to "Christianize and civilize" Hawai'i in accordance with the charge to the first company, so her parents, her uncles, and particularly her uncle George Norton Wilcox, were part of the watershed generation. The hardships they experienced in their youth and the road they followed to economic success had a profound influence on Elsie Wilcox's view of the world and especially of Hawai'i.

The pattern in the Wilcox and Lyman families was not atypical of most missionary families in Hawai'i. As they reached adulthood, the second generation had to decide whether they were going to live in the land of their birth or return to the land of their parents' birth. In most families, some did each. In the Wilcox family, Charles moved to California, returning to Hawai'i occasionally. The other Wilcox children chose to live in Hawai'i. Three Lymans—Emma, Frederick, and Rufus—stayed in Hawai'i.

Just as her grandparents' lives were important in molding Elsie Wilcox's values, so the great wealth amassed by her uncle, George Norton Wilcox, provided her the means to implement those values in her adult life. In 1857, George Wilcox, later called "G.N.," went to work at William Rice's Lihue Plantation store during the summer to help meet expenses. Rice was one of the owners of Lihue Plantation, and this was one of G.N.'s earliest experiences in growing and processing sugar. As a bookkeeper for Rice, Wilcox was introduced to the hazards of farming. The plantation was in debt at least $100,000, with little hope of changing the picture.[21] The summer between his junior and senior years in high school, G.N. worked on Jarvis Island supervising guano digging and doing bookkeeping.

Abner Wilcox was particularly anxious that the boys attend college. This was something of a problem because there were seven of them, and his income was $300 a year. In 1859, G.N. started two years of study at Sheffield Scientific School at Yale. Many of the missionary children, particularly the boys, went to the United States to obtain an education that would be useful in making a living. Wilcox studied engineering. Perhaps more than anything else, this early decision to obtain advanced, practical education separated the missionary sons from many other Caucasian children raised in Hawai'i and from the children of the Hawaiian *ali'i,* none of whom continued their formal education past high school.[22] When men like Wilcox returned to Hawai'i, they had the skills that made possible the technology needed to create the large plantations. Without these skills, they probably would have been little different from the first generation of Westerners who tried to make large-scale farming in Hawai'i successful and, to a person, failed.

Not all the Hawaiian plantations were owned by missionary descendants. Claus Spreckels, an American, was a major player in both sugar and politics for several years, and Theo. H. Davies, an Englishman, owned plantations and a factor, a commercial agency, which later became one of the "Big Five."

G. N. Wilcox began his sugar farming venture by working on his father's land at Hanalei with his brother Albert. They cleared fields, planted cane, hoed, and generally tried to make the land grow cane. They were not very successful. Hanalei was too wet, and the land was rocky. It was hard going and not profitable.

Judge Hermann Widemann, a German who had settled in Līhu'e and married a Hawaiian woman, offered G. N. Wilcox a surveying job. Wilcox accepted the offer, since it gave him an opportunity to earn some cash and also to use his skills. Judge Widemann was acquiring plots of land from Hawaiians who had forfeited on loans, and he wanted Wilcox to survey them. In common with others who were trying to grow cane, Widemann combined land purchased from the government after the *mahele,* the 1848 division of the lands, with land purchased from individual Hawaiians to create areas large enough to make growing cane profitable, a practice widely criticized by Hawaiians then and later.[23] In 1863, Widemann, impressed with Wilcox and anxious to move back to Honolulu, offered to sell or lease the plantation, Grove Farm, to Wilcox. Wilcox leased the plantation from Widemann, incurring a $9,000 debt to upgrade the technology used on the plantation. The most important improvement was installing an irrigation ditch to carry water to areas that previously relied solely on rainfall. He hired half a dozen Hawaiian women at 17½ cents a day to plant cane. For six months the farm produced no more than $.50 a week from the sale of mutton. He was tax collector, road supervisor, surveyor, and postmaster in Līhu'e. He took whatever job he could, in addition to working on the plantation and supervising the other workers, to pay down the debt.[24]

In 1870, Wilcox purchased Grove Farm from Widemann for $12,000, all of which he borrowed. By 1874, he had paid off the debt and was sole owner of Grove Farm Plantation.[25] He was thirty-five.

That same year, Sam Wilcox married Emma Lyman, and G.N. invited them to move in with him at Grove Farm. G.N. was sending money to his brother Luther, a translator in Honolulu, was putting his brother Henry through college, and, in a deal with neighbor Paul Isenberg, had set up Albert as manager of a Lihue Plantation operation at Hanamā'ulu, about 3 miles from Grove Farm. Sam was appointed sheriff of Kaua'i, and G.N. needed someone to take care of Grove Farm when he went to Honolulu, as he did with increasing frequency. Although Charles was the eldest son, G.N. was in the process of becoming the family patriarch by virtue of his economic situation and the fact that the rest of the family except Charles had chosen to remain in Hawai'i.

In 1881, G.N. bought a substantial amount of land from Princess Ruth Ke'elikolani, who wanted to sell her land on Kaua'i to build a palace on O'ahu. The acreage G.N. acquired in this transaction increased the holdings of Grove Farm tenfold. By 1884, G.N. was worth $300,000.[26] Elsie Wilcox was five.

She was a child at a time of expansion of Grove Farm and of G.N.'s growing concern about the political and economic situation in the kingdom. G.N.'s political activities were an important influence on young Elsie. During her childhood, Grove Farm was the scene of many political meetings. Politicians often stayed there, and dinner conversation focused on political events. Just as she was proud of her grandparents' contributions to the kingdom, so she supported her father's and uncles' political positions.

In 1880, G.N. was elected to the kingdom's legislature. In 1883, he was a member of the Committee of Nine, created to curb what the members saw as King David Kalākaua's extravagant spending. Their perception was that Kalākaua wanted to be a monarch on a par with European monarchs. Although popular with most Hawaiians, he was increasingly dependent on the sugar planters, none of whom was ethnically Hawaiian, for income to support the monarchy. It was a crisis waiting to happen.

The crisis occurred after Kalākaua died. In 1891, his sister, Lili'uokalani, became queen. For three years, she and the Caucasian members of the legislature sparred, as talk of revolution and annexation to the United States increased. One focus of the controversy was the queen's right to appoint a cabinet, and in 1893, she appointed G. N. Wilcox to head what would be her second-to-last cabinet. Wilcox lasted three months in the position before he lost the confidence of the queen and the legislature and resigned. He seems to have been among the least willing of the Caucasian members of the community to support the overthrow of the queen, but in the end, he agreed.[27] A few days after the Wilcox cabinet resigned, the legislature was closed. Within the next few days, the queen attempted to promulgate a new constitution, which would have given her considerably more power, and a group of Caucasians formed a Citizens' Committee of Safety, which became the nucleus for the overthrow of the queen. Of the group, six were subjects of the Kingdom of Hawai'i, either born in Hawai'i or naturalized; five were American citizens; one was a citizen of England; and one was a German citizen. Three were missionary descendants.[28] In 1893, a small number of Caucasian men overthrew the queen and established a provisional government.

There was some dissension among the leaders of the revolution as to whether to apply to the United States for territorial status. While most supported that course of action, some feared the extension of American labor laws to Hawai'i would curtail the relatively free hand plantation owners enjoyed in dealing with the labor force.

The American Minister Resident not only had been supportive of the revolution but had ordered United States troops landed in Honolulu during the uprising.[29] Those who supported annexation hoped, therefore, that the United States would quickly accept Hawai'i as a territory. Opinion in the United States, however, was divided. Many people, including President Grover Cleveland, were opposed to annexation, some because they did not want the United States to expand beyond the continental borders, others because they did not want more non-Caucasians joining the Union, and still others because they believed the revolutionary group and the United States consul had acted illegally in overthrowing the queen and that the monarchy should be restored. Thus, it was 1898 before annexation was approved by the Congress and 1900 before the formalities were complete and Hawai'i became a United States territory. During the interim, the revolutionaries created a provisional government and then declared Hawai'i to be a republic.

G. N. Wilcox supported annexation. Although periodically he was involved in the politics of the Republic of Hawai'i and later the Territory of Hawai'i, he devoted most of his time after annexation to his business interests. He branched out into shipping, real estate, and fertilizer. During these years, Sam Wilcox continued to help at Grove Farm and to act as sheriff of Kaua'i.

Over the years, G. N. Wilcox became one of the wealthiest men in Hawai'i. At the time of his death, he was a millionaire several times over. He also was a generous supporter of a variety of causes, primarily those associated with his parents' interests—religion and education. Never a particularly religious man himself, he nonetheless contributed to a number of churches and other religious groups. He gave money for the Salvation Army to create a home for girls in Honolulu, named "Waioli" after the Waiʻoli mission at Hanalei. He gave money to Punahou School and Mid-Pacific Institute, and both have buildings named in his honor. During his lifetime, he gave several million dollars to various charities and individuals.

The Impact of Family and History on Elsie Wilcox

This, then, was the culture Elsie Wilcox was born into and where she grew to maturity. She was part of a close family, whose members shared deep religious roots, were politically active, and believed in American and Christian values. Education was very important. Christian charity was an accepted responsibility. These values and beliefs came from her grandparents, who passed them to her through their children. What the children added, G. N. Wilcox in particular, was wealth and involvement in the political process. Christian values, an excellent education, and the opportunities provided by wealth combined in Elsie Wilcox to produce a woman of energy, wit, vision, and determination to use the political system to make Hawaiʻi a place that retained the values she cherished, but in a context different from what her parents and grandparents had known.

2 The Early Years

Looking back on her childhood from the vantage of sixty years, Elsie Wilcox reflected on her family and her youth at Grove Farm: "As a child, I lived here on Kauai in a plantation owner's home. Everything was simple. There were not many luxuries. People worked hard. The missionary tradition held, as we were of missionary descent on both sides, but with rather liberal modifications in some respects."[1]

At the time of Elsie's birth and during her early years, Grove Farm Plantation was an established enterprise but not yet the financial success it was to become later. The family had enough money to hire a substantial and growing household staff, but everyone in the family worked. This appears to have been a matter of principle and values as well as necessity; long after the family could afford to have all their work done by others, they continued to perform many chores themselves.

A Simple, Privileged Childhood

During the approximately forty years from her birth until the 1920s, when she came into prominence on several fronts, Elsie Wilcox led an unremarkable existence. Those years, however, set the stage for a wide array of activities in later life. Rich resources about her early life convey the texture of the lives of wealthy women in Hawai'i at that time. Readers more interested in Elsie Wilcox the progressive educator and political reformer may wish to skip ahead to chapter 3.

Sam and Emma Wilcox had six children in seven years. Ralph Lyman was born in 1876, two years after they were married. Lucy Etta, called Etta by the family, arrived the following year, Elsie Hart in 1879, Charles Henry in 1880, Gaylord Parke in 1881, and Mabel Isabel in 1882.

In the early years, the household staff consisted of Hawaiians. Gradually, Chinese and Japanese were added to the staff. As Elsie Wilcox recalled:

> Hawaiian women who helped with the children and the laundry were replaced by oriental men, much later by Japanese women. I can remember my Father saying that the Hawaiian nurses were not very dependable. They were kindly with their charges, but often would fail to come for the day's work, etc., so were gradually and naturally replaced by the Chinese and Japanese. Very early cooks were Chinese, but later came Sakuma of the 1868 immigration [from Japan] who remained with us for twenty-five years.[2]

Initially, Sam and Emma lived in a four-room cottage attached to the northern end of the house. G.N.'s bedroom and office were at the opposite end of the house. In an 1877 renovation, he built himself a cottage and separate two-room office several yards from the main house, set at right angles to it. Although a "presence" in his later years, G.N. seems to have been shy and retiring as a young man. He obviously enjoyed having Sam and Emma and their children living with him, but he nonetheless sought quiet and privacy. The cottage had two rooms, with a bed, dresser, desk, and bath. Few people were allowed to enter the cottage, and in later years, he refused even to let the servants in to clean, so Elsie and Mabel would do it themselves when he was not at home.

At the back of the house, connected by a covered walkway, was a large kitchen with a wood-burning stove, lockbox for perishables, sink, worktable, and a pantry. Three meals were cooked daily for the family of nine plus servants and a varying number of visitors, making the kitchen a place of great activity.

In 1915, an addition was built onto the house, but even then, the house was neither luxurious nor large for the number of people who lived there.[3] South of the house and connected by another short walkway was a two-room, two-bath guest cottage. For many years, Kaua'i had no public accommodations, and even after the first hotel was built, most families routinely housed visiting relatives, friends, and business associates.

In 1886, G.N. bought land at Nāwiliwili Bay, about 2 miles from the house, with the intention of saving it for a possible mill site for the plantation. He later built a beach house there named Papalinahoa, which the family used for many years.

As a little girl, Elsie Wilcox's life centered around the plantation grounds and her family. She played in the yard in front of the house with her brothers and sisters and occasionally the Rice children from a neighboring plantation. When she grew older, she went swimming and fishing at Papalinahoa. Even into her adult years, she spent a great deal of time outdoors—camping, hiking, swimming, golfing, playing tennis. She, Etta, and Mabel remained exceptionally close throughout their lives.

As an adult, Elsie Wilcox was a skilled agriculturist, ordering seeds and plants and corresponding with various people about trees and flowers. This, no doubt, was because when she was a child, Grove Farm, in addition to being a sugar plantation, was a working farm. The plantation grew much of the food for the Wilcox family and the workers the plantation employed. The land around the homestead and in the valley beneath the bluff where the house stood was farmed extensively. Banana, lime, lemon, papaya, orange, mango, and breadfruit trees were planted by G.N. during his early years at Grove Farm.

Cane cutters on Kaua'i, about 1899.

Elsie Wilcox at age seven.

Tomatoes, lettuce, cucumbers, beans, potatoes, yams, taro, melons, mulberry, *pohā,* and mint supplied most of the needs for fruit and vegetables. Chicken, ducks, geese, pigs, and rabbits were raised both at Grove Farm and at the ranch Albert Wilcox managed. The ranch also provided beef and mutton for the plantation. The children and the plantation workers fished in the ocean for *pāpio, ulua,* mullet, *weke, akule,* lobster, shrimp, and *uhu.* They hunted dove, pheasant, and quail. The plantation had to be as self-sufficient as possible, since transportation was slow, expensive, and uncertain. Perishables in particular did not do well in the hot, unrefrigerated holds of ships.

The primary mode of transportation on the island was horseback, although the family owned horse-drawn carriages, too. Kaua'i was a rural island, and the plantation owners' houses were separated by many miles. Communication and visiting were more leisurely but less frequent than in later times. Occasionally, the family packed a picnic and overnight things into a carriage and rode to the old Wilcox home at Wai'oli, 45 miles away.

When Ralph and Etta were ready to start school the family hired a tutor, and for several years the children were taught at home. They were joined by the Rice family children and later by Elsie and the younger children. School was held in a small building behind the house. The children learned reading, writing, arithmetic, geography, and history. Even though their grandparents had started several of the schools on Kaua'i and trained many of the teachers, there does not seem to have been any question but that the Wilcox children would be taught at home and then go to Punahou School in Honolulu when they were old enough to board there. The public school population was predominantly Hawaiian, with some Chinese and a few Japanese. As with many other aspects of life in Hawai'i, separation by race in education was widespread, although not absolute.

Punahou was an adventure for children from the neighbor islands. It represented a significant move away from the family, even though the atmosphere at the school was strict and disciplined. Students who boarded still performed manual labor, but that practice was gradually changing. It was not as extensive as it had been a generation before, when the boys worked in the fields for two hours a day. The students were mostly Caucasian, with some Hawaiians. By the time Elsie Wilcox attended the senior school at Punahou, the staff was quite cosmopolitan. Faculty came from Amherst, Cornell, Williams, Smith, the New England Conservatory of Music, and

The children of Samuel and Emma Wilcox in 1886. *Back row:* Etta, age eight, Ralph, age nine. *Front row:* Charles, age six; Gaylord, age five; Mabel, age four; and Elsie, age seven.

the New York Art League. They provided a demanding curriculum for students who, like Elsie Wilcox, chose to follow the "classical" curriculum. In 1894, for example, she studied physical geography, algebra, Latin, Bible, drawing, instrumental music, and rhetoric. In 1896, she added French. She was a good student, receiving mostly A's and a few B's. Her "house deportment" grades were 97 to 100 percent.[4]

The neighbor island children returned home for some vacations and the summer break. The steamer took about twelve hours to cross from Honolulu to Kaua'i, and the sailing was sometimes rough. The ship put in at Kaua'i twice a week, usually arriving in the middle of the night. The passengers went down the side of the ship on a rope-and-plank gangway, jumped into a lifeboat, and were rowed ashore.

Christmas at the Wilcox home was a quiet affair. Abner and Lucy Wilcox, like most missionaries, had opposed such increasingly elaborate additions to Christmas celebrations as decorated trees and gift giving. On the night before Christmas, the family at Grove Farm exchanged modest gifts—tokens, really—often handmade. They went to church on Christmas day, then had a special dinner. It was, as Elsie Wilcox described it, simple.

With no radio, television, telephone, or automobile, the family members, like everyone else of the time, created their own entertainment. They played cards, cribbage, and *kōnane*, a Hawaiian game similar to checkers, and did jigsaw puzzles. The children occasionally put on a musical for the adults, sometimes with a printed program. These musicals included singing and playing the piano. Lucy taught all her children to play the piano, but Elsie evidently did not learn well because in later years she took lessons from Mabel.

Lucy taught the girls to cook, and as an adult, Elsie Wilcox then taught the cooks who came to work for the household. Menus were based on what was available from the farm and ranch. Occasionally, the family had cakes and other items that required materials brought from Honolulu. The food was primarily prepared in American style, with additions of such Hawaiian foods as taro. Often when the family entertained, they served a Hawaiian dinner of *poi, lomi* salmon (salted salmon chopped in small bits with tomatoes and onions), *kālua* pork (roasted in the plantation underground oven, the *imu*), and *laulau* (fish, pork, and taro leaves wrapped in ti leaves and steamed). Although the cooks were Chinese or Japanese, the family rarely ate food prepared in either of those traditions.

Later in her life, Elsie Wilcox was asked to give a talk on what

The Wilcox sisters and cousins in 1897, in Oakland, California. *Left to right:* Elsie, Ella (Charles Wilcox's daughter), Mabel, Lucy (Charles Wilcox's daughter), and Etta.

race relations had been like when she was a child. In that speech, she described her perception as a child of the various groups that lived at Grove Farm Plantation and the larger community on Kauaʻi:

> [The Japanese cook, Sakuma] seemed to belong in the family as one of us, as did our faithful man nurse, Tatsu, who bathed, dressed and disciplined us through the years. Our attitude toward these devoted household helpers and to those who worked about our yard, based of course on the attitude of our elders, was kindly, friendly, tolerant, but we recognized, perhaps unconsciously, that they were of a different class. They were servants. We liked them. Our parents as employers were kind, friendly, almost patriarchal in their attitude, especially to the Hawaiians. I have only very pleasant recollections of the relationship between employers and employees in our family. We rarely played with Hawaiian or Oriental children. Occasionally the boys of the family had boy friends among them who came to play....
>
> The laborers on the plantation were of great interest to us as they came to the office, carpenter-shop or ox-cart assembly center, all of which were in our yard. All came once a month for their pay, the Hawaiians every week for copies of the Hawaiian newspapers, which were given to them free, and it was the Hawaiians who yoked and unyoked the oxen every morning and night and who did the carpentry work in the little shop when we were very young. Later they were replaced by the Japanese and Portuguese.... Negroes were few and far between. A Jewish lady, who came to teach in the public school became a friend of our mother and came to our house often, bringing her little girl. The little girl had a pony and rode every day, as we did.... We had very little contact with the early Portuguese and were rather prejudiced against them by remarks picked up in the community about their being dirty, aggressive and quarrelsome. The name "Portugee" applied to them seemed appropriate and one we could not forget. Behind the Orientals in desiring education for their children, they required hard work of even the youngest. Such expressions as "I go to grass" when going out to cut grass for the cows and "I blow your nose" in the heated argument preceding a fight amused us greatly.... The Chinese were first considered rough and quarrelsome, they gambled and insisted on their rights but were hard-working, able and trustworthy. We liked their humor and very much their generosity especially at Chinese New Years when pork, cakes, lichees, ginger and other delicacies came our way and most of all the wonderful long strings of firecrackers which were

tied to a tree on the very darkest night and set fire to as we shuddered at the big bomb explosions. Koreans and Filipinos came much later when we were older, the former queer, rather oldish men who looked as if life had been hard and bitter. They were always hunting for edible weeds along the roadsides and invariably they smelled of garlic. They seemed helpless and not adjusted to life here. Not until later years did I know their women in their charming immaculate white and understand the tragedy of their homeland. The first Filipinos were considered very dangerous characters and proved poor workers. It took experience and adjustment to prove their value to Hawaiian life.[5]

This is vintage Wilcox. It represents her honest impression about the people who lived and worked on the plantation—not apologetic about class and race differences, accepting of the status she had by virtue of being a member of the owner's family, but also, like her parents, as she put it, "kind and tolerant."

Awakenings

After graduating from Punahou in 1898, Elsie Wilcox went to Massachusetts to attend Wellesley College. Whether she or her parents made the choice is unclear, but it had a profound influence on her. Although the debate was still raging as to the efficacy and, indeed, the wisdom of educating young women past the high school level, it was not an issue with the Wilcoxes. Most of the Lyman and Wilcox women were well educated for their times. The grandmothers were teachers. Emma had attended Rockford and Dearborn seminaries in Michigan and had graduated from Dearborn in 1871. All three of the Wilcox girls, as well as the boys, went to school on the East Coast—Etta and Elsie to Wellesley, Mabel to Johns Hopkins for nursing training. The only familial difficulty regarding education was the nursing training for Mabel. Her mother was adamantly opposed to Mabel's becoming a nurse, evidently because she did not think nursing a suitable kind of work. Mabel prevailed, however, by agreeing to wait until she was twenty-five to start her training. Emma probably believed Mabel would change her mind, or perhaps that she would marry, but she did not.

The Wilcox young women were part of a small minority of women in the United States receiving a college education. In 1900, only

Elsie Wilcox in 1902 at age twenty-two.

2.8 percent of women between eighteen and twenty-one were enrolled in institutions of higher learning.[6] Of women in Hawai'i, the Wilcoxes represented an even smaller percentage.

Wellesley at the turn of the century was an exciting place for a young woman. Many members of the faculty were young. They were enthusiastic, dedicated, and committed to women's education. The college president was Caroline Hazard, and according to the dictates of the founder of Wellesley, Henry Fowle Durant, the entire teaching staff was female.[7] As Patricia Palmieri noted in her study of Wellesley during this time:

> In the Progressive era this professorate was a stellar cast: it included Katherine Coman, historian; Mary Calkins, philosopher; Vida Dutton Scudder, literary critic and social radical; Margaret Ferguson, botanist; Sarah Frances Whiting, physicist; Emily Greene Balch, economist; and Katherine Lee Bates, author of *America the Beautiful*. To outside observers this group had created a female Harvard, a "bubbling cauldron that seethed," a "hotbed of radicalism." To their students, the noble faculty provided a rich world which stirred them.[8]

Progressivism, at the start of the century the emerging movement for reform in politics, economics, and the social structure of the country, was a dominant force in higher education. Lynn Gordon, in her study of women in higher education during the period, observed, "Progressives exuded confidence that human beings could ameliorate the deficiencies of the national life, while remaining within a traditional American framework."[9] Given the culture Elsie Wilcox came from and to which she returned, it is hard not to conclude that she was greatly influenced by what she learned at Wellesley, particularly the progressive philosophy that permeated the college.

It was a heady time. The faculty were involved in many projects, both on and off campus. Katherine Coman and the younger Vida Scudder started a settlement house in Boston, Denison House. There were debates over whether the college should accept "tainted" money from John D. Rockefeller. Emily Greene Balch advocated pacifism during World War I, resulting in her termination by the college.[10]

Several studies have indicated the importance of single-sex schools, particularly during the early years of women's entry into higher education. Without the distraction of males and the problems associated with competing with them, women could develop a wide range of skills. Helen Horowitz wrote about the issue in her study of the "Seven Sisters" colleges:

> In the single-sex society of women's college, women re-created the social roles of men and women with their hierarchical relationships. But women took both parts, assuming masculine prerogatives as upper-class students. This encouraged the development of the forcefulness and direct stance of men rather than the tilts and smiles that marked female subordination. Buildings designed to protect femininity became places where women learned to act as men.[11]

In addition to the intellectual and social relationships, Palmieri also discussed sexual relationships at Wellesley:

> At Wellesley, the academic women spent the main part of their lives with other women. We cannot say with certainty what sexual connotation these relationships conveyed. We do know that these relationships were deeply intellectual; they fostered verbal and physical expressions of love. Many women who had complained of being shy, isolated individuals before coming to Wellesley became more self-assured and less withdrawn. Frivolity, intimacy and emotional interdependency often developed between senior and associate professors. Lifelong relationships of deep significance to women's careers and personal identities were common at Wellesley.[12]

By the time Elsie Wilcox enrolled at Wellesley, the faculty had established a college that was intellectually stimulating and supportive, an exciting place for women students. Wilcox majored in English and botany and studied French, German, biblical history, economics, and philosophy, among other subjects. During her senior year, she enrolled in two courses from Katherine Coman, "Elements of Economics" and "Industrial History of the United States," and a course titled "Business Methods and Business Law," taught by Caroline J. Cook.[13] She seems to have been preparing herself for a more active role at Grove Farm than that of younger daughter of the brother of the owner.

At Wellesley, Wilcox experienced an all-female community, with friendships, support systems, and a sense of purpose. She later tried, with some success, to recreate something similar on Kaua'i.

Elsie Wilcox at her graduation from Wellesley, in 1902.

A Young Lady of the House

Following Elsie Wilcox's commencement in 1902, she and Mabel Wilcox took a brief trip to Europe, then returned to Kaua'i. Over the next two decades, Elsie Wilcox changed from the typical young, wealthy Caucasian woman in Hawai'i to a leading voice of progressivism in the islands. Fortunately for her biographer, she faithfully kept a "daybook." Although she rarely wrote in the daybook about her feelings or emotions, she chronicled her activities day-by-day. We have, therefore, several years' description of her mundane activities. They show her progression from being the young daughter of the house, freshly returned from college and taking part in the many social activities of her particular group, to the beginning of her active involvement in community matters and her growing concern for the larger society around her.

For the first two or three years after college, her life was much like that of most of her peers. A close look at her activities reveals the details of a lifestyle now gone. It also indicates how much the values, behavior, lifestyle, and goals of the missionary families had changed in two generations.[14]

The earliest entries in Wilcox's daybook focus on four topics: family, social activities including outings and dances, church participation, and reading. The main focus of her attention was her family. Grove Farm was the center of the family's life. Until they married or had jobs in other places, all the children lived there.

The "cult of domesticity" was the dominant theme for the Wilcox women. They maintained a sense of system and order and took pride in a house well run. Catherine Beecher, outlining the pattern for her "model household" half a century earlier, could have been describing the Wilcox household:

> There is no one thing more necessary to a housekeeper, in performing her varied duties, than *a habit of system and order;* ... A wise economy is nowhere more conspicuous, than in the right *apportionment of time* to different pursuits. There are duties of a religious, intellectual, social, and domestic nature, each having different relative claims on attention.[15]

Entries in the Wilcox journal depict a tranquil, domestic existence. Day after day, her journal records her cooking for the family. She made cakes, cookies, mayonnaise, salad dressing, Washington pie, and salads. In addition, she taught their cook to prepare special dishes. She sewed curtains, tablecloths, and dishcloths, and she made centerpieces for the household. She made her own underwear and dresses for Etta, including the lace on her wedding dress. She also sewed for Mabel. In winter, when it was raining hard, she would sew all day. Although the temperature rarely fell below 55 degrees in the daytime during the winter, and usually was in the high 70s, the rain could be heavy—as much as 3 inches an hour—making outdoor travel or activities difficult and sometimes dangerous.

The family ate dinner together every evening. Guests often joined them. The food was rarely fancy and was served in courses by a maid. Elsie and her brothers and sisters had friends over for dinner and sometimes to spend the night, and her parents and uncle often entertained friends or political associates.

Elsie and her mother and sisters regularly went "calling." They visited ladies in their social circle and likewise were visited by them. They sat and talked, having tea. She did the same thing when she was in Honolulu. Before the arrival of the telephone, they risked paying a visit only to discover the recipient of the visit was already out visiting. In Honolulu, some women established "at home" days, when they were regularly home to receive guests, but that does not seem to have been the case on Kaua'i.

The family celebrated a number of holidays, because of the multicultural composition of the workforce. Every November 3, an entry in the daybook recorded the birthday of the Emperor of Japan, when all the help had a holiday. Sometimes, Kubo and Jonny, the Japanese cook and helper, prepared the noon meal, but the Japanese wanted to have the day free to celebrate. Although the majority of the workers were Japanese, they also celebrated other holidays, including Chinese New Year.

Christmas had become a more special occasion. Christmas Eve, the family lit candles on a tree and distributed gifts—at the Hawaiian church, among the servants, and with the family. Some years, Hawaiian bands visited various houses, playing carols. The holiday had changed from being reserved as a day of prayer to a day of celebration in a more secular vein.

Gradually, the family circle expanded and dispersed. Early entries in Elsie's daybook describe many visits with Daisy Rice, to sew, entertain, or have dinner. On October 4, 1902, Elsie Wilcox wrote, "Ralph

Elsie Wilcox, Sadie Alexander, and Ethel Wilcox at Papalinahoa, the Wilcox family beach house at Nāwiliwili Harbor, July 6, 1903.

over at Rice's for supper as usual." On November 14 of the same year, she entered, "Ralph announced his engagement to Daisy Rice to the family." The daybook for February 17, 1903, records their wedding:

> Ralph and Anna Rice [Daisy's given name] were married at noon, a quiet family wedding, Wilcoxes, Rices, Mr. and Mrs. H. Waterhouse, and Reverend and Mrs. H. Isenberg. House beautifully decorated in green and white. After lunch the two left for Kipukai in a carriage decorated with old shoes and showered with rice.

Elsie and Mabel were very close to Daisy and welcomed her into the family, as did G.N. and their parents. Daisy was the daughter of a neighbor, William Rice, and the family had known her since she was a child. In 1903, G.N. engaged C. W. Dickey, a young architect and family friend newly graduated from MIT, to build a house for Ralph and Daisy about half a mile from Grove Farm. Not having married, G.N. looked to Ralph, as the eldest son of Sam and Emma, eventually to take over Grove Farm.

During these years, Etta also married. Shortly after Elsie returned from Wellesley, she noted, "Mr. H. D. Sloggett called in evening and we were told of his engagement to Etta."[16] Her diary entries were quite formal in referring to people not part of the family or close friends, but after that entry, Mr. H. D. Sloggett became "Digby." The June 3, 1903, entry described Etta's wedding:

> Woke to find it rainy and threatening. Etta felt badly about it. Mrs. Humburg, Mabel and I went to Papalinahoa early and opened more presents from Hon. [Honolulu]. Mrs. Rice and Grace and Agnes Isenberg decorating. Native women making leis, etc. Cleared before noon so after lunch we went down again. Belle going to decorate coconuts on lanai. Then at 5 P.M. it poured. We had to leave and servants moved all into the house. Cleared about 7. Wedding at church at 7:30, reception at P. [Papalinahoa] later. Successful. Gaylord, best man, Mr. Crawford and Charles, ushers, Mabel and Alice = bridesmaids and I maid of honor. Etta and Digby left about 10:30 for Hanamaulu. Danced later.

Gaylord was setting out on his own career, as were Ralph and Charles. On January 28, 1903, Elsie recorded that "Gaylord brought home a sample of his first strike of sugar. Mr. Webber gave him a salary of $40 a month at Hanamaulu." Gaylord was earning about $1.50 a day and was evidently happy about it.

Thus, the grown children of the family started to leave home. The older sons had established their own homes, Gaylord was at Hanamaulu, and Etta was married. Yet, everyone returned to Grove Farm in times of celebration or need. Mabel and Elsie saw Etta and Daisy almost every day, and the whole family regularly dined together at Grove Farm.

Elsie and G.N. occasionally went to Honolulu together. On one of the trips, G.N. took her to Waialua to see the old family home. He was deeply interested in the family and the family's history, and on this and other occasions, he passed on his interest to the next generation. The sense of rootedness in Hawai'i was an integral part of G.N.'s personality and helps explain his political, charitable, and civic activities. Most of the family had a deeply held feeling of belonging to and being responsible for both the family and the larger community, defined by various members in different ways.

Elsie's daybook records that from time to time her family, like most, suffered varying degrees of illness and loss. Both Elsie's parents had dengue fever and were very sick. By far the worst illness, however,

Charles Wilcox's birthday *lū'au,* May 1903. Pictured are Enoka, Kaaihue, Lekua, and Samuel Wilcox preparing a pig for the *imu.*

struck her Uncle Luther. In late June 1903, he trimmed a corn on a toe. His toe became infected, and the infection spread. Too late, the toe, then his foot, and then his leg were amputated. He died July 12 of gangrene poisoning. His funeral in Honolulu was large. He had been a translator for the legislature and the courts, went on to become a judge, and was well known and evidently well liked. Of the Wilcox brothers, he was the closest to the Hawaiians. He had opposed the overthrow of the monarchy even after Albert and G.N. had changed their minds and supported it. He had married a Hawaiian woman, E. Kahuilanuimakehaikalani, and spoke fluent Hawaiian, better than any of his brothers.

To Elsie, his passing was more of a ripple than a wave. She had rarely seen him, even when she was in Honolulu, and he seldom traveled to Grove Farm. Her journal entry for July 8 noted, "Uncle George and Uncle Albert went to Honolulu by special trip to see Uncle Luther who was operated on, leg taken off below knee," and on July 14, "Received news of Uncle Luther's death from gangrene poisoning. Father and Uncle George were with him at the end at hospital [Queen's] at 8 P.M. Sunday, July 12th. Funeral next day at Kawaiahao

Church at 4 P.M. Papers full of tribute to the just judge, and honest, straightforward, fearless man."

During this time, Etta visited the house regularly to "keep Papa's books." It was more than a little unusual that Etta would be keeping her father's books rather than her father himself or an accountant or, perhaps, Gaylord or Ralph. When Etta began having children, she taught Elsie to keep the books, a task Elsie continued until her father died.

A regular entry in the daybook described Elsie reading to her Uncle George. G.N. had developed cataracts and was going blind. In 1903, Gaylord accompanied him to New York, where he underwent a successful operation on one eye. Later, he and Charles went back to New York to have the other cataract removed.[17] He wore thick glasses after the operations, but his sight was restored sufficiently so that Elsie did not have to read to him in the evenings.

On May 31, 1904, the first of Etta's children was born. Etta and Digby lived a few miles from Grove Farm. On June 10, Elsie observed that Etta was not feeling well, so they were not going to visit her. June 11 had the following entry:

> Mabel and mother went over to see Etta. She had high fever, but was better than the night before. The doctor was there. At lunch time, the doctor telephoned for father and mother and sent for Digby. Sent for Dr. Sandover of Waimea for a consultation. Frank driving to meet him. The boys came from Koloa in P.M. Father and mother returned at 9 P.M. Said the Drs. said that Etta was seriously ill—temperature 104, pulse 132. They gave her something to make her sleep, very anxious.

Etta almost died. She finally recovered, after months of rest, there being little else the doctors could prescribe.

One of the most telling and poignant continuing entries in Elsie Wilcox's diaries concerns the dances. She was a sociable person, who enjoyed going to dances and liked being with young men. However, her first couple of years' entries include many remarks like this: "To dance ... in evening. Music gramophone, not very lively and whole dance was slow but had fairly good time." Again, on New Year's Eve of that year, 1902, she recorded, "In P.M. went to masquerade ball at the Sugar room. Mabel going as Red Riding Hood and I in cap and gown. Dances slow but enjoyed meeting people." As much as she enjoyed the dances, the young men did not ask her to dance very

A riding party in 1908. *Left to right:* an unidentified person, Elsie Wilcox, Juliet King Kimball, Daisy Rice Wilcox, unidentified person, Mabel Wilcox, and Arthur Rice.

often, and that was a disappointment. Still, the entries for the most part are positive. New Year's Eve of 1903 was better than most. "Went to a dance at the Purvises in P.M. to see New Year in. A very good time." There were many "outings." On April 17, 1903, she wrote, "Belle Dickey and I left for Waimea at 8:30. Kaaihue driving us to Lawai and a team of Rigos taking us on. Reached Mrs. Hofgaard's at 12:30. After lunch rested and then ladies came in for coffee.... Played cards and danced."

During these early years on Kaua'i, the fact that Elsie Wilcox was reading voraciously differentiated her from her peers more than anything else. Initially, her reading followed no particular plan or program. She read novels and serious nonfiction by American and British authors and translations of German and French writers. The titles ranged from *Apologia Pro Vita Sua* through *Bleak House* to *The Octopus,* which she described as "a terrible but true account of Cal[ifornia] wheat growers and the S.P. [Southern Pacific Railroad]."[18] She seems to have read anything she could find.

On October 23, 1902, she described unpacking a box that had just arrived from Wellesley—everything was in good condition. "Glad to get my precious books again." That comment and the following one give an insight into her life at Grove Farm. On January 5, 1903, she wrote:

> Practiced [piano] as Mabel is giving me lessons and I must keep up in *something*. Have dropped everything so lately. . . . In evening found an old journal of Grandma Lyman's and find it very interesting. Poor dear soul, how she suffered for her sins. I wish I were ¼ as good. We are in an indifferent age or is it merely a personal matter!"

She was leading a comfortable, pleasant, undemanding life. She had plenty of social companions, and she attended dances, parties, picnics, outings, and dinners. She had household activities to keep her busy. Yet, with a certain amount of quiet, not often articulated pain, she missed the life she had led at Wellesley. An October 14, 1902, entry in her daybook, shortly after she returned home, expressed her sense of isolation. "Foreign mail. Heard from a lot of the girls at College and wish I could be there." Kaua'i must have seemed very small and dull.

She became frustrated at times with members of her family. On January 8, 1903, she wrote, "Cannot agree with Ralph. Wish I could help my temper. Hold my tongue most of all which runs away and says what I don't mean. Must learn self-control which I seem to have less and less of here." The first years back home were not always happy. This was not surprising. She was in the process of challenging many ideas and beliefs held by most of her family.

This was typical of college graduates who returned home different people from when they had left. Robyn Muncy, in a study of female reform movements, found that such women were often depressed and disoriented under those circumstances.[19] Jane Addams said there were many young men and women "whose uselessness hangs above them heavily," and who led "overcultivated and undernourished lives."[20]

At first, the only community activity in which Wilcox participated was teaching Sunday school to a group of Hawaiian and part-Hawaiian boys at Lihue Union Church, about a half mile away from Grove Farm. The Wilcox family was a financial mainstay of the church, although G.N. rarely attended and Emma was an Episcopalian.

Elsie and Mabel Wilcox and Daisy Rice taught Sunday school in the Hawaiian Sunday school, but used only English because they did not speak Hawaiian. Elsie recorded many class activities in her daybook. The most frequent entry concerning her Sunday school class described practicing for a *hoʻiki*. The *hoʻiki* was a remnant from earlier days when schools and church classes performed for a visiting dignitary or at the end of a semester. Songs, recitations, and other activities demonstrated what the students had learned. The church *hoʻiki* included plays, recitations of Bible verses, exhortations, and hymns sung in Hawaiian, which everyone knew whether they spoke Hawaiian or not. Elsie Wilcox's classes had between six and ten boys. The practices took place with increasing frequency as the semiannual *hoʻiki* approached. She took the obligation very seriously, sometimes practicing almost daily with the boys. On October 5, 1902, she wrote, "To Hoiki in A.M. All family going except mama. Boys did very well indeed. Exercises rather long and a bit tiresome."

In addition to the *hoʻiki* practices, Elsie Wilcox and Daisy Rice hosted parties for their classes at Papalinahoa, where the boys went swimming and played games. At Christmas, they had a party for the boys and gave them small gifts. Elsie recorded her first impressions of her students on September 28, 1902: "The boys are so interesting and nice." Her evaluation had changed by January 4, 1903: "My boys are so hard to manage. They seem to get more so every week." She continued to teach the class, however, and evidently had no serious prob-

Papalinahoa, the Wilcox family beach house. Here the family went swimming and horseback riding, and entertained—friends, children from the Lihue Church Hawaiian Sunday school, and children from the Līhuʻe public schools.

lems, because the class remained a high priority among her activities for many years.

Wilcox's attitude toward Hawaiians was ambiguous. Her family had been fond of but not altogether confident about the reliability of the Hawaiians who were hired to care for the children, and gradually, Chinese and Japanese replaced the Hawaiians. On January 20, 1903, she made the following comment in her daybook: "Mrs. Kahele called in A.M. to bring Mabel's holoku [dress]. She is a good genuine native of the old stamp, not afraid to work and worthy of respect as few of them are now days." This theme recurs in some of her later comments. She was not much involved with the Hawaiian community on Kaua'i. Her grandparents all spoke Hawaiian fluently, and her father and uncles had varying degrees of fluency, but she had little if any. Yet, she was very fond of her aunt Emma Mahelona, Albert's wife, and Ethel, their daughter, and spent considerable time with them. In later years, several of her closest friends, particularly among the teachers, were part-Hawaiian.

Elsie Wilcox's family was deeply involved in politics, and her daybook reflects some of that interest, although not as much as might be expected from a woman who was later a trailblazer in the area of women's political activity. Her diary chronicles the fortunes of her family members, all male, who were running for office, and of the Republican party. Several entries indicate that the men in the family went to political rallies that the women did not attend. This was probably because women were not yet enfranchised.

Periodically, Prince Jonah Kūhiō Kalaniana'ole, the Republican delegate to Congress, visited Kaua'i, and the men joined him for a political tour or an evening of speeches at a large hall. On election day, 1902, Elsie Wilcox made these observations: "Papa and Ralph at polls all day. Mabel and I listened for returns at telephone in P.M. Complete Republican victory.... Papa had 626 votes in all. More than any other candidate." A few days later she wrote: "Heard favorable political returns from Hawaii.... Hopes for good government now and we feel satisfied for the hard work." After the hard work came the celebration. "Went to luau at Mr. Rice's carriage house given in honor of the political victory. Probably a thousand people there. The Prince ... down from Honolulu. Rain very disagreeable."[21]

During her first few years at home from college, Elsie Wilcox embarked on other ventures that were to become important to her later. These involved the public schools, the Hawaiian Evangelical

Association (HEA)—the successor to the ABCFM in Hawaii—and the Mokihana Club. Her early daybook entries give no indication that the activities were any more important than those discussed previously, but in retrospect, Elsie was moving away from the confines of her family and friends and making a life for herself separate from them.

Her first school activity was as an observer of the closing day exercises in June 1903.[22] Then she began staying to have lunch with the teachers, and subsequently, she started teaching in the school herself.

In 1905, Elsie, her sisters, her mother, and several other women on Kaua'i founded the Mokihana Club, with Elsie as its first president. It was named for the *mokihana* plant, the flower of Kaua'i. The proximate stimulus for the club was a fair sponsored by a group of women to pay for a town hall in Līhu'e. It seems to have been the first time the women had gathered together over a period of several months to work on a project, and they were reluctant to disband. That feeling was understandable. The women who founded the club were either the wives or daughters of men whose income afforded them ample help with housekeeping and child care. They had leisure time and were probably feeling bored and isolated. Some years after the founding of the club, Elsie wrote to Dr. Edward Handy at the Bishop Museum in Honolulu, who was arranging for speakers for the Kaua'i Historical Society and the Mokihana Club: "We do not want to ask too much but you will realize that here in the country our opportunities are few and there are some who are most appreciative of any advantages."[23]

This was a time both in Hawai'i and on the mainland when middle- and upper-class women were forming clubs for various purposes. Many were social, others dealt with civic problems, and still others were self-improvement groups.

Until recently, women's organizations of the nineteenth and early twentieth centuries were either ignored or trivialized by most scholars and large segments of society, especially men. The founder of Sorosis, Jane C. Croly, in 1886 lamented that "A Woman's Club was naturally the object of many gibes and sneers, much ridicule, and cheap attempts at wit, during the first months of its existence."[24] Mary Beard wrote in 1915 that a new interpretation of women's organizations was needed, one that would include women "not in an incidental way, but as people of flesh and blood and brain,... directing equally with men, all the great social forces which mold character and determine general comfort, well-being and happiness," but her admonition fell on deaf ears.[25] William O'Neill's summary of the Association of Collegiate Alumnae's organizational problems in the early 1880s leaves little doubt as to his view of the organization: "The association fiddled endlessly with its admissions policies as if the fate of higher education for women depended on finding exactly the right formula. The resulting discrepancy between time spent and results secured suggests the ACA's main function."[26] O'Neill concluded that social feminism, of which the club movement was a significant part, was responsible for the failure of the feminist movement in the early twentieth century.

More recent research presents a different perspective. Karen Blair, whose book title, *The Clubwoman as Feminist,* states her thesis, asserts that the clubs were the vehicle through which thousands of women were able to leave the confines of their homes.[27] Many of the women were "feminists under the skin, developing a significant and popular strategy for achieving autonomy, however much they may have maintained their ideological cover."[28] Anne Firor Scott concluded:

> For women—cut off as they were through most of the years considered here from the political party, the bench, the bar, the Congress, the city council, the university, the pulpit—voluntary associations became a place to exercise the public influence otherwise denied them; in a sense they provided an alternative career ladder, one that was open to women when few others were.[29]

Elsie Wilcox was instrumental in the planning and development of the Mokihana Club for precisely the reasons discussed by Blair and Scott. The New England Women's Club in Boston was active when Wilcox was at Wellesley, and the Mokihana Club was patterned after models on the East Coast. The progression of club activities on Kaua'i was also similar to that of clubs on the mainland. What began as primarily a social and cultural enrichment organization, over the years became a group of dedicated women active in numerous community projects.

Initially, the group met at members' homes, but after Lihue Hall was built, they usually met there. The hall was "a long building with a veranda around it and entrances on each side. There was a good sized area for meetings, dances and other social gatherings. There also was a stage. Electricity had not yet come to Kauai, so kerosene lamps and lanterns were used in the hall and as footlights on the stage."[30]

They met on the first Wednesday of the month, unless "we have a stormy day," when they met the following Wednesday.[31] Heavy, blowing rains soaked long skirts and turned the unpaved roads to mud.

Their first year, the women voted to study Russia and Japan. They read about the subjects, wrote papers, and delivered their papers to the group. They also had musical presentations by the members, some of whom were accomplished musicians, and a magic lantern show.

The written history of the club reveals the staid and somewhat naïve nature of the women. In 1909, they put on a play for the community to raise funds. The script for the play was written by the minister at Lihue Union Church, John M. Lydgate. The play was titled *Joseph and His Brethren*. Mr. Lydgate played the part of Joseph, and a club member, Mrs. Fairchild, played Potiphar's wife. An uproar ensued when the more senior women in the club discovered that the script called for a seduction scene involving the two characters, and they demanded that Mrs. Lydgate play the role of Potiphar's wife. She did.[32] The club continued in this vein until the following decade, when the members launched into "municipal housekeeping" on a large scale.

The Old Maids

During the period 1904–1910, Elsie Wilcox began to participate in groups that were specifically and probably consciously all female. Clubs, associations, meetings, and social occasions more and more included only females. Given this, it is interesting that she was also taking lessons in a number of activities usually considered to be "finishing" for young ladies about to be married. She took piano lessons from Mabel. She learned embroidery, woodworking, and burnt woodwork. She studied French and German, putting the most concentrated and lasting effort into her study of German. She was living in a community that was part English speaking, part Hawaiian, and part German. The Rice family, having married with the Isenbergs, a family from Germany, was heavily influenced by German culture, and German was spoken at Lihue Plantation. Since the Wilcoxes were very close to the Rices, it was natural that Elsie would study German and that she would have an abiding interest in German culture.

The few people interviewed for this book who remembered Elsie

Wilcox in her early years said she was not good looking as a young woman, although in later pictures she seems attractive. For several years, she had serious skin problems. She received treatment on Kauaʻi, in Honolulu, and on the East Coast. Most of the treatment was X-ray, and she must have received a substantial amount of radiation. Considering the treatments, it may not be a coincidence that she died of cancer. She also had trouble with balding spots on her head. In addition, she spent many days in the dentist's chair, and her teeth would have benefited from braces had they been available. Much of her time was taken up with various medical problems.

In terms of marriage, she may have had two strikes against her: she was overly well educated, and she was not good looking. Higher education for women was increasingly accepted, but few women (or men) of the time completed a university education. Most men did not want a wife with more education than they had. Writing in 1895, Milicent Washburn Shinn summed up the situation:

> The college woman is not only more exacting in her standards of marriage, but under less pressure to accept what falls below her standard than the average woman, because she can better support and occupy herself alone.... I have no doubt that the remaining cause of the low marriage rate is that many men dislike intellectual women,—whether because such women are really disagreeable or because men's taste is at fault, I shall not try to determine.[33]

The marriage rate at Wellesley for the graduating classes between 1900 and 1909 was 68.3 percent.[34] Sara Evans found that half of all college-educated women in the late nineteenth century did not marry.[35] In addition, then, as now, selection of a wife was often based as much on looks as on compatibility and other criteria. Good looks were not the only ticket to marriage, but they were important, and being "plain" was not an asset. The other side of the issue of good looks, however, was, as Carolyn Heilbrun found, that unattractive girls developed strong egos and creativity.[36]

Elsie's social circle included a small group of "suitable" men. It would have been unusual, although not unheard of, had she not married a Caucasian. Years later, the story circulated that Mabel had been romantically attached to a part-Hawaiian doctor, and her mother's resistance to the idea of Mabel marrying a part-Hawaiian put an end to the romance. However, their uncles Albert and Luther had married part-Hawaiian women, as did Gaylord. Most Caucasian families that had been in the islands for more than a couple of generations had part-Hawaiian branches. Whether the story about Mabel was true, it was the case that although many men were around, Elsie probably would not have considered marrying a Chinese or Japanese, even a professional, and certainly not a laborer. Race and class lines between Asians and Caucasians were relatively fixed and not often crossed in marriage.

As time passed and the small number of Caucasian men, professionals or businessmen, her age began to marry, Elsie's chances of marriage decreased rapidly. Her situation hung somewhat heavily in her thoughts. Several times during these years she made mention of "the old maids," a group including Mabel and some of the schoolteachers from the U.S. mainland with whom she was spending more and more time. The first mention appears on April 3, 1904, when she was only twenty-five. "Charles, Miss Mumford, Miss Jordan, Uncle Geo. and I went to church Easter Sunday. The folks all left in P.M. leaving six old maids behind."

The fate of an "old maid" usually was not a happy one. As Carl Degler observed, "Despite the increase in the number of single women in the last decades of the 19th century, being single or an 'old maid' was hardly an honorable status. It was only less maligned than at earlier times."[37] Marriage was a woman's career, and pressure to marry, both from society and usually from a woman's family, was considerable. Some women, particularly well-educated women, chose not to marry. From the record she has left, this does not seem to have been the case with Elsie Wilcox. Her activities in the first few years after Wellesley are those of a young woman preparing for marriage and enjoying social activities with men.

The family continued to absorb much of Elsie Wilcox's time and energy. Considering how close she was to many members of her family and the fact that she lived with her parents, she showed an unusual ability to expand her horizons and activities far beyond the family.

She was, however, a devoted daughter, niece, aunt, and sister. When Mabel, who was in Honolulu, had an emergency appendectomy in February 1907, Elsie went to Honolulu to be with her for a month. When Daisy had a similar operation in 1908, Elsie, who happened to be in Honolulu, stayed up with her all of the first night because a nurse did not arrive on time. When Etta's third child was born on Maui, Elsie went there to take care of the other children. She stayed several weeks, visiting with various families, reading, and entertaining the children, of whom she was very fond.

Elsie's brother Charles married Marian Waterhouse in July 1909, and Gaylord married Ethel Mahelona, their Uncle Albert's adopted daughter, in March 1909. Excepting future children, the family circle was now complete.

In 1907, Elsie, Mabel, and G.N. took a three-month trip to Asia. They toured Japan, China, and Hong Kong. The trip had a significant impact on Elsie in two ways. First, she was intensely interested in the politics of the area, and second, she became caught up in the work of medical, educational, and agricultural missionaries, both Asian and foreign. She was in correspondence with people she met during this

Elsie Wilcox during a 1907 trip to Japan.

trip for most of her life. Her later internationalist activities, her deep personal and financial commitment to several mission operations, and her YMCA work with Japanese leaders all came about as a result of the trip to Asia. By chance, she met two women from Hull House, the famous settlement house in Chicago run by Jane Addams. She spent several hours talking with them about their work. In later years, this experience also came to be important as she became the de facto social worker on Kaua'i.

Also in 1907, G.N. bought his first car. Elsie Wilcox's diaries contain many entries about the joys and problems of car ownership. She had driven a car on the mainland in 1905 and responded with the notation, "great fun." She and G.N. took lessons from the salesman who came to Kaua'i with the car to be sure that everything was all right. It was the first car on Kaua'i. Everything was not all right. The roads were unpaved and full of ruts, resulting from a combination of carriage and horse traffic and heavy rains. They had difficulty with the tires and the motor, and on several occasions, the family became stranded. In one three-day period, they changed tires eighteen times. Progress came swiftly, however. In 1908, Elsie wrote that they were "macadamizing" the road in front of the homestead.[38]

Other inventions appeared, too. In 1908, she mentioned seeing a motion picture show. In March 1909, having just received her first camera, she noted, "Took picture (Kodak)."

Although the family lived well, they were not extravagant. Some years later, Elsie was described as being so frugal she had a dress that was patched and repatched. Her housekeeper called it the "patch on patch" dress.

Despite the fact that labor unrest marked the years covered in Elsie's diary, she made only two entries on the subject. That may have been because Grove Farm was a relatively peaceful plantation. G. N. Wilcox, by all accounts, was a fair employer. Plantation workers interviewed after his death generally spoke highly of his ability to deal equitably with his diverse workforce. Grove Farm was one of the smaller of the large plantations, and G.N. and Sam knew most, if not all, of the workers by name. They tolerated no violence by supervisors against the workers, a cause of much of the early unrest on other plantations. In addition, particularly in the early years, G.N. did much of the manual labor on the plantation himself, which put him in contact with the workmen on a daily basis. However, a large and growing gulf existed between laborers and owners or managers. Racial, economic, cultural, and language differences led to many disputes. As the plantations prospered, owners and managers became increasingly rich, but plantation workers' wages and benefits did not rise accordingly.

Interestingly, during all these years that were marked by repeated labor strikes, Elsie Wilcox only made note of the May 1909 strikes. On May 18, she wrote, "Strike continued at Oahu and Honolulu plantations. Ewa men returned to work yesterday. Strikers being replaced by men from town." And on May 25, she said, "Steamer late. Not going until after 8 P.M. Had early dinner and took Charles, Father, and Gaylord down. A long wait. Managers went for meeting about Japanese strike."

This period in Elsie Wilcox's life ends in September 1909, when she left Kaua'i for three years.

Europe

On September 6, 1909, Elsie Wilcox left Kaua'i, and she did not return until July 10, 1912. For three years, she engaged in an activity common for wealthy young people in the United States during that era—the obligatory trip to Europe. The genesis of the trip is unclear. On the one hand, she had a very pleasant life, centered on Kaua'i but including Honolulu, Maui, and the island of Hawai'i. On the other hand, she had problems with her teeth, her face, and her hair, all trying difficulties for a woman still young.

It is possible that, having nothing better to keep herself occupied, and missing the excitement of the intellectual atmosphere she had thrived on at Wellesley, she wished to see the cultures from which New England drew its history. Since she was a valuable member of the household, taking more and more responsibility for running the house, keeping her father's books, doing her uncle's driving, and helping with Etta's children, it is likely that the family was not enthusiastic about her leaving. Nonetheless, she did leave, and even by her rather dry accounts, she had a grand adventure.

Her touring in the Middle East was the most exciting and dangerous portion of the trip. She went with a small group of Americans that included the minister of the Park Street Church in Boston, a few married couples, and some other single women. She evidently did not know them before the trip, but they turned out to be a congenial group. The touring was organized by Clark Tours, with different guides in the various places they visited, none of them, according to Wilcox, very good.[39]

The main means of transportation in the Middle East were donkey and boat. At times, paths were so steep that everyone had to dismount and walk, at one point for 6 miles. When the sun was shining, the weather was warm but not unbearably hot. However, they experienced heavy rain showers, hail, and sandstorms, through all of which they rode on the donkeys, there being no shelter. Local Arabs carried them on and off the boats and occasionally across streams, in what Wilcox described as a "very funny scramble."[40] The goal of all this discomfort, the Christian holy places, moved Wilcox considerably. A visit to the Church of the Holy Sepulchre, she observed, "fills one with mixed feelings and questions as to what it all means and what the outcome will be." She toured through Egypt, Syria, Palestine, Algeria, and Morocco. She sailed the Mediterranean between Algiers and Gibraltar and visited Greece, Turkey, Lebanon, and Jordan.

Leaving the Middle East, Wilcox and some other members of the party visited Italy. She continued on to Berlin, her base for the rest of her stay in Europe. From there she toured France, England, Norway, Sweden, Denmark, Holland, Belgium, Switzerland, and Russia.

Her diary entries were consistent, no matter where she went. Museums and art dominated her comments on every country. She knew good art and appreciated the old masters. With the exception of the Russian museum of modern art, she made little mention of contemporary artists, even in Paris, which was at the time the heart of the impressionist movement.

Where she understood the language, she attended the theater. By far the most exciting theater experience was Oberammergau: "Words fail to describe the play which was given in a finished yet simple and reverent manner. Poignant scenes. Epic in one's life to have experienced it."[41] She attended church regularly. She noted that she had been to a service at St. John's in Cambridge and heard Archdeacon Wilberforce say that "things would remain as they are until middle and upper class should say it should not be so."[42]

While she was in Berlin, the structure of her life was much as it was when she was in Hawai'i. She studied German and French and took music lessons. She called regularly on single and married women and on a few couples, had tea and dinner with them, or went shopping. She read a great deal in German and English. Most of her friends and acquaintances were German, but on occasion people from Hawai'i and elsewhere visited.

Wilcox's response to Europe seems to have been that of a well-educated American woman of her time. She appreciated the art, architecture, and rural scenery. She attended many cultural events. She was moved by the great monuments of Europe and the Middle East. She took advantage of being there to continue her studies. The European experience seems to have elicited little political response. The diaries do not comment on the economic conditions, on the Russian peasants' situation, or on the colonial presence in the Middle East. This bland acceptance of the status quo is somewhat surprising from someone who had taken courses on labor relations at Wellesley and had studied with Katherine Coman. Even in later years, when her interest in world affairs had expanded and merged with her concern for social welfare, the focus of that concern was not Europe but Asia.

The End of the Beginning—1912–1920

The decade of the 1910s was a time of prosperity for sugar plantations in the Territory of Hawai'i. Despite the worries of some of the plantation owners, annexation had not brought depression to the territory. Labor continued to be relatively easy to obtain and to control. There were, it is true, some indications of discontent, primarily in the form of strikes. However, in the larger picture, these were minor and were easily put down and blamed on outside agitators or minority malcontents.

On the U.S. mainland, this was a time when vocal critics were outspoken about almost every aspect of American life. The Progressive and Populist parties in politics, the American Federation of Labor and Industrial Workers of the World in economics, the social gospel ministers in religion, the muckrakers in journalism, and the progressives in education all urged changes ranging from reform to revolution. The dialogue was lively.

This was much less true in Hawai'i. The political parties, the major sectors of the economy, the most powerful church (the Congregational Church, headed by the HEA), the English-language press, and the schools were dominated by a relatively small group of men, primarily Caucasian, but including some Hawaiians and part-Hawaiians. They had a shared set of values, beliefs, and goals for Hawai'i.

The Democratic party, although not moribund, and occasionally able to control the Honolulu city government, in fact did not differ substantially from the Republican party. A handful of men associated by family or historic ties exerted a major influence on the sugar plantations, as well as on transportation, communications, and banking institutions. The English-language newspapers generally supported the status quo, and the Japanese newspapers were divided on issues important to the Japanese community. The HEA was controlled both financially and politically by families with missionary ties, some of whom were now dominating the economy. The Episcopalians were at odds with each other, the Mormons were recovering from a financial and political fiasco brought about by one of their leaders, Walter Murry Gibson, and the Catholics, although growing in numbers and wealth, did not yet have much power. The Department of Public Instruction, which was responsible for all of the public elementary and high schools in the territory, was run by a combination of businessmen (most of whose children attended private schools) and professional educators. The educators and businessmen were often wary of each other and sometimes openly at odds, in large part because they had different goals for the schools.

Hawai'i was by no means the closed, authoritarian society that some authors have claimed. Historian Eileen Tamura noted that "Industrialists, politicians, and school leaders alike found that for all their prestige and power, they had much less control over educational, social, and occupational developments than they would have liked—and less than what some scholars have assumed they had."[43] There was, however, nothing like the extensive mainland debates on political, economic, and social issues.

On Elsie Wilcox's return from Europe, her life initially was much as it had been before she left. Her family still took most of her time and energy. The first break in the family, which had for the past several years been expanding, came the evening of July 12, 1913, when Ralph drowned while swimming off Hā'ena on Kaua'i. It was a terrible blow to the family. He and Daisy had just adopted Eunice Scott, Daisy's niece. Ralph was the eldest son, and his parents, now in their sixties, had been looking to him eventually to take the place in the family held by G.N. for so many years. G.N., who was seventy-four, had been training Ralph to take over Grove Farm, a prospect that pleased both of them.

Daisy and the other members of the family endured a time of intense mourning. She, Mabel, and Elsie had always been close friends, and the relationship deepened with her marriage to Ralph. Now Elsie or Mabel spent almost every day with her and many nights, too. As the months wore on, they included Daisy in their social activities and on trips to Honolulu. They visited Ralph's grave together, first daily, then weekly, and not just during the immediate months after his death but for years thereafter. Daisy never remarried, and G.N. established an annuity that supported her for the rest of her life. She died in 1948.

Gradually, life at Grove Farm returned to normal. The celebrations of Christmas and Thanksgiving, the birthday parties, the welcoming and farewell gatherings recommenced. G.N. turned to Charles, his nephew, as the heir destined to take over Grove Farm.

Elsie's busy social life focused more on women and women's organizations than in the past. She took part in fewer group picnics and mixed-group outings to Papalinahoa and more teas and bridge parties with single and married women. A subtle change had taken place on Kaua'i with the influx of a number of professional men—second-level managers, physicians, businessmen—and their wives. The expanding schools drew an increasing number of educated single women from the U.S. mainland to Kaua'i.[44] Probably because Elsie and Mabel were interested in education and knew all the teachers, they became good friends with several of the new arrivals and included them in many of their parties and some of their family celebrations. This was not usually the case on the other islands, where the Caucasian community maintained a fairly sharp social line between the owners and managers and the hired lower-level professionals.

For Elsie, the most interesting development during these years was the evolution of the Mokihana Club from a social-cultural group to a political force in the community. The progression was remarkably like developments in similar clubs on the mainland. This seems somewhat surprising, since Kaua'i was so isolated. Travel between Kaua'i and the East Coast of the United States took several weeks. The only newspaper, the *Garden Island,* appeared three times a week and published little national or international news. Nonetheless, during the decade of the 1910s, the club increasingly interjected itself in political matters.

This activity was called "municipal housekeeping." Across the country, women moved out of the home and into fields that could be construed as an extension of their domestic responsibilities. Education, child welfare, beautification, and public health were the first areas to feel the impact of women's groups because they were most closely associated with what women did at home. Historian Anne Scott described the trend:

> The term "municipal housekeeping" conferred an air of respectability upon what might otherwise have been considered unseemly public or political activity, but behind that innocuous label lay a considerable measure of "discontent with existing political and social conditions"—on the part of people who were not yet voters—first expressed in systematic efforts to improve village, town or city life.[45]

From 1913 to 1914, Elsie Wilcox was president of the Mokihana Club for the second time:

> Child life and its needs were the consuming topic of the year. Attention was called to the lack of school grounds and the very inadequate housing of teachers; domestic science was discussed, including hot lunches for the children, a thing then unknown on Kauai. The great need for books for school children to read became evident, and arrangements were made for the loan of books from the Honolulu library, to be distributed amongst the school children.[46]

Like its mainland counterparts, the club undertook data gathering as the first step toward understanding the problems and finding solutions. Scott described the trend: "Municipal housekeeping had often been built on careful fact-finding; now, as college graduates moved into positions of responsibility in women's organizations and in the professions, there was an increasing emphasis on research and statistical analysis as the necessary preliminary to action."[47]

The Mokihana Club members spent considerable time during 1914–1915 interviewing school officials. Elsie met with local and territorial school officials and wrote a report for the Mokihana Club endorsing plans for a new school building in Līhu'e and making suggestions about its construction and design, with which the school officials agreed.

The following year, "Miss Wilcox, chairman of the Work Committee, gave an outline of the year's work and stated that inasmuch as this is the tenth anniversary of the organization of the club the committee had decided to celebrate the same by raising a fund for playground apparatus."[48] Subsequent minutes indicate that the funds were raised and the equipment bought. Next, the club decided to give a play, "the proceeds to go toward the transportation of the athletic teams of the schools in their various games."[49] Elsie was part of the four-woman committee for the project. They raised $175 for the teams.

In 1916, Elsie was president for a third time, and during that year she and Mabel put forth several public health issues. They raised $2,500 to hire a district nurse to perform public health work. This was an experiment for one year, with the hope that if it proved successful, the plantations would take over the responsibility. Interestingly, no one proposed that the government pay for the nurse.

Obtaining a nurse proved difficult and frustrating. Many nurses who might have been interested in the position had already volunteered for the war effort. The first nurse they hired, Miss Fanny Kuhlig, had been at the Children's Hospital in Honolulu. As Mabel said, "I told her frankly I was afraid she would come down and get restless and leave us in the lurch."[50] Miss Kuhlig promised to stay a year and get the work set up if the conditions were right. She received $100 per month and $25 for her automobile, which was provided by the Mokihana Club. The club also gave her a free room at the hotel and $25 toward her board. Her responsibilities were varied:

> The nurse will work in cooperation with the Doctor. She will work primarily from the schools and hospital out into the homes of the laboring classes. She will be expected to take an interest in the families, teaching hygiene by demonstration as applied to individuals and homes and surroundings.... The nurse will receive no money consideration from patients for her services.[51]

Miss Kuhlig reported many children with "defective teeth," and the club hired a dentist for three afternoons a week at a salary of $100 a month. After seven months, Dora Isenberg gave an account of the nurse's work:

> Miss Kuhlig's work cannot be summed up in a few words, for she has done PIONEER work and as we all know every BEGINNING is difficult. Added to this most of the work has been done in a rainy winter, which has certainly not made the work easier. We have been fortunate in having a lady take up the work of such thorough going energy coupled with fearlessness and untiring devotion. Miss Kuhlig has had to over come

much prejudice among a large variety of nationalities. When the CLUB decided to establish a District Nurse I think none of us realized the neglected condition of many of the children in our midst.⁵²

Miss Kuhlig left after seven months to go to the war front. The club prevailed upon Lihue Plantation and G. N. Wilcox to undertake subsidizing the nurse's salary, with the club paying for the hotel, part of the board, and the auto.⁵³ They had a difficult time finding a replacement who would stay, and the minutes of the club mention at least four nurses within the next two years. One nurse wrote the following commentary:

> During summer vacation the work has been rather hard. Have visited 15 different camps faithfully once a week. The names of most of the camps are unknown to me, many small, scattered here and there in out of way places. I find most of the children suffer from infections which are very contagious and due mostly to dirt and improper diet. If we could teach mothers the importance of cleanliness half of the battle would be won. It has been quite amusing to watch mothers sometimes rush in to their kitchen and come back with "would be washrags" and try to wipe off the youngsters faces. The wash cloths look more like floor mops, so black and dirty. Some time ago I saw a little Filipino boy in one of the small camps. The child was so filthy it was almost impossible for me to get near him. His head was a mass of sores and scales. It took me almost one hour to wash and clean that head. . . . If the camp work is to be continued, I may be bold as to ask that something be done to make matters easy for the nurse—small dispensaries, if possible, be built near large camps so that the nurse may have a place to work. Most of the homes are so filthy that I could not possibly enter them and was obliged to work in the street.⁵⁴

The club intervened in other areas of community life in addition to public health. In 1916, its members created a garden committee "for the purpose of beautifying the town."⁵⁵ In the next couple of years, they supplied hundreds of papaya, coconut, and hibiscus plants to the schools. When the war created food shortages, they gave vegetable seeds to schoolchildren and awarded a $25 prize for the best vegetable garden.

Also in 1916, they became involved in the "good film movement" and put considerable pressure on the Honolulu company that distributed movies to the neighbor islands to provide better films, especially for children. They gave Christmas trees to the schools and Christmas candy to the schoolchildren and the hospital. Their activities reflected those of their counterpart groups on the mainland. Direct community action combined with benevolence gave the women a focus and room for activity outside of their families and filled in gaps in community life, something no other group was prepared to do.

War

On November 26, 1912, Elsie Wilcox made the following entry in her diary: "News of threatened war, 130,000 German reserves called out. Russians and Austrians mobilizing." The next entry on the subject was not until August 3, 1914: "Heard of war in Europe bet. Russia—Aus and Germany,—also threatened with Eng and Fr joining Russia. To tea at Mrs. Rohrig's"; August 4, "Eng declares war ag. Ger."

Although on the other side of the world, the war was no far-off event for Elsie Wilcox. She had only recently returned from Europe. She had visited almost all of the areas caught up in the fighting. She had friends and acquaintances on both sides.

On Kaua'i, more than on any other island, the situation was complicated by the fact that a large group of Germans lived there. Some of them had intermarried with other Caucasians or with Hawaiians, and many of them were well liked. Paul Isenberg, for instance, was a successful businessman, and although he had spent most of his time in Germany since the death of his wife, Maria Rice, he returned often to Hawai'i. For three generations, the Rices and the Wilcoxes had been, first, colleagues in the mission and, later, neighbors. Before the U.S. entry into both World War I and World War II, the *Garden Island* ranged from pro-German to neutral so far as it reported or editorialized on international events, which was not much. Thus, Elsie Wilcox was surrounded by a generally pro-German atmosphere even as the United States edged closer to war and finally joined the other side.

Abner Wilcox had adamantly opposed his sons' fighting in the American Civil War, and none of them had. It had become an issue with G.N., who evidently contemplated giving up his studies at Yale and joining the Union Army. Charles and Gaylord did not join the army during World War I. Charles was thirty-seven and had two children, and Gaylord was thirty-six, with one child.

The Wilcox family did, however, make a significant contribution to the Allied effort in the person of thirty-five-year-old Mabel. She had finished her nursing training at Johns Hopkins and returned to Kaua'i to do what in later years would be called "public health" nursing. She worked with schoolchildren and pregnant women, but most of all she worked with the TB Association trying to reduce or eliminate tuberculosis on Kaua'i. She volunteered to go to France with the Red Cross and served in both France and Belgium. She was involved in some of the heaviest fighting of the war and was decorated by both countries.

Whatever her feelings about the war, Elsie Wilcox entered into the patriotic activity in 1914 as head of the Kaua'i branch of the Territorial Food Commission's Women's Committee and also regularly made bandages, cut shirts, and engaged in other kinds of home front tasks.

When the war ended, Mabel returned home, and she and Elsie embarked on dual careers, Mabel in public health nursing and Elsie in education, social work, and, ultimately, politics.

3   The Good Years

In many respects, the decade of the 1920s was the happiest time of Elsie Wilcox's adult life. She was busy, productive, and respected. While it seems probable that she wanted to marry when she returned to Kaua'i after college, by the time she was in her forties, she had carved out an interesting and fulfilling life for herself. She traveled, she worked, she spent time with her family, including a growing number of nieces and nephews, and she socialized often with teachers and other female professionals on Kaua'i.

Hawai'i in the 1920s

The 1920s were a decade made for someone like Wilcox. The economy of the territory was healthy, people in positions of power recognized more and more that changes were needed (even if they were not willing to support them yet), and organized labor posed little threat. Americans still believed that, having fought the war to make the world safe for democracy, peace through mutual understanding was a genuine possibility. A progressive like Wilcox could be at the forefront of many social and political issues without seriously jeopardizing her economic and social position.

The decade did not start well for the Wilcox family, however. In 1920, Charles and his sixteen-year-old niece, Elizabeth Waterhouse, were killed and several other members of the family injured in an automobile accident. It was another setback for the eighty-year-old G.N., who then turned to Gaylord to take over Grove Farm. Gaylord, however, was happy with his position as vice-president of American Factors (AmFac) in Honolulu and was reluctant to move to Kaua'i. It was not until 1936 that he left his AmFac position and accepted the day-to-day running of the plantation.¹

Suffer the Little Children: Education

Nowhere did Elsie Wilcox's missionary background, her concern for the future of Kaua'i and Hawai'i, and her professionalism in the civic activities she undertook come to the fore as in the field of education. In 1920, she was appointed Commissioner for Education from Kaua'i. Commissioners established the policies of the Department of Public Instruction (DPI), the territory-wide body responsible for all the public elementary and secondary schools. She served in that position until she ran for the territorial Senate in 1932.

She was appointed under unusual and difficult circumstances. The former commissioner, Eric A. Knudsen, was forced to resign because of a brouhaha in the town of Kapa'a that seriously divided the community. It started when some teachers brought charges against the school principal, Mrs. Burke. One of the charges alleged that she whipped a boy who refused to get a vaccination. According to Bernice Hundley, the supervising principal for Kaua'i, Mrs. Burke admitted she had whipped the boy and then, in her words, "The fiend kicked me."² Another allegation was that she used students for nonschool work for herself. On the basis of the charges, with the approval of Knudsen and Hundley—and without a hearing—Mrs. Burke was ordered transferred to a small school on O'ahu with reduced rank and pay.

Letters and petitions flew back and forth. Senator Charles Rice wrote the governor: "My sister Mrs. Ralph Wilcox, informs me that Mrs. Burke has been transferred to a little school with a reduction of salary.... What is the meaning of this? From a previous talk with you I was given to understand that Mrs. Burke would not be transferred without consulting me."³ The Mokihana Club sent a petition protesting the change and requesting a hearing for Mrs. Burke.⁴ A number of prominent people from Līhu'e, including Elsie Wilcox, signed a similar petition. On the other side, there were hundreds of signatures on petitions to keep Knudsen and Hundley and fire Mrs. Burke. Most of these were from Kapa'a.

The Superintendent of Public Instruction supported Knudsen and Hundley on the ground that they were the people in charge. At one point, he told the commissioners that he would like to fire Burke, but was afraid to do so. "If we were to take that step, we would be besieged with letters from the Mokihana Club and other prominent Lihue people." Finally, however, he relented and held a hearing, where it became apparent that Mrs. Burke's main accuser had lied. Burke subsequently was transferred to another principalship at her original pay. That, of course, made no one happy.

Governor Charles J. McCarthy asked for Knudsen's resignation because he thought Knudsen had mismanaged the whole affair. When he did not receive the resignation, he sent a letter to Knudsen saying, "Not having received your resignation as Commissioner of Public Instruction for the island of Kauai, I beg to inform you that you have been removed from such position as of this date and the same declared vacant."[5]

The next issue was who would be appointed to take Knudsen's place. Many people wrote in with nominees, including A. H. Waterhouse, who nominated Etta Wilcox Sloggett:

> Mrs. Sloggett, in my opinion, is the best fitted for the position of anyone on Kauai, excepting only her sister, Miss Wilcox. She is not connected with any political faction. The Anti-Rice people cannot object to her as it is well known that her husband is Anti-Rice. On the other hand, Chas. Rice favors her appointment.[6]

The governor chose Claire Brandt from Waimea, but she turned him down because of what had happened to Knudsen. "Old political grudges, land disputes, and social jealousies have all played a greater part than a desire to improve the schools," she wrote McCarthy.[7]

Things remained in a state of some confusion. Finally, in December, the Kaua'i Chamber of Commerce wrote, "After careful consideration and investigation we have unanimously selected Miss E. Wilcox and have consulted with her and secured her consent. We beg to recommend her for that position."[8] On December 27, the governor appointed her.

A small group from Kapa'a protested her appointment.[9] Other than that one protest, however, Wilcox seems to have been enough removed from the fray that her appointment did not polarize the situation further. Thus, after a somewhat inauspicious beginning, Elsie Wilcox commenced twelve years as Commissioner for Education.

She took her responsibilities seriously, belonged to several education organizations, and in 1922 was a delegate to a National Education Association conference in Chicago. She threw herself into all kinds of activities with the schools. She was chair of the Kaua'i public school Athletics League, she chaired the Thrift Essay Committee, and she gave parties for the schoolchildren.[10] She was anything but removed from the day-to-day activities of the schools, and it is no wonder that so many of the teachers became her friends.

During the 1920s, education in Hawai'i became the battleground for a classic conflict between two fundamental American principles—capitalism and democracy. Elsie Wilcox was a central figure in this conflict, which forced her to define her vision for Hawai'i and her role in achieving that vision. On one side were the capitalists—the plantation owners and a few other businessmen. On the other side were the plantation laborers, their children, some school officials, and a few progressives, including Elsie Wilcox. Despite her familial ties to the capitalists, she pressed for progressive, democratic programs during the twelve years she was a commissioner.

Plantation owners and managers felt they needed a supply of cheap, docile agricultural labor to maintain the economy of the territory.[11] Since they could not continue to import that kind of labor, they wanted the children of immigrant laborers to become workers like their parents. Cutting cane did not require much, if any, education. The large majority of jobs in the territory did not require more than bare literacy. Businessmen recognized that there were relatively few white-collar jobs in the agricultural economy and that the need was for laborers in the fields and mills. Education beyond literacy would be counterproductive: the students would not be able to use the additional skills in the fields and mills, and with education they would be unwilling to do manual labor.

The business leaders also did not want to spend more money on public education than was "necessary," however that was defined. The fact that almost all of their children attended private schools removed any personal incentive to spend on public education. Miles Carey, the principal of McKinley School in Honolulu, was very critical of these leaders. In his opinion, "The uproar about cost of education really hides the social conditions—those in favorable positions are not interested in seeing their circle entered by young people of the immigrant laboring class."[12]

This was not a time when people who spoke for capitalism were embarrassed about their philosophy. They felt no need to appear public-service minded. It was not a "public be damned" attitude—the only public that mattered agreed with them. Thus, R. A. Cooke, president of the Hawaiian Sugar Planters Association (HSPA), was speaking for his peers when he stated, "As has been emphasized again and again, the primary function of our plantations is not to produce sugar but to pay dividends,"[13] and Royal Mead, also of the HSPA, was doing the same when he said, "Up to the present time the Asiatic has had only an economic value in the social equation. So far as the institutions, laws, customs and language of the permanent population go, his presence is no more felt than is that of the cattle on the ranges."[14]

If nothing else, the demographics should have warned the people who controlled the territory that times would change. In 1860, there were 816 Chinese and no other Asians in the Kingdom of Hawai'i. By 1920, Japanese comprised 42.7 percent of the population, and the Japanese, Chinese, Koreans, and Filipinos together constituted more than half the population.[15] Most Asian immigrants were ineligible for American citizenship, but their children, having been born in the territory, were citizens and would have all the rights of citizens, including the vote, when they became adults.

Paradoxically, the businessmen also supported the "Americanization" programs designed to inculcate American ideas of democracy and other accoutrements of American culture in first- and second-generation children. The Americanization programs were fundamentally subversive to the goals of the business leaders, particularly in the hands of the many New England teachers who were brought to Hawai'i in the 1910s and 1920s. These women were steeped in the American traditions of equality, democracy, individualism, and freedom. That these goals themselves were not always compatible was not as apparent then as later generations would discover. Thus, throughout the islands, teachers encouraged students to read basic documents in American history—the Declaration of Independence, the Bill of Rights, Jefferson, Thoreau, and Lincoln. Principals like Miles Carey organized student governments and clubs where students could practice what they had learned in their texts. "The public school system perhaps without realizing it . . . created unrest and disorganization," said a University of Hawaii student of that time.[16]

These students were expected to live the lives of their parents, working in the fields or mills for low wages, marginalized in the political system, and excluded from the social organizations of the larger community. At the same time, they were encouraged to consider themselves part of the "American Dream," where the poor could become wealthy and anyone could become president. Naturally, the children and their parents looked to the latter formula. They wanted to succeed on America's terms.

In 1920, the U.S. Office of Education conducted a major survey of schools in Hawaiʻi and issued a report that became the basis for many of the actions taken by Elsie Wilcox and others during the following decade. The survey called for sweeping change: more junior high schools on the outer islands; free transportation to them and to the high schools; free public kindergartens; more vocational education; expansion of the normal school's library by four or five times; improved lighting in almost all the schools; a requirement that teachers have a high school diploma plus two years at normal school, even to teach in rural elementary schools; better living conditions for teachers in rural schools to encourage them to remain longer than one or two years; better materials and a new course of study; and increasing enrollment at the high school level.[17] The additional cost of these proposals was not included, but obviously they would be expensive. Critics of the survey pointed out that the territory had already spent large amounts of money to establish three new high schools within nine years—Hilo High in 1905, Maui High in 1913, and Kauaʻi High in 1914.[18]

The survey disapproved of the low economic and social status of the laborers and of the policies of the community leaders:

> It is a spurious education, an education unworthy of the name that teaches, even by implication, that in this democracy of America there are necessary occupations unworthy of any but the ignorant and the illiterate or that there is room anywhere in this country for a group of men, however small, who shall be forced to their occupations through dire need. Men who work in occupations deemed unworthy, and who do so only because driven to it by the biting lash of necessity, are in reality not free men. They work only in the spirit of the slave. There is no place in America for such, and it is as much the business of education to teach men this as it is to make them literate.
>
> Children in Hawaii should realize there is service in cutting cane just as in other jobs. Reciprocally, they should likewise recognize that they have a right to follow such occupations under fit and tolerable conditions and to receive as a tangible reward for service rendered a wage that is more than an existence wage, more than a thrift wage, in fact,

that it shall be a cultural wage, one which may be defined as a wage which not only brings relief from worry but provides a margin sufficient for recreation, self-improvement, spiritual uplift.

[When this happens,] there will disappear from the minds of the men of Hawaii the thought that the great enterprises of the islands are dependent for success upon successive waves of cheap, ignorant, illiterate, alien laborers who stick at their jobs only through fear of want and through inability to do anything else.[19]

However, the success of the territorial economy appeared to depend on exactly that kind of labor.

The issue of vocational education was controversial. Business leaders wanted schools to instill in children a desire to work in agriculture, so they generally supported vocational education. The survey recommended that "every junior and senior high school in the Territory should have nearby a well-stocked farm in charge of a practical, progressive, scientific farmer and his wife who herself should be an expert in all those matters properly falling within the field of the duties of a house wife on a farm."[20] The report would have required all children, no matter what their future plans, to spend some time each day on a farm.

Throughout the decade, various vocational education programs were instituted, modified, and dropped. In 1925, the Smith-Hughes Act was extended to the territory. It provided federal money for vocational education courses and was initially hailed as an important addition to the territorial education system. "However, introduction of this program met with prejudices of students, parents, and plantation interests. Both students and parents showed a reluctance toward training for agricultural work. In 1928 only six percent of the boys over 14 years of age were enrolled in vocational agriculture."[21]

The problem centered on the fact that the few skills necessary for cutting cane were not the same farming skills being taught by the vocational education teachers. They were teaching diversified farming—truck farming, orchards, animal husbandry. Floy Gay, in studying the situation, reached the following conclusions:

> Diversified farming was generally opposed by plantation interests in the early 1920's. Plantations held the best farming land and were able to realize a higher profit per acre than were those who farmed in a diversified way. It was not until the depression of 1929–34, and the Agricul-

tural Adjustment Administration Legislation in 1933, which limited the production of sugar, that agricultural leaders in the Territory began to give their support to diversified agriculture.[22]

As a member of the Commission for Education, Elsie Wilcox consistently supported the creation of vocational education programs, although this does not seem to have been as significant a concern to her as some other issues. Perhaps that was because she had a better view of the goals of the plantations and of the laborers' desires on behalf of their children and did not regard vocational education as a long-term solution to the needs of either group. The children wanted white-collar jobs, and plantation owners did not need many workers trained in the skills taught in vocational education classes.

The problems in vocational education raised another issue, which turned out to be divisive. Children were required to attend school through eighth grade. There was a precipitous decline in enrollment between eighth and ninth grades as a matter of school policy in order to reduce the number of students in high school. The goal was to cut costs and provide only enough high school graduates to fill the small number of white-collar jobs likely to be available in the foreseeable future.

The DPI wanted to extend the mandatory school attendance policy to the ninth grade so that more students would remain in school an extra year. They surveyed the schools to see what the effect of such an expansion would be and found that only about 25 percent of the students would stay in school the extra year, but 75 percent would stay if they could continue through high school.[23] A large proportion of students wanted the opportunity to graduate from high school.

Elsie Wilcox was supportive of the move to increase the number of high school students, and predictably, this put her at odds with most of her peers, who believed that "if boys are to be induced to go back to the plantations, they must be taken before they enter high school."[24] Or, as the supervising principal of rural Oʻahu wrote to the Superintendent of Public Instruction, "The plantation managers and lunas . . . in the main stand for the arbitrary cutting off of schooling at the eight or ninth grade."[25] At every opportunity, Wilcox voted in favor of expanding the schools and keeping students in school longer.

Another issue, but one where she was in sympathy with most of the non-Asian community, was what to do with the foreign-language schools. Starting about 1900, Japanese-, Korean-, Chinese-, and Portuguese-language schools were created with the goal of teaching the immigrant children the language and culture of their parents. This was similar to what the missionaries did when they created Punahou School to educate their children to American standards. The major debate about the foreign-language schools focused on the Japanese-language schools, probably because they had by far the largest enrollment and because of some of their policies. At first, the schools were run by Christian missionaries from Japan, but soon most were sponsored by Buddhist temples.

Several complaints about the schools arose. The additional two or three hours a day in school were wearing for young children. They went from Japanese-speaking homes to public schools, where few children spoke English as their first language, then to language school after the public school, and back home again to Japanese-speaking parents. How, under those circumstances, could the children learn English? What were they being taught in addition to Japanese language? There was great concern that Japanese values were being inculcated, particularly emperor worship. The one comprehensive study conducted of the schools' curriculum found that, with the exception of emperor worship, the values and behavior outlined as goals of the curriculum were very much like those of the public schools.[26] The concern remained, however.

In 1920, the territorial legislature passed comprehensive legislation regulating the schools and turning implementation of the regulations over to the DPI. The DPI mandated that all foreign-language schools be licensed and that all teachers take and pass an examination on American history and culture in English. The Japanese Counsel requested that the teachers be able to use an interpreter and retake the exams in five years in English. He estimated that 90 percent would fail if they had to take the exams in English at that time.[27] He argued strenuously that the purpose of the law was to regulate the schools, not abolish them, and that they would be extinct in a few years anyway. The commission decided that the teachers could have an interpreter for the American history and ideals of democracy part of the exam, but that they had to pass the English-language exam in English.[28]

In 1923, the DPI discovered that some teachers in the schools had not passed the examination. The DPI tried to close some of the schools and stop the teachers from teaching. The Japanese-language newspapers and the language schools took the DPI to court, and eventually, the schools won a complete victory in the United States Supreme Court, which declared all regulations of the language schools unconstitutional.[29]

In retrospect, the language school issue was an unnecessary debacle for the DPI. It created considerable ill will in the community on both sides of the question. A public school teacher commented in the 1920 survey:

> As the English language becomes the easiest means of communication, the Japanese language will give way as mist before the wind. Very few of the offspring of our present school population will learn two languages, and the surviving language will undoubtedly be English. It is far better to let the Japanese language die a natural death than to cause the friction necessary in killing it.[30]

She was correct. It is difficult to know what would have happened had World War II not occurred. However, it seems likely that even without the anti-Japanese stimulus of the war, the third generation would have learned English as its first language, and only those people having a particular interest in Japan would have learned Japanese. Elsie Wilcox initiated or seconded several of the proposals to limit and regulate the language schools.

Somewhat the reverse of the foreign-language school debate was the English standard school controversy. The English standard schools were begun because parents of children whose first language was English objected to their children being in classes where the large majority of children did not speak English as a first language. Many parents who could not afford to send their children to a private school feared that their children's progress would be hampered in such a situation. The 1920 survey had recommended that children be grouped according to ability in the English language. A subcommittee report, not published with the final survey, was more specific:

> Whenever the demand by parents who have been citizens of no other country than America is sufficient to justify it, establish schools of the same grade and kind as the Territory has established or shall establish for children of other peoples and restrict the attendance upon such schools to children of such American parents except as further provided herein.

Allow a reasonable percentage of the enrollment, perhaps 15 or 20 percent, to begin with, to be drawn from the various groups, having other national origins, living in the attendance district, the individuals to be selected on the basis of scholarship and facility in the use of the English language. No special school to be established in a given community, however, unless proper provision has been made for the giving of equal educational facilities to the children of all other racial groups living in that community.[31]

After much debate, this proposal was adopted by the DPI with the exception that admission was to be on the basis of a language examination, not on parental citizenship. Naturally, children whose parents spoke standard English would pass the exam, but the change left the door open for other children as well, not limited by the 15 to 20 percent quota.

From the beginning, the English standard school system generated debate. Proponents said that it was unfair to place children of parents whose native language was English in classrooms where the majority of children were learning English as a second language. These parents were taxpayers and deserved to have a public educational system that would not jeopardize their children's educational progress. This was probably the view of most of the English-speaking community, which included Caucasians from the United States and Great Britain and many Hawaiians and part-Hawaiians.

The only group to object to the DPI about the plan was the Portuguese, who, with good reason, feared that many of their children would not be able to pass the examination and would be kept in the district schools.[32] The Portuguese were in an unusual situation. Although elsewhere in the world they were classified as Caucasian, in Hawai'i most demographic studies included a separate category for them (and sometimes for Puerto Ricans and Spanish, too), with the remainder of the Caucasians being classified as "other Caucasian." On plantations, the Portuguese often occupied the lowest rung of the management classification, and some were laborers. They resented being classed with laborers from Asia, however, and wanted their children to be part of management, not part of the working class. Access to the English standard schools was important to these parents.

In addition to the Portuguese, there was always some opposition to the English standard schools from other groups, opposition that grew increasingly vocal during the 1940s and resulted in the gradual abolition of the system, starting in the late 1950s. Opponents had two major objections. First, given the goal of integrating second-generation children into American culture, it was counterproductive to keep them away from children who were already "Americanized." There was very little other opportunity for contact with "American" elements in the community except in the schools since churches, temples, and plantation camps were usually separated by language group. Second, opponents charged that the main reason parents wanted separate schools was that they did not want their children associating with children of different races. This was particularly true of the increasing number of people in the military and from the southern United States, who began coming to Hawai'i during these years.[33]

Wilcox was a strong supporter of the English standard schools.[34] Her position was perhaps contradictory. She was a follower of John Dewey and quoted him so often—"What the wisest and best parent wants for his child the whole community wants for all its children"— that the quotation appeared in her obituary.[35] Dewey, however, viewed the schools as the most important institution of upward mobility for all children through the interaction of various classes and races in the classroom. The Dewey quote seems unambiguous, but in the real life of Hawai'i in the 1920s, the competing needs of the English-speaking and non-English–speaking children were diametrically opposed, and accommodating both appeared impossible.

With the coming of the depression, the business community's opposition to spending for education increased. For example, E. E. Green, chairman of the education committee of the Chamber of Commerce and manager of Oahu Sugar, said in a public address, "The laudable desire to make the public school system, not simply an institution for mental training but a great center for intellectual, moral and social activity in the community, ministering to all the needs of childhood, is almost limitless in its possibilities for increasing the expenditures of the taxpayers' money."[36]

The Superintendent of Public Instruction, Will Crawford, replied that the extras Green criticized—child welfare, vocational training, dental hygiene, and nutrition—had been thrust on the schools because no other institution was willing to offer them, and the community thought they were necessary.[37] Teachers entered the fray by arguing that high schools should accept all children up to the age of eighteen, and they should "contribute definitely to insight and control in the whole range of their activities and interests, civic, domestic, health and others."[38]

The business community in 1931 responded by putting together another study of the schools, but this time the investigating group was controlled by the businessmen. They hired an outside expert, Charles Prosser, whose specialty was vocational education, and created their own study groups. The report of the Prosser committee, while acknowledging many legitimate educational needs, found the financial plight of the territory overwhelming and recommended against spending more money on education. It also said that the goals of the parents as expressed through the schools were in conflict with the reality of the agricultural-based economy. It suggested that the parents and teachers needed to change:

> Many parents seem to rely on the hope that by spending many years in school their children will automatically gain both high social and high economic standing. The Committee believes that these hopes of the schools and the parents have not been realized, and we see no grounds for the belief that they will be realized in the future. We feel that the continuation or expansion of such a scheme of schooling will lead great numbers of youth to build up ambitions and aspirations which are predestined to frustration.[39]

Just as the 1920 survey had been used by supporters of public education, so the Prosser Report was used by those who wanted to cut education spending. Not all businessmen were happy with the report, however. According to historian Edward Beechert, R. A. Cooke, as a representative of the sugar industry, thought it went in the wrong direction. "Clearly, what Cooke had in mind was to simply close down or scale down drastically the available schooling—not build a new system."[40]

Wilcox was outraged by the Prosser Report and said so publicly. She received many letters in response to her statements, one of the most impassioned from the minister at Central Union Church in Honolulu:

> I have repeatedly commended you in my mind in recent weeks for the valiant stand you have taken on educational affairs against what are evidently reactionary colleagues.... Thank heavens one persons [sic] dares to stand out from among them and contend for the basic rights of citizens.... This slashing of the educational budget while the other branches of politically rotten fruit are not pruned at all or very little is evidence of distorted thinking and stupid reaction to current needs.

> Those men better come alive from their feudalistic backwardness. They are not representative of liberal America.[41]

When Wilcox resigned from the Commission for Public Instruction to run for the territorial Senate, she was presented with a declaration titled "A Tribute," which said in part: "Because she has earnestly striven to see that every child in Hawaii has the encouragement to express in fullest measure the spirit within which is the final endowment of every human being; we the teachers of Kauai express our heartfelt Aloha." During the next decade, Elsie Wilcox spent much of her time in the territorial Senate trying to prevent implementation of the Prosser Report.

What You Do to the Least of These: Social Worker

By 1920, Elsie Wilcox was already established as *the* social worker on Kaua'i. She was disparaging of the idea, and in 1920, wrote to respected University of Hawaii sociologist Romanzo Adams that she was "entirely untrained in Social Work of any kind and [had] no gift for writing."[42] However, her correspondence and activities show that people on Kaua'i, in Honolulu, and later on the U.S. mainland regarded her as the leading person in the field on Kaua'i and a key person in Hawai'i. At the time, the field was not large. Wilcox's comment to Adams acknowledges the growing professionalism of social workers, but it was still possible to be accepted as a social worker because of one's practice and experience rather than formal training. In 1929, in part to remedy her lack of formal training, she enrolled in a social work correspondence course.

From the early years of the missionaries, much activity had taken place in the area that would later be called "social work:"

> The first institution created to help the needy in the Western style of charitable organization was the Seamen's Bethel founded in 1833 to assist sailors. Next came the Stranger's Friend Society in 1852, started by a group of women to give aid to the sick, destitute, and to strangers. In 1869 the YMCA was started in Honolulu to work with youth. The Hawaiian Humane Society was established in 1883 to give care to both animals and children.... Also in 1883 the Lunalilo Home was founded for poor, destitute Hawaiians, with preference being given to the eld-

erly. Then, in 1892 the Kindergarten and Children's Aid Association was created to provide kindergartens, health care and a home for dependent children.[43]

Generally, the plantations took care of their own. They had started doing this out of necessity. When plantations were first created in the rural areas, basic support services such as housing, water, food, or fuel often were not in place:

> The Hawaiian communities were able to provide these and other necessities for their members but were not organized to do so for large numbers of other people on a continuing cash or barter basis. The immigrants spoke no English or Hawaiian and were not prepared to fend for themselves in a rural environment in addition to working for the plantation.[44]

The paternalism of the plantations, begun as a necessity, continued both as a way of making plantation life attractive and as a form of social control. By the 1920s, many plantations were deeply involved in social work projects, providing health and child care classes for mothers, sponsoring interplantation athletic teams, building swimming pools and parks, holding dances and parties, plus building single-family houses for employees. This was not disinterested community building. Beechert found that following most labor disputes, conditions on the plantations improved significantly. He also agreed with a claim made later by the unions—that paternalism was a significant vehicle for control of the laborers. "Housing was ... converted into an instrument for labor control. Indeed, the absence of alternative housing made evicting a potent weapon."[45] In addition, as historian Ronald Takaki pointed out, earlier Japanese immigrants came from desperate circumstances. "Thousands of farmers lost their lands and hunger stalked many parts of the country."[46] Hawai'i was appealing, regardless of the circumstances of life for the plantation worker. Things had changed by the 1920s, and the plantations had to make an active effort to keep their workers.

Unemployment was low, and generally, at least on Kaua'i, the plantations did not abandon the ill, injured, widowed, or orphaned. On other islands, however, men were simply being let go when they were too old to work, and not everyone lived on the plantations. In addition, the plantations were unwilling to help their employees in some cases, especially where the cause of the problem seemed to be an individual's lack of morality. Thus, men with gambling debts or drinking problems and girls "in trouble" did not meet with much sympathy or receive much help.

In 1899, the Associated Charities were organized, out of which came the Child and Family Services, whose goals were to keep children from becoming paupers, to end begging, and to encourage self-reliance. Before the Associated Charities, no one in Hawai'i had developed an approach to take care of people in need. Families, churches, and wealthy individuals were the sources of whatever help people in need received. The problem was worst in Honolulu, where many people were in need for whom no one except the community at large had any responsibility.

In 1915, Margaret Bergen, head of the Associated Charities in Honolulu, went to Kaua'i and presented several lectures at the Mokihana Club and other groups on the role of the Associated Charities in Honolulu and what needed to be done on Kaua'i. Her visit propelled Elsie Wilcox into more activity in the social work area. Wilcox began providing information and advice to Bergen when people from Grove Farm ran into difficulties in Honolulu. She also worked with other agencies and individuals, including the Susanna Wesley Home for unwed pregnant girls, the prison on O'ahu, and attorneys for individuals in trouble. In addition, she was trying to address some more general problems on the plantation—maternal and child nutrition, recreation, English-language classes, and public health. She knew the workers and their families at Grove Farm. Through Mabel's Tuberculosis Association activities and her own work in the schools, she was acquainted with many people outside the plantation system, and she knew the managers of all the plantations on the island. The result of her particular position, her interest and concern for helping those in need, and her growing expertise, especially in the area of women's and children's problems, was that she became Bergen's contact on Kaua'i and her good friend.

As social work became more "professional," married women who had been involved in those kinds of activities found it more difficult to participate. Increasingly, during the 1920s single women took over the work, either volunteers like Wilcox or paid professionals like Bergen.[47] This trend appeared on the U.S. mainland as well.

In 1920, Grove Farm hired Estelle Roe as a professional social worker. She was young and enthusiastic. Elsie or Mabel wrote to her about Grove Farm when she was about to start working there:

There will be work helping the mothers and cooperating with the District Nurse in that line. At the big new camp, where the majority of the people live, there is a Day Nursery now run by a Japanese woman and run very poorly. That will have to be reformed. The building for it is nice and could be used for a sort of clubhouse for women and girls as well as for the nursery. A YWCA is now conducting a women's and girls' sewing-class and English class once a week. Adjoining is an open place for ball and other games, used by the young men, and a social hall for Movies, entertainment.[48]

A 1919 survey had found that plantations had widely ranging facilities and services for their workers. About Grove Farm the survey concluded, "This plantation had the newest and most elaborate village, Puhi Camp, as well as two camps almost unfit for habitation. ... As to activities in the category 'Group Life,' the report observed: 'There are none.' " The report acknowledged recreation and amusement at Puhi Camp, but nowhere else at Grove Farm.[49] This report was disturbing to the Wilcoxes; hence, the hiring of Estelle Roe.

Wilcox's sense of proportion set the tone for a letter she wrote to a woman in the Philippines who had supplied her with materials for the Filipino women at Grove Farm. Wilcox had already obtained a loom, and now she needed material for weaving and a "larger shuttle catted barkilla. I hope I have the above correct. My inexperience in these matters is terrific."[50] She was earnestly trying to find practical ways to help immigrant women plantation workers.

Attempts to deal with social problems on an individual basis throughout the territory were not working. Thus, during these years a move arose to institutionalize assistance and to create vehicles for people working in similar areas to meet, share ideas, and bring pressure to bear on plantations, other employers, and the legislature to solve the problems. As the *Garden Island* put it in a 1919 editorial, private charity could be sporadic, and the territory needed better organization for its welfare activities.[51]

On Kaua'i, a Child Welfare Association was formed in 1919, with Elsie a member of the board. It grew out of the Council for National Defense, which disbanded at the end of the war. By then its members had become interested in child welfare issues. At the territorial level, Wilcox was a member of the Child Welfare Committee and the Social Services Association. By 1921, she chaired the Social Services Association. That same year the social workers of Kaua'i formed their own organization, which Wilcox also chaired. Membership was open to people in charitable, philanthropic, institutional, and educational work. The organization set goals to develop cooperation among workers in various related endeavors, to act as a clearinghouse for information, and to develop community interest in the work.[52]

One of the major functions of the organizations was to organize conferences, and during these years Elsie Wilcox attended many, both on Kaua'i and in Honolulu. Her primary participation was in panels or sessions dealing with the issues of paramount concern to her: education, child welfare, rural life, and family relations.

In preparation for a 1924 conference, Wilcox and Bergen corresponded on one of the key questions facing social service agencies—how much should be provided to families that were unable to care for themselves? Bergen wrote Wilcox:

> Another topic would be on the ultimate purpose of the mother's pension;—is it physical, moral or character building? The school age of the children of the families is a good discussion. Should there be more distinction in the financial requirements of the families as to whether the man is in prison or incapacitated for other reasons from supporting his family?[53]

Ethel S. Baldwin wrote Elsie from Maui on the same subject:

> I guess we all have about the same kinds of problems to work out with our Child Welfare cases—such as what we should really call sufficient incomes to live on; how much we should allow an average family for out-side expenses (outside of food and house rent, for instance); whether or not a family that has a wee bit in the bank saved for a "rainy day" should receive help from us or not; should children under 15 ever be obliged to work to swell a family budget, and so on.[54]

Elsie Wilcox's handwritten notes made in preparation for the conference indicate the kinds of questions she was interested in addressing. How does the agency compute the amount of food a family needs—calorie, percent, quantitative, or unit basis? How much more should a family receive if there is a TB case—25 percent as in Oakland, 20 percent as in San Francisco, 10 percent as in Detroit, 20 percent as in New York City? Could people be taught about food values? Should they be taught how to make a budget? Would providing mothers an expense sheet for record keeping help? Are working mothers away from home too much?[55]

These seem to be straightforward questions that could be answered with factual information, but in fact they were explosive topics. In the case of trying to determine how much a family needed to live on when the male earner was unable to provide an income, the social workers had to determine what constituted a living income for a family. The business community was adamant that this should not be more than a person could earn by working either in the city or on a plantation, otherwise the incentive to work would be severely undermined. Other people felt that plantation wages were, in fact, not living wages. A 1926 report done for the HSPA concluded that wages were "bare subsistence wage. . . . The unwritten policy of the industry of a wage level beyond which it is undesirable to pass manifests a tacit acceptance for its workers of a standard of living far below American ideals."[56]

It was an old dilemma and one the 1920s did not solve. It was also one some people in the 1920s much preferred not to discuss at all. Bergen made that clear in her letter to Wilcox:

> Mr. Richard Cooke is much interested in the study of the budgets and if anyone discusses it, I should like to suggest him. This is a dangerous sort of subject to discuss, because you will get into a wage discussion. Someone will be sure to state that the plantations do not give sufficient wage to cover a living budget and I know that Mr. Cooke is studying this all the time in regard to wages. He may not want to discuss it in public.

Social workers were given a difficult task. In December 1921, Romanzo Adams told them that within six or seven years, Honolulu would have absorbed as many second-generation, white-collar workers as it could. Social work therefore had two aims: to make the workers happy with plantation work and to give them American ideals so that they would be motivated to better themselves. These goals were contradictory in the eyes of many of the laborers. In a 1927 speech, Adams explained why the Americans of Japanese Ancestry (AJA) youth did not like plantation work:

> Their reasons were fairly obvious: low wages, long hours, the burdensome character of the work, the lack of opportunity, racial discrimination in job assignment, mistreatment of workers by overseers, camp police, doctors, and, "in general, a type of plantation discipline which denies what the workers regard as a reasonable freedom."[57]

Overcoming these negative attitudes of the workers posed a tough assignment for social workers.

Child nutrition was another major concern for social workers and groups like the Mokihana Club. In fact, the Mokihana Club began a program to measure the growth of schoolchildren and to provide free milk to the schools. It found that the children of Japanese ancestry were generally underweight and underheight. Some people believed that the traditional Japanese diet, even in families with sufficient income, was relatively deficient in protein, and regarded education of the mothers as the key to improving the children's diet. Others observed that the Japanese were sending money back to their families in Japan, a practice severely criticized by those who said that they should be spending that money on food for their children. Whatever the reason, by American standards, some Japanese children were not getting adequate food.

Considerable irony marked the school milk program. The women who founded the Mokihana Club, and many of its members in the period when the school nutrition and other studies were performed, were affiliated through birth or marriage with owners or managers of the Kaua'i sugar plantations. Most children who were the subject of the survey were children of plantation laborers. Dr. W. R. P. Emerson, with some acerbity, put his finger on the heart of the matter in 1922 when he said that measuring and providing milk were helpful, but they did not get at the basic problem—children were living in poverty and they were living in poverty because their parents were not being paid enough.[58]

The same issue arose on the mainland. Mary Beard, discussing the problem of poor mothers working so long that they were unable to nurse their babies, said, "The question of poverty, that skeleton in every social closet, looms up here with an insistency that nothing will banish. No kind of philanthropy will solve the requirements of infant welfare when poverty or labor conditions are the root of the problem."[59] Establishing a minimum wage would have helped, but labor was not yet powerful enough to accomplish that, and even in much more progressive communities on the mainland, such direct governmental intervention in the economy faced strong opposition.

Other community organizations were also engaged in social work. The Salvation Army, for example, was for years the organization that helped unwed pregnant girls. In 1930, the home in Honolulu had thirteen girls and five babies. The minimum age of the mothers was thirteen. As Brigadier Layman of the Salvation Army wrote Wilcox, "Very few of these girls are really *bad girls,* only very weak, and we believe the training they receive in this Home, helps to strengthen them, to go out and face the world and make good."[60] An enclosed report observed that "In nearly every case, the girls who have been in the home were there through ignorance." Wilcox was on the board of the Kauaʻi Salvation Army and supported the Susanna Wesley Home in Honolulu generously.

Elsie Wilcox threw herself into these activities with enthusiasm. She conducted studies, wrote reports, chaired panels, and gave papers. She was at home with the professionals—social workers, university professors, physicians, nurses. She was accepted because she had three characteristics: she was genuinely interested in the goals of the organizations, she was very good at what she did, and she had easy access to the people who could make real changes—the men who ran the territorial political and economic systems.

The changes, however, were slow in coming and incremental. For all her concern, Wilcox did not propose radical changes in the economic system. She no doubt wrestled with a considerable amount of conflict over the situation. On the one hand, she was working full time to improve the situation of women and children in poverty. On the other hand, she was the direct beneficiary of the status quo. Although this has been the case throughout the history of reform movements, it did not lessen Wilcox's dilemma.

Let Not Thy Left Hand Know: Charity

Elsie Wilcox continued the family's charitable activities. She was usually supporting or contributing to the support of about a dozen people outside the family. Although she did this without fanfare, and privately, her generosity was well known. She received more requests for help than she was able or willing to meet, and her criteria for accepting or rejecting the requests were fairly straightforward. In general, she helped people from Kauaʻi, with a special regard for people who worked at Grove Farm.

Children were her first priority. Over the years, she and Mabel paid for the education of perhaps fifty young people, some through high school and others through college as well. Charles Fern, longtime editor of the *Garden Island,* said of the sisters' interest in students: "Nobody knows how many people Elsie and Mabel sent to college. I know of two or three I got them to send.... They were very discreet about it. They never publicized it. They had two qualifications. One was ability and the other was lack of funds."[61]

The students went to many different schools, mainly in Honolulu, since there were no private schools on Kauaʻi. They included The Priory, Mid-Pacific, Kamehameha, the Normal School, the University of Hawaii, colleges on the mainland, and, in one case, a medical school in China.

Elsie Wilcox was the legal guardian of several orphaned children. Even when she was not legally responsible for the children she supported, she took a deep interest in them. She wanted them to succeed in whatever course of study they had chosen. She paid for eyeglasses, doctor bills, and, for a student who contracted tuberculosis, a prolonged hospital stay. She sent them birthday cards and Christmas presents. She corresponded regularly with some of them for years, telling them about events on Kauaʻi and following their progress. When they completed their study, she was usually able to help them find jobs. This was not always easy, however. In 1930, Henry Tanaka wrote her from the U.S. mainland thanking her for helping him. She had asked him what he wanted to do, and he said he was thinking carefully about his future:

> As to radio, I do not believe at the present time, that on the mainland an Oriental has just a [sic] good a chance as a white man. I hate to bring up this racial matter, but we must be frank and discuss the actual conditions which exist. A great number of Japanese boys who took up electricity and made a good showing at school have not been able to secure electrical positions here in the states.[62]

Eventually, Tanaka decided to take up radio and attended the RCA Institute in Philadelphia. There followed a typewritten letter with the signature in pen in Japanese:

> As a [sic] mother of Henry Tanaka, and in whose behalf I am writing you, I wish to thank you for sending him a postal money order. Nevertheless, you have helped him a great deal and I am very grateful towards you.... Henry's success in his later life depends wholly on the splendid support you have given him and I cannot help but think that way.[63]

Sometimes the help was in the form of a gift; often it was a loan, which she forgave when some of the loan had been repaid.

In 1930, she wrote the principal of The Priory regarding two recently orphaned sisters for whom she was guardian:

> [The girls] have written home of some concern regarding their work at the Priory and I therefore write to make a few enquiries. Hilary is concerned because she can get no Science with you. She had hoped to take Chemistry. She says that Latin and French are requisite for graduation and she has had none of the former and cannot make up the amount in one year's time. We are anxious that she should graduate there as she would have here in the local High School. Is it not possible to make some adjustment for her? I believe that Latin is of very little value to our island girls, anyhow, and with the modern freedom in curriculum could she not substitute something else? For Alice, who is only a Junior, adjustments are not so hard. She is disappointed in finding no commercial work, which I think your list mentions.[64]

She rarely criticized the students, even when they let themselves and her down, but on occasion she criticized the schools. She chastised the principal of Mid-Pacific for making a student work during the school year when she was paying for his room, board, and tuition. When she received a request for $25 from a student who was graduating from Kamehameha, she enclosed it with a letter to the principal deploring the poor English. The principal wrote back that he had passed it on to the student's English teacher.

She did not restrict her help to students only. Several of the people she supported were young pregnant girls whom she sent to the Susanna Wesley Home in Honolulu. In a couple of instances, she evidently accomplished this with a court order because the father of the child was the girl's own father. Usually, however, the family asked her to help and she did. After the baby was born, she sometimes got the girl a job on Kaua'i or in Honolulu if she could. She did not respond positively to every appeal, however. A well-known Kaua'i politician wrote asking her for money to help his pregnant daughter. Wilcox replied that this was the responsibility of the father of the baby, and the politician should enforce that responsibility rather than appealing to someone outside the family.

In addition to children, Elsie Wilcox supported or assisted several women. How they all came to her attention is unknown—some were from Kauaʻi, and most had been widowed or deserted. Generally, the assistance was for a specific problem. For instance, she took over payment of doctor and hospital bills, occasionally anonymously. She tracked down legal and financial advice about mortgages and investments. As with the students, she also remembered birthdays and Christmas with a note and a gift. She was a remarkably kind as well as generous person.

Again, however, she did not respond positively to every request. She received a plea for money from a woman she had met in the Philippines some years earlier that she turned down, but even then she provided a measure of help. The woman closed her letter outlining her husband's desertion after taking her money, "I am frightened, Miss Wilcox, terribly frightened. God will bless you as one of his angels of mercy if you can help me and my little girl with this money and I shall be your servant for time and eternity." Wilcox wrote to Nell Findley at the Associated Charities in Honolulu asking what to do, and on Findley's advice wrote to the Portland Public Welfare Bureau enclosing a copy of the letter and stating, "This is the first and only communication I have had with her. I have no responsibility in the case, but the woman does need her affairs straightened out, I am sure and I hope you can help her."[65] She also wrote the woman, telling her not "to become panic stricken. Other women have been in similar positions and have worked their way through. It seems to me that it is not money that you need, so much as help and advice and there are people and organizations whose business it is to help those in trouble such as yours." She gave her the name of the Welfare Bureau director and urged her not to be discouraged. The woman evidently thought money would have been more helpful, because there is no acknowledgment of Wilcox's letter and no further correspondence in the file.

In addition to young people and women, a third group of people, much smaller than the preceding two, who received financial assistance from Elsie Wilcox were individuals who showed particular promise. These included Japanese, Chinese, and Hawaiian ministers and artists. She arranged for the pastor of Kawaiahaʻo Church, a Hawaiian church in Honolulu, to spend a year on the mainland for study and rest and recuperation. Of special interest is Isami Doi, who later became a well-known artist. Wilcox regularly sent Doi and his wife money while they were living in New York City and he was trying to establish himself in the art world. Mrs. Doi wrote thanking

Elsie and added, "Isami does not have any work now. He goes looking around for work and I pity him coming back looking weary and yet not discouraged."⁶⁶

Your Home Shall Be My Home: Americanization

Elsie Wilcox cared passionately about Kaua'i and Hawai'i. This explains in part her wholehearted participation in the Americanization movement. The Americanization movement had special appeal for her because it combined working with young people and the field of education, both of which she enjoyed. She was not nearly as wed to the status quo as many of her contemporaries, but she valued the basic structure of the society and saw a severe threat to it in the demographic changes that were in progress. The laborers from Asia brought "foreign" cultures, which they passed on to their children. This was part of the reason Wilcox opposed foreign-language schools. She and other Americanizers felt it was crucial to give the children American cultural values.

In an excellent history of the first- and second-generation Japanese in Hawai'i, Eileen Tamura discussed Americanization, acculturation, and assimilation. She found that "During the first three decades of the twentieth century the term *assimilation* was used rather than *acculturation*. Further, *assimilation* was used interchangeably with *Americanization* to refer to what historians and sociologists now call Anglo-conformity."⁶⁷ Most people in Hawai'i used the term *Americanization* to refer to a variety of activities that, interestingly, sometimes had contradictory goals. Tamura criticized the Americanizers, claiming that on the one hand, they wanted the second generation to adopt American ways, while on the other hand, they structured the society so that it was closed to the legitimate aspirations of the second generation under the American system. Elsie Wilcox seems to be an exception to Tamura's findings, as were some of Wilcox's friends and colleagues in various agencies working on Americanization issues.

Americanizers in Hawai'i were following a path similar to what was occurring on the mainland. They viewed language, culture, and customs as keys to fitting newcomers into the American mainstream. Various groups, ranging from the Daughters of the American Revolution through the General Federation of Women's Clubs to unions and employers, sought to help or force immigrants to become "Americanized."[68] On the mainland, this often included encouraging them to vote. That was not the case in Hawai'i, because when the large immigration from Japan was under way, first-generation Japanese were ineligible for U.S. citizenship.

A series of strikes further stimulated the Americanization movement in Hawai'i during these years. The strikes were generally race based, and the overt appeal to racial groupings was in some ways disturbing to the Caucasian and Hawaiian leadership, even though the centrality of race resulted in a splintering of the labor movement because the various groups had a hard time getting together.

Elsie Wilcox's activities are so intertwined that it is artificial to divide them into categories, and certainly she did not. For some of the people who were helped, her social work provided an easing into the local way of life. Wilcox's church activities included much that was specifically Americanizing and labeled as such. The YMCA (Young Men's Christian Association) and YWCA (Young Women's Christian Association), however, were the leading Americanization vehicles, and Wilcox gave a considerable amount of time and money to the Kaua'i and Honolulu YMCA and YWCA. In 1921, she founded the YWCA on Kaua'i and served as its president for five years.[69]

In 1925, her friend Lloyd Killam, the YMCA secretary in Honolulu, wrote asking if she would endorse the Y's work, which focused mainly on second-generation young men. He indicated that he was under pressure from businessmen in Honolulu to do more and that her support of the Y's work would be helpful:

> Your endorsement of this work means a great deal more than the money involved. We constantly have the feeling that businessmen like Galt, Dillingham, and Mr. Al Castle want to see what they call "concrete results." The work that we do with these students is absolutely indefinite and difficult to report to them. I believe, however, that it is among the most important that we are doing and it will surely bring valuable results for the future of Hawaii.[70]

In response, Elsie wrote a piece that appeared in a small pamphlet titled "Endorsements of County YMCA Work in the Territory of Hawaii":

> I consider the Young Men's Christian Association one of the best assets in Welfare Work which Kauai has. Next to the public schools it reaches

more boys and young men than any other organization. Its programs, worked out through years of experience in the islands and elsewhere meet the real needs and interests of our boys. So well rounded is it, emphasizing all sides of personal development, that every youth has a chance, not only the athletic boy, but the boy with intellectual interests, the boy with character which denotes him as natural leader, the socially minded boy. All find opportunity for character development under the YMCA. It presents a wholesome attitude toward life, responsibility, and happiness in the pleasant activity of daily life. So far, the YMCA seems to offer the best training in morals which our generation has produced in both its group and individual types of work. It is simple and direct in method and in the ideals it presents to young manhood. When we bear in mind that "it is among the young that the issues of the future are decided," any effort we can make to produce their welfare is well worthwhile.

Elsie Wilcox respected expertise, and in 1919, when the Americanization movement was at its height, she went to Honolulu to learn what she could about dealing with the problems of immigrants and the young second generation. She spent about a week there talking with people at the YWCA and observing their programs, and when she returned to Kauaʻi, she brought with her the women who were running the programs for the YWCA in Honolulu. She invited them to meet with interested people on Kauaʻi, and they gave talks to the Mokihana Club and school groups as they helped set up YWCA programs on Kauaʻi.

During the following years, Wilcox served the YWCA on Kauaʻi as president and in other offices. She entered into the real activity of the Y with the girls. Much of the process was learning by doing. The principal of Kauai High School had lamented the fact that students declined invitations to private homes because they were not used to Western-style food and social manners.[71] Wilcox and her YWCA and Mokihana Club cohorts gave many parties for the young men and women and the children, to make them feel part of the community and help them become more at ease in Western social settings. They gave Christmas, Valentine, and Halloween parties, and sometimes they gave a party for no particular occasion. Camping was another activity that lent itself to helping the students learn American songs, dances, and games. Wilcox enjoyed camping and on several occasions was a camp leader with the YWCA. She was the person who urged the

YWCA to purchase Camp Wahiawa on Kaua'i, and she contributed generously to the camp as she did to other Y programs.

One of the personal benefits of the work she performed as a "professional volunteer" was the chance it gave her to spend time and become friends with people outside her immediate social circle. An example was Neil Locke, who came to take over the YMCA work on Kaua'i in 1921. The Y was in sad financial and organizational straits, and Locke set about with vigor and enterprising creativity to resurrect it. He was very successful, especially with the second-generation plantation children, who responded enthusiastically to his exuberant leadership. Membership increased and, as was often the case, success brought him to the attention of the Y leaders in Honolulu, and he was lured away. Elsie Wilcox missed him. He was not intimidated by her, and they shared a dry wit and similar views on many matters of the day. Their letters to each other are those of close friends. In 1925, she wrote and asked him to visit Kaua'i:

> When you left Kauai it was with the express understanding that you would return at stated intervals to look after our moral progress. No excuses from Oahu will be acceptable for we know you have lots of extra young secretaries tucked away there who need to be on *extra* work. That is a real country attitude, isn't it? Anyway, it will do us all good to have you come down and cast an eye again on our merits and defects.[72]

She was also good friends with Grace Channon, the executive secretary of the YWCA in Honolulu. Wilcox did not suffer fools gladly, and she had an understanding of the situation of working girls and young women equaled by few of her peers. She was also willing to take on the male establishment when necessary. A good example of this involved the Honolulu YWCA. In 1921, Frank Atherton had offered to trade the half acre of land owned by the YWCA in the center of downtown for 2 acres on Alapa'i Street, about a mile from the city center. Miss Channon was very much opposed to the idea, but several of her board members (mainly wealthy women) supported it. Channon wrote Wilcox for help, and Wilcox wrote back a letter meant for wide circulation:

> I am quite surprised to hear that the Alapai Street property is even considered for the new Y building. Certainly if some of your good Board members would discard their automobiles for a short time and foot it

around town in hot weather, they would soon have no taste for the walk out there and back at the noon-hour. I *walk* when I am in town and know whereof I speak. Tired shop and office girls will be much less inclined to do it than are we who are less occupied. If you want to ruin your business, move out and let some other organization come into town and do your work for you. I thought the site was out of the question before Fernhurst was built, even. Why revive it?[73]

She spent more time with the girls, but she was also concerned about the young men and the women. Worried about the growing alienation between some of the second generation and their parents, she encouraged the Y to start English-language and other classes at night for mothers. She was disturbed by the increasing gap between parents and children, as the required public education inevitably led the children down paths their parents had a difficult time understanding and in some cases did not like at all.

A problem on the neighbor islands was how students outside the main town, where the only public high school was located, could continue their education after eighth grade. One of the significant projects of the YWCA on Kaua'i was to establish a home in Līhu'e, with a housemother, for those girls. Elsie Wilcox wrote the Reverend Norman Schenck, secretary of the board of the HEA, stating specifications for the housemother as the YWCA started the home:

> This must be someone not too old, not too young, the former better than the latter, for the position will be even more confining than Miss Johnson's [a woman who ran a boarding school at Lihue Japanese Church for "Oriental boys"].... I do hope we can secure someone who will make a happy and well regulated home for the girls and also be of value to our general community life.[74]

In 1920, Elsie Wilcox wrote to Charles Loomis at the Honolulu YMCA suggesting that he start a newsletter for Filipino youth. He replied that he had been thinking about the same idea.[75] Loomis evidently pursued the proposal but ran into stumbling blocks because of funding. Lloyd Killam wrote Wilcox about the problem in December that year:

> The influence of such a paper as it touches the schools, churches and future industrial life on the Islands would certainly justify the Board of Education, the Hawaiian Board and the plantation agencies in making

its publication possible. There is some question, however, as to whether we could ever get them to provide the finances unless the paper were under their direct control. We feel that the present generation of boys need high Christian ideals presented to them from the Association's point of view. We question whether a church paper as such will fill the need and also whether a paper largely subsidized by the corporations will be just what is needed. We feel that the boys need ideals presented to them which, while the corporations would not oppose them, are not advanced enough in their thinking to pay for them.[76]

The plan was eventually dropped.

In 1926, Locke wrote to her about an idea proposed by the YMCA worker on Kaua'i. The plan was to bring a man from Japan to be trained in working with country youth and return to Japan. Locke explained the proposal:

When you were in the Orient you may have sensed as we have from nearly every passer thru that the time has passed when foreign leadership will be recognized as it has been. If this be true, our biggest contribution can be made in training workers here in Hawaii where racial and organizational conditions are so favorable, and in doing this we will realize quicker and more effective results than could possibly be secured by sending our own folk.[77]

Wilcox agreed readily to the idea, and Noboru Kubo came to Hawai'i for many months, part of the time on Kaua'i and part in Honolulu. In addition to paying for his passage to Hawai'i, Wilcox also provided the funds for sending him to California for further training. She wrote Locke at the YMCA that Mr. Kubo's "English is so good and his spirit so modest and sweet I think he is going to make a real contribution to the work among the Japanese here as well as gaining knowledge for himself."[78] Locke wrote with high hope in response:

I believe this initial experiment in training men from other countries is going to lead to a larger out-reach, after we have demonstrated the possibilities for men coming from other countries bordering the Pacific. Others will be sent and we can add our small bit to the efforts of other institutions that are trying to bring friendly relationships among the people of the Pacific.[79]

She visited Kubo when he became ill, and he wrote, thanking her for the visit, "I shall never forget Kauai, it has taught me many things."[80]

Wilcox rarely used sharp words in her correspondence, even when she might have been annoyed. An exception was her response to what she viewed as interference with a highly valued YWCA worker on Kauaʻi who worked with Filipino girls. On September 16, 1926, Norman Schenck at the HEA—someone Wilcox knew well—wrote to Edith Hansen, secretary of the YWCA in Līhuʻe, castigating her for hiring the wife of one of the HEA's Kauaʻi ministers:

> Mrs. Cortezon was here this morning, and told me that she had been engaged by the YWCA on Kauai to work for them four days of the week. I am very much bothered to learn of this arrangement because I think it is especially important for Mrs. Cortezon to confine here [sic] activities to Koloa. I wish you had given me a chance to explain this to you before any final arrangements were made with her. But inasmuch as this has not been done, I beg of you to keep searching for a permanent worker, and to regard Mrs. Cortezon's services as temporary only.[81]

This might have been intended to squelch Miss Hansen, but Wilcox, a member of the YWCA board of directors, blistered back at Schenck:

> We had been somewhat surprised by the tone of your letter to Miss Hansen, and thereby indirectly to the Kauai County YWCA committee, regarding the employment of Mrs. Courtezan by our Board. [Wilcox and Schenck spelled the name differently.] I understand that the Hawaiian Board is paying Mrs. Courtezan no salary and has no claim on her other that [sic] that which any church or community has upon the wife of its pastor. The day has long since gone when a woman was so much a part of her husband that she could not establish a separate individuality—and vice versa....
>
> As you know, it is almost impossible to secure good Filipino workers. We must use what is available, and it seems far and away the best thing for Mrs. Courtezan, who is a fine influence, to extend her work as far as possible. If we could easily secure someone else, you might have some argument to present, but you know from your own experience that work among the Filipinos advances slowly because of our lack of trained people speaking their languages. At present Mrs. Courtezan's

work is all planned for her, the backing of Plantation managers secured, etc., and we cannot withdraw without great detriment to the respect in which our work is held. Also, I think we ought not to withdraw when I consider the work to be done. This will be a great aid and blessing in your own Filipino work and you ought to thank the Lord that he has granted you a bit of organizing ability in Miss Edith Hansen, free gratis, by the way, to get in back of some of your work. When you come to Kauai we shall be glad to talk this over with you. For the present we must continue as we are, and I beg you not to intimidate our worker.[82]

Wilcox and Hansen had been working hard against difficult odds to reach young Filipino women, and Wilcox did not intend to lose a worker who not only spoke their language and English but was an experienced nurse as well. The Wilcox family's association with Mrs. Courtezan continued for years after she left the YWCA because she became a public health nurse and worked with Mabel Wilcox in TB and maternity activities.

Toward the end of this time, the YMCA's efforts were showing success. Neil Locke wrote Elsie in 1926 that his boys had won all the elective offices in Honolulu's McKinley High School elections, an indication of the boys' organization, cooperation, and hard work.[83] As the people who were teens in the period 1915–1920 became young adults, they continued their support of the YMCA, and Elsie Wilcox wrote Paul Marvin, executive secretary of the Nuuanu YMCA, with some relief:

> It is most encouraging to find that the Oriental students who have had so much done for them by the YM and YW are responding to the extent of taking on some of the responsibility for the work, by both personal service and financial aid. It looks as if we have reached the "second mile" and should go ahead now at an increased pace.[84]

In May 1930, the YMCA fired Neil Locke. According to a letter from U. Watada, Locke and the general secretary, Merle Scott, had a personality clash, and Scott had asked the board to fire Locke for being too aggressive. The board had done so, giving Locke six days' notice and six months' leave of absence.[85] Watada was a Locke supporter, as was Wilcox. Time passed, and in September, Wilcox received a letter from Scott inquiring about the Wilcox family pledges to the Y, which by that time were overdue.[86] She wrote back:

One sometime wonders what to say when an organization throws out one's friends whom one knows to be invaluable in its work. Reiterations of claims of greater efficiency do not make up in any way for one's disappointment, regret and shame that such things can happen in a Christian organization. I am slow to condemn or criticize, but we have held off our money to show in some degree what our feeling toward your organization now is. Today I send you the amount pledged but I cannot give any assurance of a return of this amount for next year. We have lots of work to do down here, too, on this little island of Kauai and perhaps our money should go here.[87]

She continued to support the Y but at a reduced amount.

One of the most interesting people Wilcox came into close contact with through her Americanization efforts was Takie Okamura, minister of Makiki Christian Church in Honolulu. Okamura had converted to Christianity as a young man in Japan. After a visit to Honolulu, appalled by the miserable physical, moral, and spiritual conditions of his fellow countrymen in Honolulu and on the plantations, he gave up a career in Japan and moved to Honolulu to minister among the Japanese laborers. Okamura was the leading spokesperson in the Japanese community for the Americanization of the Japanese youth. Although he was attacked by some segments of the Japanese press for his position, he was adamant that the second generation, and, as much as possible, the first generation, should learn American ways if they were going to be successful in Hawai'i. He wanted young people to learn English, do well in school, continue their education as far as they could, and move into the mainstream of life in Hawai'i, not remain on the fringes as their parents had. His own children did just that. All of them became professionals, including his daughters, several of whom were teachers and the rest nurses. While women in Japan at that time were still struggling for the right to college education, Okamura believed that Japanese American girls as well as boys needed to be encouraged to educate themselves for work and to be able to function effectively in the society where they were going to live. Thus, one of the projects for which he asked and received Wilcox support was a home for Japanese American girls at the Normal School in Honolulu. The house would provide a place for girls who lived in rural O'ahu or on the neighbor islands, so they would not be denied the opportunity to become teachers just because they had nowhere to live while they were attending school.

Like the YMCA and YWCA Americanizers, Okamura believed that teaching American culture had to include converting the young people to Christianity. This put him at odds with a large part of the Buddhist community, some of whom seemed to view him as a traitor. As he wrote Wilcox in 1919, however, his position was firm:

> Americanization is now being pushed forth with great force. But I have come to feel that Americanization apart from Christianization is useless. We must Christianize and Americanize the girls who are to be the teachers and future mothers in Hawaii. If not we will surely hamper the future of Japanese as citizens.
>
> We can not expect the girls placed under the care or influence of [a] Buddhist temple to be the real influence in Americanizing the Japanese.[88]

He remained convinced and was successful in converting large numbers of Japanese to Christianity.

Okamura was by all accounts a dynamic, persuasive man. He convinced the Caucasian leaders of the HEA to let him build Makiki Christian Church, modeled after Kochi Castle in Japan, and raised hundreds of thousands of dollars, primarily from the Caucasian community, to build it; he raised more money, this time from the Japanese, to build the Japanese Hospital, later Kuakini Medical Center; he started homes for girls and ran a dormitory for boys.

He and Elsie Wilcox became good friends, although how this came about is uncertain, since, as his youngest son pointed out some sixty years later in an interview, Okamura spoke almost no English.[89] His oldest son, Umetaro, often traveled with him, acting as his interpreter and on occasion also serving as his secretary. Probably part of the reason Wilcox and Okamura got along so well was that they shared a common set of values, and in many ways, he was in a better position to encourage Americanization than she was.

Over the years, Wilcox not only gave thousands of dollars to Okamura's various endeavors but also attended and supported the New Americans conventions he held annually. These were large convocations for second-generation teens and young adults where various business and political leaders addressed the group and then met more informally with them in smaller sessions. Okamura wanted to provide a means by which the young Japanese could meet some of the leading figures in the community, and those leaders could talk with the young people. There was a gulf between the two groups, and the conventions were one of the few opportunities for them to meet.

Some commentators, including Eileen Tamura, had a negative view of Okamura. Tamura portrayed him as something of an elitist because, she claimed, he believed second-generation Japanese should stay on the plantations, yet he educated his own children to become professionals.[90]

By 1922, people were already beginning to question the advisability of so much emphasis on Americanization. In November, Wilcox wrote Clinton Childs, chair of the Program Committee of the Conference of Social Workers, regarding the program for the upcoming conference: "The best response has come from Rev. R. G. Hall of Koloa who feels that we should discuss the problem of Assimilation [Americanization]. He thinks that our attitude is wrong and that we are overemphasizing the subject. He has discussed the subject with Professor Romanzo Adams who agrees with him."[91] Americanization faded as a concern by the end of the decade.

Peace Be with You: Internationalism

An ardent internationalist, Elsie Wilcox invested considerable time and money supporting various organizations whose goals were to bring people from different countries together in pursuit of world understanding and peace. Her interest developed out of her visits to and correspondence with Christian missionaries in Asia. The trip she, Mabel, and G.N. had taken in 1907 made a lasting impression on her.

She went to Asia again in 1926 with Nell Findley and members of the Institute of Pacific Relations (IPR) and met many more people with whom she kept in contact until World War II disrupted her correspondence. It was a working vacation. She wrote C. F. Loomis, "Since our interest was mainly in comparing Hawaiian and Philippine conditions and in becoming acquainted with the sources of our Hawaiian/Filipino labor supply, we spent most of our time in the provinces."[92] They also went to Hong Kong, Canton, Shanghai, and Peking. Wilcox was especially impressed with the mass education movement in China and wrote its director, "I am thrilled when I think of it all and realize that it is one of the great world movements. What it will do for China, socially and economically, is immense. And to the Christian cause, as I have gathered from my friends on the American

Board, it is giving a new way to work and a new hope for usefulness."[93] Subsequently, she supported it and many other church organizations she visited in China. She was convinced that missionary work in Asia would help secure peace for the region and the world.

Her internationalist interest soon expanded beyond the missions, and during the 1920s, she was actively involved with the Pan Pacific Union (PPU), the IPR, and the Pan Pacific Women's Association. The PPU was founded in 1917 with the goal of bringing "all nations and peoples about the Pacific Ocean into closer friendly commercial contact and relationship." The IPR was created in 1925 as a vehicle for private individuals to engage in the "study of economic, educational, social, political, moral and religious conditions with a view to their improvement."[94] In 1927, she was elected to the executive council of the IPR. A strong believer in education as the solution to most problems, Wilcox embraced both organizations, contributed to them, served on committees, planned meetings, and provided contacts with her increasingly large number of friends and colleagues in Asia.

The Pan Pacific Women's Association grew out of the PPU. Its goals were similar to the other two organizations'—to promote understanding and, through understanding, peace. It sponsored several large conferences, including one in 1928 where Jane Addams was the main speaker. Wilcox hosted that and several other conferences. When asked to host one in 1930, she wrote back saying she would not be able to attend but sent money to cover the expenses of five delegates. She was one of the organizers of a YMCA Pan Pacific Conference in 1923, and she was a member of the National Council for the Prevention of War for many years.

Her stature with the internationalists was captured in a letter sent from the director of the PPU, A. H. Ford, to Wilcox in 1928: "My Dear Miss Wilcox: For you to ask is to command and I of course will at once refer your letter to Miss Hinder with the suggestion that she make the trip."[95]

This Is My Father's House: Religion

Elsie Wilcox was intimately involved with the operation of Lihue Union Church. She continued her Sunday school teaching and also conducted classes for Sunday school teachers. She acted as a mentor for at least one young woman, who then transferred the work she had done with Wilcox to the Honolulu Bible Training School for credit. She had a close relationship with the pastors and their wives, taking them to meet people when they first arrived and looking after their needs, particularly in regard to housing. She held various offices in the church and was usually on the church board of directors. She also held positions of one kind or another with the Kauai Evangelical Association (KEA). Because of her special interests, she gave most of her attention to the KEA's Americanization and education efforts. She chaired the KEA education committee and worked hard trying to update and strengthen the curriculum for the Sunday school teachers. The KEA included churches for congregations who spoke English, Hawaiian, Chinese, Japanese, Tagalog, Ilocano, Korean, and Okinawan. With such a diverse ethnic and language population in the KEA, developing the curriculum was no easy task. On several occasions, she turned to the Methodists and to the HEA in Honolulu for help in obtaining appropriate materials.

Wilcox became more and more involved with the workings of the HEA and traveled often to Honolulu for meetings. She was a member of the board of directors—the policy-making group of the HEA—and she was secretary-treasurer for a time. Most important, she was an advisor to the general secretary and other ministers about conditions on Kauaʻi. Her correspondence contains several blunt letters where she exchanged ideas on how to handle delicate problems in the Kauaʻi churches. The letters tell of race and generational problems. In 1929, she wrote to the minister at Central Union Church in Honolulu:

> The problem . . . is similar to those met with in other country communities on the islands where a Japanese-born minister of the old school has built up his church among older people, using the Japanese language and methods of a generation ago in Japan, and now finds himself confronted with a group of young people who want English used, who want the church to keep step with modern recreation, social life, etc., and who will not conform nor submit themselves to authority as represented by the minister and older members of the church. They are not interested and it is beyond the minister's power to interest or hold them, and he can't see why, and blames other organizations because they are giving the boys and girls what they want, or at least trying to do so. This has the elements of tragedy in it, hasn't it!

She suggested hiring young assistant ministers but urged that they be protected, or "the older ones will snuff them out like the Hawaiians had done until just recently."96

Although her primary concern was for the Congregational churches, she helped other denominations as well. She gave money to the Reverend P. T. Fukao of the Methodist Trinity Mission in response to his request for help in bringing his daughter and mother-in-law to Hawai'i from Japan. She became a good friend of the Episcopal bishop, Joseph Restarick, in part because her mother and Etta were Episcopalians, but mainly because she and Restarick had many interests in common. They shared long discussions about religion, history, politics, and Hawaiiana when he stayed with the Wilcoxes during his visits to Kaua'i. Even after he had left Hawai'i, they remained in close communication.

A certain amount of rivalry marked all the organizations Wilcox worked with, an unfortunate situation given the fact that there was more than enough for everyone to do. In January 1924, she wrote a long letter to Brigadier Bourne of the Salvation Army in Honolulu suggesting that the Army, the Y, and the church combine their forces at Puhi Camp at Grove Farm rather than duplicating each others' efforts. As she put it, "Both schools [the Salvation Army and the Sunday school] have been very disorganized, undermanned and underequipped."97

The Salvation Army's Major Coe replied and said they would try, although reluctantly:

> Take Koloa for instance, it looks as if certain interests would desire to crowd us out entirely—after 30 years of self-sacrificing work on the part of our officers.
>
> Again, at Lihue where nothing was being done as you say for the Filipinos—Capt. Haan took hold and has accomplished wonders, now I understand a worker has been appointed who will of course reap the benefit of Capt. Haan's work, when the Army could handle the situation alright.
>
> However, the Salvation Army is concerned about the salvation of young and old and if this plan works out we will be as pleased as any other interests.98

Wilcox was a member of the board of directors of all four organizations—the Salvation Army, the YWCA, the YMCA, and the Kauai

Sunday School Association. She tended to become the court of appeal in jurisdictional disputes.

Elsie Wilcox in the 1920s

Elsie Wilcox had matured into a leading figure in most of the territorial institutions that dealt with women, children, religion, social welfare, and Americanization. Her private life reflected her changed circumstances. Marriage for her was unlikely. Nor was she going to pursue the life of leisure her means could have provided.

This was not entirely unusual. A few women on the U.S. mainland lived similar lives during these years. Jane Addams is perhaps the best known, but many communities had single women whose lives focused on service to other people. As scholars have observed, for women who were intent on stepping outside the family circle, the issues with which Wilcox became identified in the 1920s were relatively acceptable.[99] Children, teens, women, and the "betterment of the community" fit comfortably within the context of the extended family.

By the end of the decade, Wilcox was working full time in her role of community volunteer. She had defined her vision for Kaua'i. She wanted a Christian, Americanized community with shared values and beliefs. Although her means were different, her goals were not far removed from those of her grandparents. She was convinced that if the second generation of immigrants was not Americanized, the territory would undergo tremendous, negative changes when they became adults. She believed strongly in the power of education, whether through the schools or other institutions like the YMCA-YWCA. She wanted to provide all children with an education appropriate to their abilities, not tied to their family's social and economic status.

The decade of the '20s was a good one for Elsie Wilcox and the values she espoused. She was secure in her economic, social, and personal circumstances. She was respected in the community, and hers was a voice that carried authority in a wide range of circles. The hope for world peace seemed attainable. Depression, war, strikes, union organizing, and the growing power of the Democratic party were all in the future. They each, in turn, would threaten the life she had crafted for herself.

4 The Plunge into Politics

Elsie Wilcox's correspondence conveys the impact of the 1930s depression in Hawai'i. She and her family supported many individuals and charities, and almost every file at Grove Farm reflects the decline of her income and her concern about the future. As more people who normally gave to charity either ceased or reduced their contributions, appeals to the Wilcoxes increased.

The Depression

In 1931, Elsie Wilcox wrote Brewer Eddie, head of the ABCFM, with whom she often corresponded: "It looks as if we should give away every cent we have. If people were but warmhearted enough to do but a fraction of that, but alas, too many that have do not give and others have not where with to give. I do not envy you, your job of assembling money, but I fancy you like it so my sympathy is wasted."[1]

In August, she sent him extra money, "as sort of emergency relief to you and the [ABCFM] board in this year of such accumulated 'pili-kiyas' [troubles]. One stands aghast at the poverty, unemployment, debt, ignorance and general helplessness of the world."[2] Brewer Eddie, like other heads of charitable organizations, was having great difficulty. In August he wrote, "This has been the worst year of my life for health as I have just avoided a serious breakdown last fall. I am very much better but will be greatly relieved when these dark days pass."[3] In 1933 he wrote, "The devastation worked in financial trusts, and wills and future plans has been terrible. I know that hundreds of wills have had to take out legacies to the American Board and the present reductions of gifts from our churches are becoming very critical."[4]

Hawai'i charities also were in trouble. Elsie Wilcox in 1933 responded to a request from the chairman of the finance committee of the First Chinese Church of Christ in Honolulu asking her for money. She acknowledged the heavy burden the church was carrying, but considering the "many demands made upon us, just now it is impossible for us to consider giving you any aid. As soon as conditions improve financially, I should think your Church should deserve first consideration."[5]

The year 1933 seems to have been the worst year for the Wilcoxes. In September, she wrote Dr. W. H. Frye at the Methodist Episcopal Mission:

> I understand very well the difficult position in which your Methodist mission finds itself. You share this in common with many other organizations in this era of Depression, only your situation is perhaps worse than that of most in that your income has been cut to one-fifth of what it was 10 years ago. Every welfare or religious organization which I know about on Kauai is behind, our Salvation Army over a $1,000 short, our own church with only enough funds to meet this month's expenses our treasurer tells me, etc. It is the same everywhere, as you know, and I write of this here only to let you know that until we have affairs here at home on Kauai in going shape it does not seem that we should as yet give elsewhere. I also have some gifts to China missions coming due next month and that limits me personally just at present.[6]

Reluctantly, she turned down her old missionary friend in China, Frank Rowlinson, who edited the *Chinese Recorder* in Shanghai. "It would be impossible for me to give you the $3,000 you asked for. Our own magazine, *The Friend,* is in a precarious condition and should come first, I think, with Island people. Also, the financial condition in general is none too good and we hesitate to take on new projects in a modest way."[7]

She continued most of her donations, some in reduced form. The range of her interests is indicative of her value system. She and others quietly subsidized the salary of the Lihue Union Church minister because the church was unable to pay him what they had promised.[8] She gave to several churches in Hawai'i, including $1,000 to Makiki Christian Church.[9] She provided funds for many teaching, preaching, and agricultural missionaries in China, Korea, and Japan. She supplied a missionary in Peru with a radio so he could keep in contact with the rest of the world because, as his brother wrote Elsie, he was "going off to the Amazon to live with a bunch of head hunters."[10] She not only supported the missionaries but in at least one instance sent $400 to the widow of a Chinese missionary.[11] She gave to the China Flood Relief fund, the Napoopoo parsonage, and the Peking YMCA.[12] She continued to support many students in various Hawai'i schools. One of the students wrote to thank her:

> Miss Wilcox, you have done so much for me; I will never forget you loaned me that large sum when I needed it badly, to be returned as I pleased and without interest; and now you have canceled the rest which is quite a sum yet. I can't express what I really want to say, Miss Wilcox, what you have done for me I know, is just a little of so much that you have done for other girls.[13]

She gave to the YMCA, YWCA, National Council for the Prevention of War, Pan Pacific Union, Pan Pacific Women's Conference, Salvation Army, Girls Reserve, the Anti-Saloon League, and the Association for Improving the Condition of the Poor. Contributions ranged from $25 to $4,000.

During these trying times, Wilcox's social work activities, if anything, increased. She became a member of the speakers bureau for the White House Conference on Child Health and Protection.[14] She assumed legal guardianship for several children, including those of her dead brother, Charles,[15] and a nineteen-year-old girl at the Susanna Wesley Home in Honolulu.[16] She made arrangements for a man with TB to be taken into the TB hospital and warned his son to have the family checked periodically. She wrote letters on behalf of unemployed clerks, teachers, and nurses.

Wilcox expanded her deep involvement with the local church and the HEA. She served on several HEA committees and consulted regularly with HEA officers in Honolulu about problems in Kaua'i churches. In one instance, she wrote to Henry Judd at the HEA, explaining how a third party had brought about a reconciliation between two ministers who were fighting over who controlled what territory: "In this effort he has been successful and to both gentlemen have been presented the little figures of the three monkeys, 'Hear no evil, Speak no evil, See no evil.' It is to be hoped that simple philosophy presented by the monkeys will accomplish what Christian admonishing seems to have failed to do!"[17] Evidently, Wilcox had done the admonishing.

She continued her work with young people but on a considerably reduced scale. Although most of her activities were with children of immigrants, on one occasion she had a party for *haole* (Caucasian) boys. Her comments, written to a missionary in China, illustrate her views about different groups and how she related to young people:

> Boys of that class . . . are inclined to feel themselves somewhat superior than those of other nationalities and therefore need a good deal of broadening and guidance. I had the fun of entertaining these 50 boys in our mission home at Hanalei a few days ago. Much to my surprise, they seemed very interested in the old things in the house and the history of the bygone days.[18]

Historic Preservation

In 1931, Elsie, Etta, and Mabel undertook the moving and renovation of the Lyman house in Hilo. The city had condemned the property to widen and straighten one of the main roads in town, and the old Lyman house was slated to be torn down. The sisters had it moved several yards and refurnished it in period furniture. The project required not only substantial funding—provided in large part by the Wilcox family—but also research on the family and the surroundings, mainly accomplished by Elsie. Subsequently, a museum and archives were opened to the public.

The Lyman house project coincided with Elsie and Mabel's longstanding interest in the history of their family and of Hawai'i. They were reputed to own the largest collection of Hawaiian artifacts and books outside of museums and libraries. In 1917, Elsie had written a history of Hanalei, a detailed recounting of the early history of the area, representing extensive research. She wrote various other histories over the years. The Lyman house in Hilo, the Wilcox house at Wai'oli, and eventually, following Mabel's death, Grove Farm homestead were all turned into museums either by Elsie and Mabel, or Mabel alone. Before it became a recognized field, both sisters were active in historic preservation.

In 1932, Elsie Wilcox was leading a full life. She had accomplished what she set out to do—create an interesting and productive existence on Kaua'i. Not wanting to live in Honolulu or on the U.S. mainland, she seemed to have the best of all worlds—a stimulating intellectual life lived at home on Kaua'i.

Grove Farm house in 1938. The house was expanded from the single-story wing at right to include a two-story addition built during Elsie Wilcox's childhood. It remained essentially the same after that. The large tree in front of the house is a false *kamani*.

Campaign and Election

In the summer of 1932, Senator Charles Rice approached Elsie Wilcox and urged her to run for the territorial Senate, with his backing. This move was surprising because speculation held that Rice was grooming his son-in-law, Fred Wichman, a territorial representative, for the race.[19] The timing was excellent for Wilcox. She was fifty-three years old. She had established a reputation as a staunch supporter of the schools, a leading social worker, and a champion of women's rights and child welfare. She was well known not only on Kaua'i but on O'ahu and Maui. Her personal life, however, raised a few problems. Her Uncle George was ninety-three, and her mother was eighty-three. Her father had died in 1929. The household had adequate assistance, but she and Mabel were in charge of running it, and she was reluctant to leave Kaua'i for long. On the other hand, she was not burdened with the obligation of children, and Mabel did most of her public health work on Kaua'i, working out of an office at Grove Farm. Elsie Wilcox was vigorous, anxious to be active in the affairs of the community and to have a hand in deciding the direction the territory would take. She could have remained on the Commission for Public Instruction, but in the legislature, she would have more of an impact on territorial life.

Rice evidently asked Wilcox to run in an effort to block John T.

Moir Jr., manager of Koloa Sugar Company and a critic of Rice. Wilcox had been contemplating entering the race for some months, but she remained undecided until Rice's encouragement. She said later that she would not have run had Moir announced, and Moir chose not to run against her.[20]

In May 1931, following a special session of the legislature in which the House of Representatives refused to pass legislation sponsored by Senator Rice, the *Garden Island* newspaper wrote Charles Rice's political obituary: "It is to be regretted that the sun of Senator Charles Rice's political ascendancy has been doomed to set by his stand in the present legislative muddle. A king, once dethroned, never returns to power."[21] The "obituary" was premature. Charles Rice was the most politically powerful person on Kaua'i and one of the most powerful men in the territory. With his brother William, the sheriff, he had created a political machine that, while not unchallenged, was usually stronger than any opposition.

Part of the reason for Charles Rice's success in politics was that he brooked little disagreement from those he supported. In 1932, he withdrew his support from Henry K. Aki, whom he had put in the Senate in 1925, because on several occasions Aki had voted against Rice in the 1932 special session of the legislature. Aki was dismayed. "The Rice political machine has supported me all these years. Why desert me now? I am the people's man," he said.[22]

Aki was not the only person who wanted the Senate seat. John B. Fernandes wrote Wilcox in May 1932 saying that he was being pressed to run on the Democratic ticket but that he would not announce if she planned to enter the race.[23] In July, she wrote him telling of her decision: "At the earnest felicitations of my friends, [I have] decided to run. I am therefore letting you know at once and I hope that I may rely on you for your support, which, I assure you, that I shall appreciate very much. I would like you to know that you are the first person I am informing."[24] In addition to Wilcox, Moir, Aki, and Fernandes, Clem Gomes, then a Republican in the territorial House of Representatives, said in August 1931 that he might try for the Senate, but he later changed his mind.[25]

The Honolulu *Star Bulletin* judged it a mistake for Wilcox to enter the race with the backing of Rice. "The presence of the names of Senator Charles A. Rice, Rep. Fred Wichman and others of the so-called Rice faction on Miss Wilcox's nomination papers is said by political observers to have considerably marred her chances for election."[26] Others also commented on the Rice tie. Horace H. Leavitt, minister at Central Union Church in Honolulu, wrote to her: "My only regret is that I am not a registered voter on Kauai, so I might cast a ballot for you. Of course, if I thought that the Honorable Mr. Rice from your fair Island was going to control your vote, I would feel very different, but knowing you is sufficient answer to any such subject."[27] She responded with her appreciation for his support, adding that even though she might not always do what people wanted or expected her to do, she would remain independent.[28]

Charles Rice was a man who generated extreme reactions. He was a big, cigar-smoking man, with a large following among the working class on Kaua'i. He was colorful, dramatic, and something of a latter-day populist. During one campaign, he was accused by his opponents of being the "czar" of Kaua'i. At the next rally, he appeared in a czarist costume, brandishing a sword.[29] In the 1932 election, he described the ingratitude of those he had supported, probably referring to Aki. He turned his back on the crowd several times, "calling them to witness the imaginary wounds which certain individuals whom he had befriended inflicted upon him." The crowd loved it.[30]

An anti-Rice faction in the Republican party appealed to the same constituency on Kaua'i. It was headed by Clem Gomes and A. Q. Marcallino, who in 1931 were both in the territorial House of Representatives. The antagonisms, which were intense, appeared to be more a question of personalities than of policies. In August 1931, Gomes announced that his faction would field candidates for every office on Kaua'i to challenge the Rice machine.[31] He accused Rice of trying to run both the territorial House and the Senate.

The plantation managers on Kaua'i comprised a second Republican anti-Rice group. Although his grandparents had been missionaries, Rice was often at odds with his missionary-related peers and others who dominated the factors in Honolulu and, through them, most of the plantations on all the islands. Partly it was his style, which offended his more reserved and restrained associates. Partly it was his politics, which were more liberal than theirs. Partly it was because he disliked several of them for what he viewed as a conspiracy against his father that had almost ruined the family. One of the large factors in Honolulu had extended his father credit well beyond his father's ability to repay, resulting in debt for the family holdings for years. Because of this, the Rices became poor cousins, relatively speaking, in relation to the Wilcoxes, Alexanders, and Baldwins.[32] The *Star*

Bulletin reported, "Plantation managers of West Kauai particularly and other prominent businessmen of the island" supported Gomes because Rice was too domineering and needed to be "put in his place."[33] On several occasions, J. T. Moir Jr. accused Rice of running a corrupt political machine. Rice responded that "Honolulu interests" were behind the opposition to him, in particular American Factors, Alexander and Baldwin, and C. Brewer, whose political advisers, he claimed, were Gomes, Marcallino, and John Kealoha.[34]

Elsie Wilcox was not averse to Rice's support. They had grown up together and their families had intermarried. She was confident of her ability to remain independent of Rice and all others.

Luckily for the Republicans, the Democrats were badly divided. This was particularly unfortunate for the Democrats in 1932 because the national ticket was so strong the local party actually had some chance of winning. Before then, as the *Garden Island* observed, "One automobile was more than enough to take all the [Democratic] candidates to their meetings over the island."[35]

The campaigning was colorful. Candidates held stew and rice dinners and *lū'au* for their supporters. Hawaiian bands played, dancers performed *hula*, entertainers sang Hawaiian, Portuguese, and Japanese songs, orators draped in *lei* gave speeches in Hawaiian, Portuguese, Japanese, and English, children ran among the crowds, and bootleg whiskey flowed freely. Wilcox's 1932 "election box" records show expenditures for music, food, transportation, cigars, and lunches. Her campaign manager was paid $50.

Elsie Wilcox proved to be an effective campaigner. This may have come as a surprise, since by all accounts the Wilcox family was restrained and not particularly talkative. Long silences were common at family gatherings, and Mabel and G.N. often said little if anything during an entire evening.[36] Elsie Wilcox, however, enjoyed campaigning. She claimed that she did not like to speak in public, but she was a good debater. Like everything else she did, she took the campaign seriously. She was well prepared for every debate and spoke forcefully and authoritatively. More than her brothers and sisters, she had experience speaking to large groups of people.

She did not attack Aki directly, but dwelt on her past experience, especially in social work and education. "She [stated] that she has been deeply interested in education, health, public welfare and better living conditions... that she was qualified to fight for any good cause."[37] Although Rosalie Keliinoi, also from Kaua'i, had been elected

Elsie Wilcox's 1932 campaign photograph. It was reproduced on three-by-five-inch cards and passed out all over Kaua'i during her campaign.

to the territorial House of Representatives in 1925, Wilcox made special appeals to women voters by pointing out that she was the first woman to run for the Senate.

Aki praised Wilcox for her work as Commissioner for Education and "urged voters to leave [her] at home to take care of the schools and he would go to the senate and watch Senator Rice."[38] His campaign was directed more against Rice than Wilcox.

Elsie Wilcox beat Henry Aki in the primary by a vote of 2,204 to 1,456.[39] Gomes and Marcallino also won, along with Tom Ouye and Fred Wichman. Because people presumably did not hold out much hope for the Democrats on Kaua'i, attention turned to the national and territorial political scene.

The major territorial race was for delegate to Congress. It pitted Republican Victor Kaleoaloha Houston against Democrat Lincoln "Linc" McCandless. The Republican platform opposed any new taxes and called for spending cuts.[40] The Democrats proposed public works for the unemployed, bonds for each Filipino immigrant sufficient to ensure return passage to the Philippines if he became a public charge, establishing an income tax similar to the federal income tax, old-age pensions, restricting real and personal taxes, and ending all education fees.[41]

McCandless beat Houston 29,431 to 27,017. Houston carried the neighbor islands, but McCandless won heavily on O'ahu. Democrats also elected three senators and ten representatives, up from one and two in 1930—the Roosevelt coattails reached across the Pacific. Historian Donald Johnson observed that the Republicans "inherited all the dissatisfactions that went with the depression, unemployment, wage and salary cuts, legislative bickering over tax reform, and suspicion of leadership that had failed to avert all these.... Considering the public mood in the nation, it is surprising that so little changed in Honolulu politics, or that change came so slowly."[42] The same could be said of the whole territory.

In the general election, Elsie Wilcox trounced her Democratic challenger, D. Louis Agard, 2,952 to 858. Her victory was not a surprise because she was popular and well known, and Agard ran a modest campaign. The big surprise on Kaua'i was that both Gomes and Marcallino lost. Republicans Wichman and Tom Ouye and Democrat John Gomez won a six-way contest for three House seats.[43]

Elsie Wilcox received many letters of congratulations, the most exuberant from Mary L. Cady, general secretary of the YWCA of

Honolulu: "I am thrilled that you are going to be in the Senate. It will seem good to have you as our near neighbor during the session. Hurrah for the women!"[44]

In August, a group of sixteen people, including several management-level people from Grove Farm, had written Governor Judd recommending that John T. Moir Jr. or his wife replace Elsie as Commissioner for Education, since she had already announced her campaign for the Senate, but the Governor wrote back saying that was premature. Henry Aki had also written, nominating Mrs. Adrian Englehard, the niece of Robert Hind, to replace Wilcox.[45]

On November 1, 1932, Wilcox resigned her position as Commissioner for Public Instruction. Also on November 1, Charles Rice wrote the governor recommending that Elsie Wilcox's sister, Etta Sloggett, replace her on the commission and that Mabel Wilcox be appointed a member of the Board of Child Welfare for Kaua'i, also to replace Elsie. On November 3, the governor wrote the senator: "Acting on the suggestion contained in your letter of November 1, 1932, I have today appointed Mrs. Etta E. Sloggett as School Commissioner of Kauai and Miss Mabel I. Wilcox as a member of the Board of Child Welfare of Kauai."

Etta served only one year because in December 1933 she suffered a heart attack and died. It was a great shock to the family. She was only fifty-six and had not previously experienced heart trouble.

Also in 1933, G.N. died of cancer. He had withdrawn from most of the day-to-day running of the plantation, but had continued his charitable activities. In his lifetime, he gave away more than $3 million.[46]

During the early years of the depression some people on Kaua'i and in Honolulu regarded Elsie Wilcox as a private loan company. She received an astonishing number of requests for loans or outright gifts, with an extra-large number coming in 1932. A man stranded in Honolulu because he could not pay his hotel bill wrote Wilcox, as did a woman whose husband told her to write for money to pay for his boat. There is no indication in the record that Wilcox responded favorably to these requests. Perhaps the depression created extra need, although the fact that she was running for public office and presumably wanted support may also have been a consideration. A few of the loan requests included information on how many voters were in the family.

1933 Legislature: How Can We Get There without a Map?

In January, Elsie Wilcox took the overnight boat to Oʻahu and settled into the Alexander Young Hotel on Bishop Street in downtown Honolulu. It was the tallest building downtown, looming six stories over the one- and two-story businesses and shops surrounding it. Wilcox took most of her meals in the hotel dining room and went almost everywhere by foot or streetcar. She had many friends in Honolulu and led an active social life, attending teas, lectures, meetings, and dinners when she was not occupied with legislative work. She was particularly in demand as a speaker for women's educational and child welfare groups.

The legislature met at ʻIolani Palace. Although somewhat modified since the time when it served royalty, the building still resembled the September 24, 1881, description in the *Pacific Coast Advertiser*:

Members of the 1933 Senate, seventeenth legislature, of the Territory of Hawaii. *Standing, left to right:* Joseph L. Sylva, William H. Heen, Charles A. Rice, Lester Petrie, Henry Freitas, Harold W. Rice, James Campsie, Francis H. Ii Brown (vice-president), and Robert Hind. *Seated, left to right:* William H. Hill, Harry H. Holt, Elsie H. Wilcox, George P. Cooke, (president), David K. Trask, and Stephen L. Desha Sr.

The design of the exterior cannot be described in a few words or referred to any recognized order of architecture. If a name is to be coined for it we should favor "American Florentine" as the nearest approach to a correct one. The facade of the front is in two stories, 140 feet long, and 54 high, with a tower . . . in the center and one at each end. Each tower is capped by a square campanile having the concave outline so common in the Italian architecture of the late Middle Ages; and the central tower having a third story rises to a height of 80 feet.[47]

Eleven Republicans and four Democrats were in the Senate. (See Appendix for the names of the senators.) Nine senators, all Republicans, were from the neighbor islands; six senators, including all the Democrats, were from Oʻahu. Wilcox was a member of the Judiciary, Health, Education, and Public Lands committees.

As in preceding decades, the major business leaders in the territory sought to control the legislature either by their actual presence as legislators or through second- and third-level employees who generally could be counted on to support business interests. This did not begin to change until 1938, and only after World War II did a reinvigorated and reconstructed Democratic party break the plantations' and factors' hold on the legislature.

The opening day of the territorial legislative session was always a festive occasion. Legislators were draped with *lei,* often so many that their faces were scarcely visible. The flowers created a profusion of color and fragrance—a moving garden as their bearers walked around the chamber. *Hula* dancers performed, various bands played Hawaiian songs, and the session opened with a prayer, often given in Hawaiian by the minister of Kawaiahaʻo Church.

Despite the fun and the party atmosphere, the economic situation facing the new legislature was serious. The governor, Lawrence Judd, wrote in an opening letter to the legislature, "The financial outlook for the coming biennium is exceedingly discouraging," and indeed it was.[48] More businesses had declared bankruptcy in 1932 than at any time in the territory's history.[49] Many companies reduced their dividends, and for the first time in twenty-four years, Hawaiian Pineapple paid no dividend.[50] Projected territorial income was down 14.3 percent. In December 1932, Governor Judd cut $3.5 million from the 1933–1935 biennium budget. The income tax, poll tax, and business excise taxes were all up because of new laws, but they did not make up for the decline in property tax revenues from $2,919,040 in

1931–1933 to an estimated $807,124 in 1933–1935. Between 1920 and 1932, the total net valuation of property on Oʻahu had risen from $121,556,890 to $213,952,977; in 1932, it was down to $178,274,562. Territorial and county requirements from the real and property taxes were $2,789,552 in 1920 and $7,150,070 in 1932.[51] In 1932, the HSPA sent 7,200 Filipinos back to the Philippines to reduce unemployment and open jobs for local youth.[52]

The Republicans were trapped in the conservative, laissez-faire mode of thought that had brought prosperity to the islands and sections of the mainland in the previous three decades. Their dated rhetoric and lack of a plan checkmated the opportunity they had because of the territorial Democrats' problems. The Republicans had campaigned against most New Deal ideas—they could hardly have supported them after the election even if they viewed them as economically sound, which most Republicans did not.

The Democrats were bitterly divided among themselves and were unable to capitalize on their newfound national power. Governor Judd's term was to expire at the end of June 1933. After Linc McCandless was elected to Congress, three other Democratic candidates remained, vying to be appointed governor by President Franklin D. Roosevelt: former federal district judge Joseph B. Poindexter, John Wilson, mayor of Honolulu, and Delbert Metzger of Hilo. In November 1932, the Democratic Central Committee voted to recommend Metzger, but the defiant Oʻahu Democrats said they would support Wilson anyway because the Central Committee was stacked against Oʻahu in favor of the neighbor islands. To add to the confusion, McCandless announced in December that he would resign from Congress and accept the governorship if Roosevelt offered it to him.[53] Some of the would-be governors sent their own delegations to Washington to importune Roosevelt and Secretary of the Interior Harold Ickes, who both became annoyed at the Democratic backbiting in Hawaiʻi.

Wilcox appears to have supported the Democrats' ends and the Republicans' means—not a happy combination. It would have been an easier legislative session for her had the reverse been true. Her heart was with the Democrats. Having been a teacher, she knew the needs of the schools and did not want to see their operations cut. Having been a social worker, she knew full well the real impact of unemployment on a family because for years she had dealt firsthand with families in crisis. Her head, however, was with the Republicans. She supported some tax increases, but opposed a fundamental reordering of the tax structure. Many territorial businesses had a negative cash flow, and she believed higher taxation would push them into bankruptcy. She was also convinced that the territorial budget had to be balanced if the territory was to meet its monthly payroll, since the territory seemed to be without a source for borrowing money. Wilcox, like most other legislators, floundered during the 1933 session. She was trying to protect her vision of the future of Hawai'i, the fundamental economy of the territory, and her own economic future in a situation that did not seem to admit an easy resolution of those conflicting goals.

With the Republicans stuck in a time warp and the Democrats organizing their firing squad in a circle, it would have been too much to hope that the 1933 legislature could solve the pressing problems facing the territory, and in fact, it did not. In hindsight, the people of the territory were fortunate the depression was never as severe in Hawai'i as in some areas on the mainland, because their leaders were too divided and unclear as to what to do to deal effectively with the issues.

Those issues were basic ones that called into question the entire political, social, racial, and economic structure of the territory. Did the government have an obligation to intervene in the economy to help end the depression? Who should be taxed and how much? Should territorial employees be laid off? If so, which ones? What kind of assistance should the unemployed receive? How long should children be educated and what kind of education should the community provide?

The answer to the first question, that of governmental intervention in the economy, was an equivocal and reluctant "yes" from the Republicans and a resounding "yes" from the Democrats. The fundamental problem did not loom large in terms of the local economy because the major employers—the plantations—did not go bankrupt or shut down for long periods of time, nor did the banks collapse. New Deal programs were another matter, however. In principle, Republicans in Hawai'i, like those on the mainland, were supporters of laissez-faire economics. In practice, they were just as vociferous as Democrats in demanding that Hawai'i receive its fair share of the New Deal largesse. By April 1933, federal moneys were beginning to flow into the territory. The first amount was modest, $87,000 from the Reconstruction Finance Corporation. By summer, however, the territory was receiving millions of dollars, primarily for construction of roads, harbors, and defense systems. By September 1933, the amount totaled approximately $40 million.[54] No Republican proposed returning the money to the federal government. Wilcox in particular began rethinking the role of government in the economy during this session, a process that led to her introducing or supporting legislation in subsequent sessions that would have been anathema in earlier years.

The questions of who should be taxed and by how much were more divisive and did not cut strictly across party lines. Many Republicans opposed any new taxes. Others, including Charles Rice and Elsie Wilcox, supported some increases. Most Democrats favored raising property and excise taxes, but some were opposed.

Proposals abounded. Establish a poll tax of $5 on women earning more than $200. Impose a 1 percent tax on all income, including unearned income. Change that to .5 percent. Create a graduated income tax on the U.S. model. Tax businesses more. Raise the property tax.[55]

A bipartisan group organized in 1932, the Honolulu Taxpayers Association, fought against increasing the property tax. The group was headed by Democrat Joseph Poindexter, with Republican S. N. Castle as vice-chairman. They argued that the property tax had come to represent too large a share of the territorial taxes, all of which were too high. In 1912, the property tax had contributed $1,706,000, or 35.54 percent, of the $4,427,000 taxes raised that year. In 1931, it provided $13,698,000, or 63.57 percent, of the total taxes of $21,549,000.[56] In twenty years, the budget had increased fivefold and the property tax eightfold.

Raising income for the territorial government was half of the equation; cutting expenditures was the other half. Education was the natural focal point for much of the debate because the DPI took about half the territorial budget.[57] Proposals were introduced that would eliminate teacher positions, force teachers to retire at age sixty-five rather than seventy, cut salaries, and require teachers to pay extra if a spouse or parent lived with them in their territorial-supported cottage.[58]

For some leaders, the depression presented an opportunity to halt what they viewed as the excessive spending that had begun in the 1920s and to focus education on more practical matters, that is, educating to make plantation work attractive to local children. The arguments of the 1920s continued into the 1930s, and for the same reasons. The *Advertiser* editorialized about it:

> Hawaii's plantations offer boys and young men something better than grubbing in coal pits or glass works. They offer work in the open, rent free homes which the others do not, and a chance to become lunas, engineers, members of the office staff and even managers. . . . [An executive] who eventually owned his own plantation began as a blacksmith's helper.[59]

Pressure to limit most students to an eighth-grade education was strong. Alvah Scott, manager of Honolulu Plantation, in October 1932 had called it "little short of criminal to encourage pupils to follow studies that could be of no practical use to them."[60] To head off a direct assault on the high schools, Superintendent of Education Will Crawford proposed a plan giving principals authority to determine who could continue past the eighth grade; young men who went to work on the plantations would be offered a cooperative education program.[61]

Reacting to tremendous public pressure to cut the education budget, Crawford recommended that people be let go in the following order: "those who had come to Hawai'i in the past five years; wives of government employees who earned at least $3,000; wives of government employees if their joint salaries were $3,000; wives of non-government employees who earned more than $3,000."[62] In opposition, Elsie Wilcox pointed out that if all those positions were eliminated, the new University of Hawaii graduates would have no jobs. She argued that the proposed cuts were too drastic—they would "cripple the school Department." She also objected strongly to the attack on wives and introduced an amendment to change "wife" to "married person."

In large part, class size determined the number of teachers. During the 1920s, class size had been gradually reduced in line with the recommendations of the 1920 Survey. Several people proposed raising the class size to a ratio of 50:1. Wilcox countered by submitting a minority report setting the ratio at 35:1 in elementary and high school and eliminating forty-one positions, for a saving of $140,000.[63]

In this atmosphere of what seemed to be dire fiscal conditions and pressure to keep local youth on the plantations, the budget submitted by the DPI was cut by $1.2 million, and a $10 high school tuition fee was approved.[64] The final school budget was $8,353,777, representing 51 percent of the budget.[65]

Hawai'i was spending less on education than thirty-six states. The states spending less than Hawai'i were all in the South. Between 1929 and 1933, Hawai'i spent $71.56 per pupil and $15.29 per capita; New York spent the most, $149.84 per pupil and $28.45 per capita; Georgia spent the least, $31.89 per pupil and $6.39 per capita.[66]

Elsie Wilcox made several public statements during the legislative session, usually to oppose cuts in education, to support funding for the library system, and to fight elimination of the pension system. She was vehement in her arguments on education. She contended that firing teachers would only add to the unemployment problem, because teachers had to have enough money to provide for a place to sleep and food to eat. She urged that if pension funding were reduced, the cuts be only the same percentage as the reductions in salaries for current employees. Her argument was the same one she used against firing teachers—elimination of income for retirees would only add to the welfare roles unless the territory wanted the retirees to starve.

Reluctantly, she agreed to the $10 fee for high school students.[67] This compromise caused her considerable trouble later, but she always defended the decision on the basis of the intense pressure to cut the education budget and on her fundamental belief in balancing the territorial budget.

Education was not the only area under attack. Some legislators were demanding an across-the-board reduction in territorial personnel or salaries, or both. They put forward several proposals on the subject. The one that finally passed cut all salaries 10 percent. Some people wanted to eliminate the territorial pension system.[68] The idea of firing all married women who earned more than $3,000 or married women with spouses also employed by the territory enjoyed widespread support. These measures were a nationwide response to the depression. Women, especially married women, were urged not to compete with men for scarce jobs. On the mainland, many school districts, state governments, and companies refused to hire married women.[69]

On the question of who should receive unemployment assistance and what form that assistance should take, the territorial legislature was breaking new ground. By mainland standards, the territory had never experienced a serious unemployment problem. Until the 1920s, the economy of the territory was almost entirely rural. The plantations generally looked after their own, or if a labor glut developed, sent workers back to their home country. During the 1920s, Honolulu, Hilo, and Wailuku had grown. More small entrepreneurs had opened shop, the building trades boomed, and substantial numbers of workers were lured to the cities from the plantations. Hundreds of people became destitute because of the depression—city-dwelling men, many families, and some self-supporting women. Half of the unemployed men in Honolulu worked in the building trades.[70] Throughout the territory, 3 percent of the unemployed were sugar plantation laborers, 26 percent were construction workers, 18 percent were government workers, and 15 percent were pineapple workers.[71] By February 1933, sixty people had been cut from government jobs and were receiving unemployment compensation. As Charles Rice pointed out, the territory could not cut expenses without cutting people who then were supported by welfare.[72]

Nell Findley, head of the Social Service Bureau, was candid in her appraisal of the problem. The private charity organizations that had taken care of the indigent in the past were overwhelmed and could not handle the deluge. They had never before had to deal with such numbers, and to make matters worse, private charitable donations declined as more and more affluent people watched their incomes shrink. Many people gave a tithe (10 percent of their income) to some form of charity, but with reduced income, the tithes were less. Wilcox agreed with Findley's analysis. She was beginning to believe that large-scale government intervention was necessary. She was one of the few people in the legislature actively involved on all sides of the situation. Her own income, dependent on dividends, was dropping; she was director of several charitable organizations whose incomes were falling precipitously; and she was meeting regularly with Nell Findley, who was sinking under the weight of the mounting demands for help from the community at large.

In 1933, Governor Judd established an Unemployment Commission and asked Richard A. Cooke, president of C. Brewer and Company, to head it. Several views on welfare were circulating at the time. Cooke was a strong advocate of work rather than "soup kitchens," which, in his view, were cheaper but did not take long "to make a chronic loafer out of a potential worker." Senator Harold Rice suggested lowering unemployment support from $2.50 per day to $1.00 per day, a move that Cooke opposed because $2.50 was as low as it could go "in fairness" to the men who were receiving it. Senator William "Doc" Hill opposed the entire idea of unemployment support, calling it "a dole," but Honolulu Mayor George Fred Wright observed that only 10 percent of the men on unemployment were "bums" and the rest wanted to work. Cooke expressed the need for immediate assistance to the unemployed but opposed raising taxes, saying it was better to feed hungry men than to "put intellectual fodder in the minds of the youth." He advocated shifting money from education to pay for welfare.

Elsie Wilcox challenged Cooke on that point: "To return to the so-called intellectual budget, if we cut down that intellectual budget we will begin to throw people out of work here; you will have a mob on your hands who cannot live on $12 a month for food; they are making the situation worse instead of better." Cooke retorted that the territory had been spending less on education ten years earlier, and education had been good then.[73] While that was true, post–World War I inflation had resulted in a significant increase in the cost of living for teachers, construction costs for school buildings, and the cost of supplies.

The Cooke-Wilcox debate was a remarkable exchange, but it went unnoticed. Two missionary descendants, both with wealth and power, debated the future of the educational system and with it the future of the territory. That one of the debaters was a woman made the encounter even more intriguing. That so little attention was paid to it probably indicates the extent to which Elsie Wilcox was accepted as part of the political scene in Honolulu. The press generally treated her like a man.

Closely tied to the unemployment question was the issue of working people's wages. Business leaders did not want someone on unemployment relief receiving as much as someone who was earning a wage, because that would undermine the work ethic. In August 1933, Harry L. Hopkins sent the territory a memo ordering that after August 1, 1933, all wages paid under Federal Emergency Relief Administration (FERA) had to be at or above $.30 an hour ($2.40 per eight-hour day), and no one under sixteen years could be employed.[74] The September 1933 minutes of the Unemployment Work Relief Commission show the wage scales in effect at the time:[75]

Honolulu	$2 a day, eight-hour day
Hawai'i	$.85 a day for Filipinos
In Hilo	$1.50 a day
Outside Hilo	$1.25 a day
Maui	$1.25 a day

None of them met the FERA minimum.

Although the legislative session focused mainly on the economy, it addressed other issues. Prison directors asked for legislation permitting the sterilization of "mentally defective persons." Harold Rice introduced the bill.[76] A good deal of testimony favored it, including statements by sociologist Stanley D. Porteus, Dr. Harry Arnold, and Nell Findley. The Holy Name Society, a Catholic group, opposed the bill.[77] It passed in the Senate by a vote of 10 to 3, with Wilcox voting yes, but it died in the House.[78]

The issue of reapportionment was raised and tabled. Oʻahu, with 62 percent of the registered voters, had 40 percent of the legislators. The neighbor island Republican legislators had no intention of giving urban, Democratic Oʻahu more legislative representation, and with Republicans controlling the legislature, they defeated the proposition.[79] Senator David Trask petitioned Congress to reapportion Hawaiʻi according to population, but the U.S. House of Representatives was itself malapportioned (and destined to remain that way until 1964 and the *Westberry v. Sanders* case), and it did nothing.[80]

The issue of Hawaiian homestead lands surfaced more than once during the session. These were lands set aside in 1920 for native Hawaiians in an effort to promote self-sufficiency for Hawaiian farmers. The idea harkened back to the missionary vision of "pleasant farms," but much of the land set aside for the program was marginally suited to farming, and the program was never adequately funded. As early as the 1930s, people raised the concern that the lands were being leased to large plantations and ranches, thus defeating the act's purpose. Despite the discussion, nothing of substance came of it, although a joint resolution was sent to Congress petitioning for more land in and around Honolulu to be included in the program.[81]

In May, Charles Rice resigned from the Republican Territorial Central Committee and the Executive Committee of the Central Committee, and then from the party itself, although he subsequently rejoined the party.[82] He evidently had been smarting over the opposition of party regulars on Kauaʻi to his brother William's 1932 campaign for the office of sheriff. He hinted that he might become an independent.

Rice's decision had serious implications for Wilcox. She was more or less tied to him, since he had been so prominent in pushing her candidacy. His leaving the party left her in a difficult position. Not a man to overlook differences with people whose careers he felt he had advanced, he was unlikely to take kindly to opposition from her.

However, she felt a strong loyalty to the party, and that meant the regulars. The situation caused a marked tension between Rice and Wilcox that seemed to persist for the rest of their lives and was never resolved. For the time, however, she said nothing publicly.

The session ended as it had begun—in confusion. The legislators accomplished little of substance; they were frustrated with each other and with their inability to solve the economic problems. They left the territory with a $5 million deficit and no way to fund it.[83] In the last days of the session, the House killed Rice's revenue bill because, the Democrats claimed, it taxed small-business people, not the rich and wealthy corporations. William Crozier, increasingly liberal, led the attack. He was joined by seven Republicans and most of the Democrats. At the demand of the House, Rice's unemployment tax was cut from 1 percent to .5 percent.[84] Rice seemed to have lost whatever control he once had of the House.[85]

Governor Judd threatened to call the legislators back for a special session, but most people regarded a special session as a waste of time if the legislators could not come to some prior agreements. Judd was a lame-duck governor. The Democrats were still fighting vigorously among themselves on the question of who would replace him. Roosevelt was so angry at the locals that he requested a change in the Organic Act so that he could appoint someone who had not been a resident of the territory for three years. One of the few points everyone agreed on was that they did not want a "carpetbagger" for governor.

In later years, when Wilcox discussed her contributions to the 1933 session, she pointed to her support of expanded appropriations for the Teachers College to enable more local students to become teachers; an additional appropriation for Mahelona Hospital on Kaua'i; dental hygienists for the schools; a vocational division in the school system; money for crippled schoolchildren and the adult blind; provision for exchange of teachers; unemployment relief; and her vigorous opposition to reducing the teaching staff during the depression.[86] These efforts represented her priorities—education and social welfare. Her venue had changed, but her interests and values had not. She was establishing herself within the political system as the spokesperson for these issues.

During the summer, controversy arose over the National Recovery Act (NRA) minimum wage requirements. Hawai'i stood to lose federal funds if it did not enact and enforce minimum wage laws, but most Asian business owners were adamantly opposed to the idea. Hawai'i had 10,906 businesses—7,506 Japanese, 1,379 Chinese, and 2,021 Caucasian and others. Mainland standards were likely to put many of the Asian-owned establishments out of business. Japanese-language newspapers were divided. The *Hawaii Hochi* supported the single standard. The *Nippu Jiji* was opposed: "To make the Orientals accept the same standard as the haoles suddenly at this time would be practically impossible." The paper said it was not against NRA but that too many small family firms would be bankrupted if forced to pay minimum wages right away. Some Caucasian employers had a double standard also, paying Asians and Asian Americans less than Caucasians, and they too opposed the NRA. To meet the NRA requirements, in September 1933 the territorial government set the maximum hours for a work week at forty-eight and the minimum wage at $12. The U.S. minimum was $14, and both the *Advertiser* and the labor unions thought the Hawai'i minimum should be $14 also.[87] For the moment, however, that ended the debate about the NRA.

Because of the increasingly desperate economic situation, in October Governor Judd called a special session of the legislature to begin on November 1. The territory was out of funds. It had issued warrants in lieu of checks, the city of Honolulu had refused to accept them, and the banks had declined to help.

The governor proposed using money from the territorial sinking fund and the employees' retirement fund to back the warrants. The Senate approved the proposal nine to four, with Wilcox voting in the majority. The Senate also unanimously passed a .5 percent business tax, designed to be in effect until $3 million was raised, when it would expire. A proposal to cut the school budget by $1 million put forth by George Cooke was rejected, with Wilcox one of the six who defeated it. The plan would have instituted a "platoon" system to double up some classes and would also have tested teachers' knowledge of English and dismissed anyone who failed.

The House balked at the Senate tax plan, preferring a personal property tax. Charles Rice warned that if the House did not pass the Senate version, home rule might be taken away, and the territory would be governed by a congressionally appointed commission. The House ignored him. Fatigued and frustrated, the senators accepted the House bill, not because they thought it was a good idea but because, as Rice said, "We can't stay deadlocked here for ever. I want to get back to Kauai."[88] Elsie Wilcox also reluctantly supported the measure.

During the special session, the renomination of Will Crawford as Superintendent of Public Education was defeated by a 7–7 tie. Wilcox supported Crawford.[89] She had worked closely with him when she was on the Commission for Public Instruction, and she understood the pressures he faced. He had, unfortunately, made enemies on all sides by supporting educational programs the wealthy opposed and conceding issues on which Democrats believed he should have held firm.

The legislative special session ended January 12, 1934. The *Advertiser* editorialized on the problems caused by the division between the two legislative bodies:

> Racial and non-business versus other racial and business groups makes for conflict in the body. Jealousies amongst the island delegations figure in it somewhat. Conflicts of interests between large centers of population and smaller centers of population are part of it. . . . The whole situation seems to be drifting toward more and more inefficiency, rather than less; . . . Why should not our legislature be expected to make good on our constant boast that we can rule ourselves?[90]

The paper was somewhat unfair. The session accomplished more than the previous one had. It solved the immediate crisis that had occurred in November when banks would not honor the territorial warrants; it passed a balanced budget by enacting a personal property tax and gross sales tax; and it passed legislation regulating the manufacture and sale of liquor.

This last issue, arising with passage of the Twenty-first Amendment to the United States Constitution, which ended prohibition, created much acrimonious debate. As originally introduced by Elsie Wilcox and H. A. Baldwin, the legislation would have required that liquor be sold only with a full meal, in a package, or delivered to a hotel room. The goal was to avoid the return of saloons. The *Advertiser* judged that it read like "a bill sponsored by interests who can not take defeat [of prohibition] like sportsmen." People complained that it would only help private clubs. In light of the vigorous public criticism, the Senate established a committee composed of Wilcox, David Trask, and William Heen, the last two being Democrats and supporters of liberal regulations, to redraft the legislation. At the end of the session, they emerged with a compromise easing the sale of beer that was passed unanimously.[91] Wilcox supported the compromise. The issue of temperance was not one that aroused deep concern in her. Her grandparents would have been disappointed and perhaps shocked, but it was another example of the more secularized life the third generation was leading.

A bill to have old-age pensions administered by the county Boards of Child Welfare rather than by the county Boards of Supervisors passed over the strong opposition of Senator Trask. He said Hawaiians, the primary beneficiaries, found the child welfare boards too cold, and the bill would mean the "importation of more 'high priced experts from Berkeley and waystations.' " Wilcox supported it as part of her general stance toward making social work more professional. A move to institute parimutuel betting failed, and on that note the legislature ended.[92]

The debate over minimum wages continued. In December, Richard A. Cooke resigned as head of the Civil Works Administration (CWA) because Washington had ordered Hawai'i to establish a wage scale of $.45 per hour for unskilled laborers and $1 per hour for skilled, with a forty-hour maximum work week. Cooke had argued for $.25 and $.35, respectively, and a forty-eight-hour work week. Cooke and Washington were far apart. The *Star Bulletin* supported Cooke, and the *Advertiser* supported Washington. Cooke said people would be getting relief without work. "It seems to me that this is putting a premium on being a bum." He claimed that labor in Hawai'i was the best paid in the country, yet they did not receive $.45 an hour. He pointed out that the unemployed in rural areas were people the plantations had let go, and if welfare paid $.45 an hour, it would be difficult to get plantation workers. The plantations had operated at a loss for the past two years, had kept on workers they did not need, and had shipped three thousand to four thousand Filipinos back to the Philippines that year to give jobs to local youth. The Democrats were vigorously opposed to paying less than the mainland rates and called Cooke's idea "pernicious."[93]

A study by the U.S. Department of Labor, Bureau of Agricultural Economics, found that mainland cash farm wages per day without board varied between $1.06 and $1.25 depending on the month. In Hawai'i, they were $1.42 for unskilled labor. That did not include the housing, medical services for the worker and his family, fuel, and water provided by the plantation, plus a guarantee of continuous employment throughout the year. With the "turnout rate" of 10 percent if the worker reported to work twenty-three or more days, the average was $1.56.[94] For the employed, an unemployment rate of

$.45 an hour probably was attractive, although it was difficult to compare with the $1.56 a day because the housing, medical care, fuel, and water were not included.

In January 1934, President Roosevelt named John Poindexter governor, ending the speculation and indecision. There was general acclaim for the decision, if for no other reason than the appointment of a "carpetbagger" had been avoided. Poindexter, a Wilsonian Democrat, was more conservative than many of the New Dealers. As James Lane concluded in his study of the Poindexter administration, Poindexter actually got along well with the Republicans, a situation that became troublesome for the Democrats.[95]

In the summer of 1934, the territorial Republicans held their biennial convention. Elsie Wilcox was chair of the Kaua'i Republican Central Committee and delegate to the convention. When another delegate was asked why Wilcox was elected from Kaua'i when so many men could have been elected, he replied, "She's a good sport and nothing of interest to Kauai is too small or too big but it gets her attention."[96] This expressed both her attitude and the perception of her attitude. Kaua'i was her home. Her attention focused on it, and it was an attention informed by forces that made her different from many other politicians in the territory.

The Republican platform called for statehood for Hawai'i; an "adequate public school system for our citizens with emphasis upon training which best fits our youth for good citizenship and for earning a livelihood in Hawaii"; restoration of the pay of public employees as soon as government finances permitted; county rather than territorial support of welfare recipients; a sound retirement system; work for everyone who could work and adequate care for those who could not; employment of Americans at fair wages; diversified farming; and condemnation of the Democratic sugar quotas, which limited the amount of sugar Hawai'i could ship to the mainland under the Jones-Costigan Act. Considering what had transpired in the past four years, it was a conservative platform.

The Democratic party platform backed Jones-Costigan, saying it had helped Hawai'i, and condemned an HSPA lawsuit challenging Jones-Costigan. It supported statehood; reapportionment of the territorial legislature; regulation of all utilities by the Public Utilities Commission; an income tax like the federal government's; better workman's compensation supplied by the territory; and exclusion of cheap labor. It opposed fees for high school and university students.[97]

The 1934 election resulted in losses for the Democrats, who could not seem to translate the New Deal monies, which had undeniably helped the territory weather the depression, into votes. Part of the difficulty was Jones-Costigan, perceived by most people in Hawai'i as detrimental to the territory's economy. Also, the Democrats continued to be bitterly divided. They fought bruising primary battles and were unable to regroup adequately for the general election. On Kaua'i, the result of the 1932 national Democratic success was a large increase in Democratic party members. The *Garden Island* said Democratic party leader, D. Louis Agard, "was probably as surprised as anyone to learn that there were so many Democrats on the island, but he managed to keep control of himself and enroll the members as fast as they appeared."[98] Agard, however, had become so accustomed to making all party decisions himself that he was unable to effectively integrate newcomers into the party structure, and they ran opposition candidates in most of the primary races in 1934.

Race was a significant element in the elections. Linc McCandless was quoted as saying, "I regret seeing the big stick being used among the sugar plantations; that free American citizens are not allowed to attend Democratic meetings and to express their honest opinions. Why should Scotchmen [supervisors] tell us Hawaiians how to vote?" That picture was somewhat clouded by the fact that McCandless had been born on the mainland and was not ethnically Hawaiian, while the Republican opponent who beat him, Samuel King, was part-Hawaiian. McCandless filed a grievance with Congress, asserting that managers had intimidated voters. Claims surfaced about people losing jobs because they supported the Democratic party and about plantation managers having told workers to vote Republican. William Heen, a part-Hawaiian, made a similar plea: "I'm appealing to my own people for support, the haoles have their own people who look after their interests." On the Big Island, Japanese voters outnumbered Hawaiians for the first time, and even with part-Hawaiians, the voting numbers were about equal. Eight out of ten eligible Japanese voted, six out of ten Hawaiians, and four out of ten "Americans." An editorial declared, "Here is a permanent loss of Hawaiian strength." Another editorial claimed, "According to those who have followed this growing situation and who presume to know, the Japanese voter will never center upon candidates of its own racial group."[99] Events following World War II would prove those supposed experts wrong.

Neither party made a concerted effort to attract the Japanese

American or the Chinese American vote. Donald Johnson has pointed out that Japanese and Chinese candidates in the Republican party generally were associated with the plantations or factor firms, and that the old guard of the Democratic party were similar to the Republicans in their racial views. "No one in the Republican old guard had on record more blatantly anti-Oriental statements than Lincoln L. McCandless."[100] Lawrence Fuchs concluded that when faced with the choice between Democrats and Republicans, most Japanese American voters chose the Republicans because they were the dominant party, and it did not make sense to support the losers.[101] The second-generation Asian-ancestry voters did not vote in a block, as they later would, because there was no comfortable home for them yet. In 1932 and 1936, Wilcox appealed to all racial groups and felt at ease doing so. That was not the case in 1940, a reflection of the great change in issues and concerns among the Japanese American voters during the decade.

The NRA controversy continued into the steamy fall months. John Waterhouse, president and manager of Alexander and Baldwin, described having had forty jobs on the wharf but only ten people to take them, because they could "play at work" a few hours and make money out of all proportion to the effort. The NRA, turning down pleas from Asian businesses, still refused to have separate wage scales, but in Waterhouse's opinion, the wages were too high even for Caucasian businesses.[102]

Another issue that kept arising during the fall was the high school tuition problem. Five hundred students had been turned away from high school because they could not pay the tuition, and a growing number of people felt this was unfair and bad public policy.

Before the start of the 1935 legislative session, Governor Poindexter appointed an advisory committee to review the territory's taxation system and recommend changes. William Borthwick, chair of the committee, commented after studying the matter, "Our new income tax law is a fraud, a delusion, a snare and should be killed as soon as possible." He claimed that some people making more than $300,000 paid no income tax, and that the burden fell on those in the $3,500–$8,000 bracket.[103] In large part, this was because the territory, unlike the federal government, did not tax dividends. The committee recommended repeal of the business excise and personal property taxes and adoption of a tax on gross income.

Industry was split on the matter. Sherwood Lowrey, treasurer of

AmFac, supported the gross income tax because too many businesses were avoiding the other taxes, burdening the honest businesses. C. C. von Hamm, on the other hand, said his profit was .5 percent on gross sales, and if the tax were levied at the suggested 2 percent, he would be out of business. Some Japanese businesses also opposed the tax, citing how their business taxes had gone up between two and five times in recent years, and that was enough.[104]

Signs that the economy was doing better were beginning to appear. In 1934, the net taxable corporate income was up three times over 1933, although income from individuals was down $264,000. Evidently, while corporate income was recovering, salaries were not being returned to their pre-1932 levels. Charles Rice predicted a million-dollar surplus in 1937. Ten thousand people had been assisted by FERA, and the federal government had poured $3,693,392 into the territory.[105]

The 1933 legislative session was a turning point in Elsie Wilcox's life. For years she had been a highly skilled professional volunteer, focusing on Kaua'i. Now she was becoming a professional politician, forced to deal with a much wider range of people and issues. The transition seems to have been a smooth one. By the start of the 1935 session, Wilcox was becoming part of the leadership group in the Senate. Her committee assignments put her in a position to control legislation in her areas of concern. She was more vocal. Most important, she was changing her view of the government's role in economic and social issues. The depression had severely eroded the laissez-faire philosophy that had been a cornerstone of her father's and uncle's views, and of her own. More and more, she was willing to use the government to solve the problems facing the territory.

5 Lady Politician

The 1935 legislative session opened with the worst internecine battle in the history of the territory. Five Democrats were now in the Senate, but the composition was similar to the 1933 legislature; initially, all the Democrats, again, were from Honolulu. (See Appendix for the names of the senators.)

The 1935 Legislature: Treading Water

Charles Rice had lost the confidence of the Republican caucus, and Oʻahu Democrats proposed to join forces with the Republicans to overthrow him. This put some members in a difficult position. George Cooke from Maui, for example, was planning to run for reelection in 1936 and did not want to alienate Rice's brother, Harold, a powerful politician on Maui. Elsie Wilcox's dilemma continued. At the Republican caucus organizational meeting, Harry Holt nominated Rice to be chairperson of the Senate Ways and Means Committee, but the nomination died for lack of a second. In the full Senate, Joseph Sylva was elected chair of the Ways and Means Committee and George Cooke president. David Trask nominated Henry Freitas to be vice-president. Freitas withdrew and moved Wilcox be elected unanimously, which she was.[1] She was also chair of the Education Committee.

Responding to a Kauaʻi newspaper article asserting she had been discourteous in not seconding Rice's nomination, Wilcox, in her usual straightforward manner, attributed it to "his activities in the recent election when he supported L. L. McCandless against Samuel Wilder King, the Republican nominee for delegate." Rice, she believed, was disloyal to his party:

> Under the circumstances it is rather difficult to see just how anyone could expect the party to grant him any favors. As the executive committeeman of the Republican central committee, I could hardly countenance Senator Rice's campaign activities for Mr. McCandless by supporting him for one of the most important committee chairmanships that the Republican majority in the senate has to offer its members. I believe in party government and am a loyal member of the Republican party.[2]

If anyone had doubts about the division between Wilcox and Rice, this put them to rest.

The fact that Wilcox was elected vice-president and chair of the Education Committee indicated the esteem her colleagues afforded her. Another indication of the senators' high regard was that she was appointed by Cooke to a five-person committee to investigate allegations against Republican Senator Ernest Akina that he did not live in his Hilo district and that he had asked for $300 to engineer the transfer of a public schoolteacher from Moloka'i to O'ahu. After extensive investigation, the committee gave a split recommendation. Wilcox, Joseph Farrington, and Joseph Sylva—all Republicans—recommended expulsion, and Democrat Lester Petrie and Republican H. A. Baldwin recommended a reprimand. By an 11 to 3 vote, the Senate voted to expel Akina.[3]

Several minor issues came up during the session. Reapportionment was raised and "squelched again." All the O'ahu senators, regardless of party, voted against tabling the measure but lost to the nine senators from the neighbor islands.[4] The question of establishing a civil service in the territory was raised and killed. Hawaiians opposed it because, according to the *Advertiser,* they held many of the positions that would be covered by civil service and feared they could not compete in the examinations.[5]

The Hawaiian homesteads issue came up again, this time with a complaint from Ho'olehua homesteaders on Moloka'i that they were not receiving enough profit from the pineapple companies leasing homestead lands. The pineapple companies were giving the homesteaders supplies and labor, but the homesteaders had to help pay for roads the company used. Rice investigated the complaint and recommended that the problem be given to Secretary of the Interior Ickes because the legislature could not do much in the fifteen days remaining in the session.[6]

A Wilcox bill to increase the number of circuit court clerks and raise their pay passed both houses of the legislature.[7] A Wilcox Senate concurrent resolution to create a holdover committee to study single-salary schedules for teachers also passed.[8]

A big debate centered on how the Kaua'i supervisors should be chosen. The House had passed a bill sponsored by Clem Gomes to divide the island into five districts, with the members elected from the districts choosing their own chair. Charles Rice, on the other hand, supported the existing system of five at-large seats, with the winners choosing the chair. Rice was angry with Wilcox because she wanted the Senate to vote on Gomes' bill, which she supported. Rice claimed that "election by districts would deprive the taxpayers of the right to vote for county government, leaving them merely district representatives and leaving elections on the island open to 'colonization' of the districts."[9] He feared "coercion by big interests." However, all the Kaua'i House members were for Gomes' bill. Wilcox argued that some "districts on Kaua'i were not represented at all on the board but they should be." The Senate approved the Gomes bill.

After all the debate, the governor vetoed the separate district bill, saying the island was small, and supervisors who acted for the whole island should be elected by all the people of the island. In small districts, the dominant element could lead to "invisible government," something everyone wanted to avoid. He also vetoed a civil service plan the Democrats labeled as a Republican attempt to take away the governor's power to replace people he did not want in government.[10]

The legislative session had not been particularly productive. However, with the depression receding, issues other than economics had at least been debated. A sense of relief that Hawai'i had been spared the worst of the depression permeated the session. The education budget was raised 12.8 percent to $9,093.725, an indication of better times.[11] With no mid-term elections, the legislators returned to their districts until January 1937.

Commenting on her contributions to the 1935 legislative session, Wilcox highlighted her support for additional money to the Child Welfare Boards; territorial money to secure federal funds; more money to vocational education; a senior high school established at Waimea; restoration of teachers' and other employees' salaries; a $3.00 minimum wage (which did not pass); and changes in the workmen's compensation law.[12] Again, her emphasis was on social welfare and education.

In June 1935, the United States Supreme Court declared the NRA unconstitutional. The *Advertiser* opined that progress toward a single wage standard had come about because of the NRA and that more would follow, although more slowly. Second-generation Asian children were becoming Americanized, and they would aspire to an American life-style. "Because they want these things there will be a gradual pressure for American-style wages and that pressure will eventually make itself felt."[13]

Through the end of 1935 and into 1936, the economy continued to improve. The sugar industry had a profitable year in 1935, the first in several years. Tax receipts in 1935 were 29 percent higher than in 1934. In July 1936, the governor announced a pay increase for teachers and other territorial employees, restoring their salaries almost to the 1929 level. In November, the HSPA recommended a 5 percent bonus for all workers.[14]

The New Deal made a significant impact not just on the economy of Hawai'i but on other aspects of life in the territory. In August 1936, the HSPA announced it would initiate an eight-hour day for skilled workers. Even the Republicans embraced social security in their party platform.

Statehood was a major issue in the territory. For the first time since 1896, the national Republican platform did not mention statehood for Hawai'i. The national Democratic party platform had never supported statehood. The national AFL-CIO (American Federation of Labor and Congress of Industrial Organizations) announced its opposition to statehood, fearing it would "add a Japanese state to the union."[15] Wilcox and most Republicans were strong supporters of statehood; they believed that the needs of Hawai'i would be better represented in Congress by a full, voting congressional delegation. Hawai'i would receive more attention and support as a state than as a territory. The desire for statehood increased as the national government inserted itself more energetically into areas of life that traditionally had been the states' domain. With the increase in federal money came federal regulation, but at least in the beginning, the regulation was modest compared with the resources available from Washington. In addition, Wilcox and many others in Hawai'i considered themselves Americans and resented their second-class status.

Despite the popularity of the New Deal programs, the territorial Democrats did not make significant electoral gains because they remained badly divided. The McCandless and Wilson factions seemed to be more interested in fighting each other than the Republicans. One thing they could agree on was that Governor Poindexter was too slow in getting rid of Republicans and giving patronage jobs to Democrats. To make matters worse, William and Clarence Crozier announced they were forming an Independent Labor Party because neither existing party was serving the people. William Crozier had particularly harsh words for the Democratic party, which he accused of doublecrossing him. The *Advertiser* commented that it was entirely possible a third party would be successful in the near future in Hawai'i because the Democrats fought among themselves so much, and "there are growing free-thinking groups" in the territory who might not support the Republicans if the Republicans were unable to maintain the prosperity of the territory. The *Advertiser* also pointed the finger at old-timers who continued to control the Republican party and the unwise party stance opposing many New Deal programs, including the AAA (Agricultural Adjustment Administration) and NRA.[16]

In May 1936, the territory began preparations to qualify for Social Security. Each of the counties had an established old-age pension board. Following the national pattern, these were reconstituted as child welfare boards, and their chairs became the territorial Hawaii Child Welfare Board. Elsie Wilcox, chair of the Kaua'i board, was selected to chair the territorial board. Nell Findley was the director.

There Is More to Life Than Politics

During the summer of 1936, Elsie Wilcox took a three-month trip to the mainland, a combination of business and pleasure. She visited Mexico and Guatemala City and traveled through the Panama Canal to New York. She was a delegate to the National Conference of Social Work in Atlantic City, which she attended with Nell Findley. Wilcox concluded that many opportunities for social workers would arise as a result of the Social Security Act.[17] She also commented on the increasingly public nature of social welfare work and said that the private personnel were "somewhat perplexed as to their future field of activity."[18] That was eminently true in Hawai'i, where the government had taken over much of the work previously funded by private charities.[19]

While in Atlantic City, Findley received a cablegram from Governor Poindexter asking her to go to Washington to determine what kind of laws Hawai'i needed to bring the territory into line with federal mandates. Wilcox joined Findley and spent several days with people from the Social Security Administration learning how to obtain old-age pension and child welfare grants for Hawai'i.

Wilcox was an observer at the Republican National Convention in Cleveland and was quoted as saying, "Governor Landon has a strong support among the younger elements especially in the middle West, and the feeling seems to be that he has a good, fighting chance in the coming election."[20] She remained a party loyalist.

That year she was elected corporate member-at-large of the American Board of Commissioners for Foreign Missions (ABCFM) for a six-year term. It is interesting to note her continued support of the ABCFM. Brewer Eddie had commented earlier on the fact that G. N. Wilcox supported the organization, even though he was one of the "men who had suffered through the Board's neglect, perhaps, in their boyhood."[21] Despite Abner Wilcox's bitterness about his treatment by the ABCFM, his children and grandchildren held the group in high regard and gave it substantial amounts of money.

Elsie Wilcox continued the family's philanthropy, in 1936 opening Wilcox Hall at Punahou School. Wilcox's response to a request that she be present at the building's dedication was typical of her attitude toward publicity: "Is a ceremony of dedicating necessary? If you feel that there should be one it should be extremely simple in character."[22]

Back to Politics

In March 1936, Henry K. Aki had announced he would run against Elsie Wilcox in the October primary. The speculation was that Rice "would not actively support Sen. Wilcox in her campaign for reelection." Aki said that unlike Wilcox, he would support Rice for chair of the Ways and Means Committee. Aki pointed out that he had always supported Rice, except during the 1931 session and special 1932 session. The *Advertiser* said, "It was this break that brought about his defeat by Sen. Wilcox in 1932."[23] In a July 26 editorial, the *Honolulu Times* wrote, "Kauai knows Henry, for he served one term as senator. He is a jovial, personally likeable fellow, fond of luaus and other divertissements, but as a senator, he is a good craps shooter. During his incumbency he was just one more vote for senator Charlie Rice, who did his thinking for him—as, indeed, he did for other senators." The paper predicted a "calamity" would result if Aki were elected.

The actual campaigning began in late September. In a typical speech, Wilcox, speaking in Hanalei, said she felt right at home, because her family had lived there for a hundred years. "I have stood by you," she said, listing her committees and other activities. She stressed the importance of education and her knowledge of education needs. Aki said, "If you send me back I will cooperate with Sen. C. A. Rice. Sen. Rice needs someone down there to help him."[24]

Wilcox and Aki sparred often on the subject of education. At a rally in Waimea, Wilcox reminded listeners she was responsible for restoring the teachers' salaries. Aki accused her of supporting the $10 tuition (which she had done) and promised free education, books, and bussing. Wilcox pointed out that she was responsible for the new school in Waimea.[25]

Whenever Wilcox visited a community and gave a speech, she highlighted her talk with her accomplishments for that area: money for a water resources study at Kalāheo; electric power for Moloaʻa; $2,000 for a drainage ditch in Anahola; $5,000 for a river opening at Hanapēpē; $13,000 for vocational equipment for intermediate and high schools; and county dentists to care for indigent patients. The "pork" was duly noted everywhere.

Given the fact that she was a seasoned campaigner and had been delivering speeches for at least fifteen years, Wilcox's response to a request from the Hawaii Education Association to present a speech at their convention is amusing. She said, "As you know I am not much of a speaker and the prospect of addressing in the microphone of KGU or KGMB as well as your many MA's and Ph.D.'s is quite terrifying to me. I am sure you can find someone far better equipped to address such a discriminating group."[26] This despite the fact that she had regularly entertained distinguished educators at Grove Farm for many years. She was occasionally bemused by her status and was inclined to downplay it.

Wilcox had a well-organized campaign. She had many supporters among the Japanese on the plantations, and she kept lists of their names with comments about their likes and dislikes, their position in the community, and whether they were good or poor campaign workers. She also worked the small businesses—ice houses, garages, bakeries, and soda water works. She had strong support among the teachers.

Elsie Wilcox beat Aki decisively, two to one.[27] Not only was she popular, but Aki had lost much of his credibility in his vacillation regarding Rice. Rice also had suffered from his defeat in the Ways and Means Committee battle and his inability to control either the House or the Senate during the previous session.

The 1937 Legislature: The Economy Gets Better

The makeup of the Senate remained similar to what it had been in 1935. There were four Democrats, one Nonpartisan, and ten Republicans. The Democrats did better on the island of Hawai'i and worse on O'ahu, but the totals were as they had been before. Sarah Todd Cunningham from Hilo joined Elsie Wilcox as the second woman elected to the Senate.

In an odd turn of events, Rice continued to be powerful in the Senate. This time around, his supporters were different and included David Trask, William Heen, and Charles Silva—all Democrats—and Republican Harry Holt. Those opposing him were Eugene Beebe, Joseph Farrington, Joseph Sylva, James Campsie, H. A. Baldwin, and Elsie Wilcox—all Republicans. The rest were "uncertain." Rice, called to explain a $1,000 contribution to President Roosevelt's reelection campaign, said, "I have never made any secret of my great admiration and respect for president Franklin Delano Roosevelt. Before I am a member of the Republican party I am an American first." He went on to claim that the bank holiday had saved America from revolution, that Jones-Costigan saved the Hawaiian sugar industry, that the Republican presidential candidate had pledged to make the Midwest and Western beet areas the sugar bowl of the United States (which would have ruined Hawai'i), and that CWA and FERA had saved thousands of people from starvation. He was accused of making the $1,000 donation in a bid to be appointed governor, a charge he labeled as "silly," because $1,000 was an insignificant amount.[28]

H. A. Baldwin was elected president of the Senate. During the session, party lines, somewhat strictly observed during previous sessions, were less decisive. Before the session, Wilcox had written to a woman who wanted to join the Senate staff: "The prospects of a really harmonious senate do not appear so very good but I hope affairs may turn in more promising shape than anticipated in some quarters."[29] With Rice at odds with the Republicans, and the Croziers in both

House and Senate at odds with almost everyone, the situation was more fluid than in past years. Elsie Wilcox was again chair of the Education Committee and was on the Lands and Health committees. Rice chaired the Lands Committee.

Elsie Wilcox was considerably more active in this session than in previous years. She introduced legislation to secure additional social security benefits, including child welfare, mothers' aid, and help for the blind and crippled.[30] Her work in Washington, D.C., had given her a good understanding of what the territory needed to do to secure federal funds. She sponsored a bill eliminating the $10 tuition for high school students. Only Trask and Brown voted against it in the Senate, but it was killed in the House. Another Wilcox bill, to credit teachers with the automatic pay raises they lost during the four worst years of the depression, passed the Senate by a 9 to 6 vote.[31] A Wilcox bill to establish kindergartens in public schools using federal funds became law. She was successful in sponsoring a bill to raise the compulsory school age from fourteen to sixteen.[32] She appeared before various public meetings and on KGMB radio to explain her position and to push her program. Despite her reservations about speaking into microphones, she used radio with increasing frequency.[33]

The issue of reapportionment came up again, this time in the context of statehood. Governor Poindexter had sent a resolution to Congress to pass enabling legislation for statehood. Neighbor island legislators were angered by the resolution's stipulation that delegates to the constitutional convention should be elected on the basis of population. Harry Baldwin of Maui pointed out that the resolution would give Oʻahu control of the territorial government, to which David Trask replied that that was a good idea. Charles Rice urged that if delegates were to be elected on the basis of population, actual voters, not registered voters should be counted, because Maui had "a lot of dead people on the rolls." The Senate passed a Rice bill to reapportion the House but not the Senate.[34]

Despite heated opposition, the Senate passed a resolution introduced by Crozier to ask Congress to make women in Hawaiʻi eligible for jury service.[35] Elsie Wilcox and other prominent women, including Leonora Bilger, University of Hawaii Dean of Women, spoke in favor of it. Wilcox pointed out that the proposal had passed the territorial legislature ten years earlier, but Congress had rejected it. However, a more liberal Congress was likely to approve it. "History shows that Hawaiian women have always been active in government and civic affairs and have amply proved they are qualified for jury service," she said. Senator Trask, in opposition, responded, "I have a wife and 9 children and if my wife went on a jury I would have to stay home and do the work. And my wife would feel sorry for every accused person."[36]

Senator Crozier introduced several minimum wage and maximum hours bills, some for women only, some for men also. Some women's clubs supported the women's legislation, because many women were working twelve to sixteen hours a day. Some professional women opposed the plan because they feared their wages would be lowered or that no one would hire them because they could not work long hours.[37] None passed.

During the session, Elsie Wilcox gave a speech to the YWCA. She spoke of her legislative program and then turned to the responsibility that the members' advantages of education, wealth, and leisure entailed. She called on the Y to research the lives of working girls, including wages, hours, safety, and other working conditions. Then she presented the women with an additional challenge:

> What of the maids in our own homes? Are not we, too, great offenders in imposing long hours, with often inadequate pay, insufficient time off for rest or recreation, unattractive and unsuitable living quarters, poorly planned schedules or *no* set schedules, abrupt changes of plans with no advance notice, no extra time off or extra pay where a girl gives *us* extra time, no effort made to allow her to improve herself educationally, but little opportunity for recreation or social life, no annual vacation. Of all the professions, household employment seems to be the one in which the least opportunity is offered a girl to be regarded as a *person,* with normal desires for self-expression and self-realization.[38]

She pointed out that bills for an eight-hour day and a minimum wage of $.25 per hour for women had been introduced, but research was needed to support them.

Despite strong Democratic opposition, the legislature passed a comprehensive civil service bill. The first attempt to establish civil service in the territory had been in 1912, when the Honolulu police and fire departments were covered by a territorial act. According to Donald Johnson, that act was not effective in isolating those departments from political favoritism, and the concept of civil service was fought by patronage interests and some employees who were afraid they might not pass the exam.[39] Included in the 1937 coverage were all but the most senior executives in the territorial and county governments. The Democrats claimed that the provision forbidding civil service employees from contributing to political causes would break the party because they "were without wealthy friends" and relied on office holders for their support. They particularly objected to including the police in the City and County of Honolulu.[40]

As was often the case, the legislature worked right up to its deadline, including an all-night session the final night. Although the legislators were exhausted, tempers were not especially frayed, probably indicating that despite the debates, the legislature had not dealt with any genuinely divisive issues. In part that was because at the last minute the leadership decided to create interim committees to work on several matters. Wilcox, Beebe, Crozier, Silva, and Heen were appointed to a committee to study the Crozier bills and other labor legislation. Wilcox, Heen, and Farrington were appointed to a committee to study education and the financial support necessary for it.[41]

The governor signed most of the legislation, but pocket vetoed the teachers' pay restoration bill, much to Elsie Wilcox's dismay. He said the cost was too high, but, as it turned out, the territory ended the biennium with a $1,315,133 surplus, a situation Rice had predicted in 1934. The teachers may have overplayed their hand. Their public, highly vocal lobbying seemed to have antagonized the governor and small businessmen, who reasoned that any surplus money ought to go toward compensating people who had lost their jobs during the depression. The governor also vetoed the civil service bill, on the ground that it was too extensive—the provision included everyone not confirmed by the territorial Senate, or, in the case of Honolulu, the county Board of Supervisors. He did not want the provision to include private, confidential clerks or stenos for judges and other high officials.[42]

As she viewed the session in retrospect, Wilcox pointed to an array of achievements: an increased school budget; more teachers; the establishment of more than twenty additional grades in rural schools; more money for vocational education; the workmen's disability compensation law; legislation protecting children; more money for Kaua'i public improvement projects; county pension systems; and improvements in the social security law.[43]

It is significant that she was so supportive of vocational education. About this time, vocational education began to lead to good jobs because of the increasing national defense buildup and mechanization on the plantations in response to the exigencies of the depression. Wilcox still had the same goals, but now the means were shifting as government, with her leadership, was becoming more involved in problem solving at the local level.

In the summer of 1937, Helen Bary from the Social Security Administration in Washington spent a month investigating the social security plan in Hawai'i. She declared it a "model system of public welfare, one with sound laws and a board and administrative personnel of extremely high caliber." She was confident that the aid to dependent children and old-age plans would be approved by Washington.[44] Elsie Wilcox's study in Washington and her prestige in the legislature were largely responsible for the quick approval of the territorial laws by Washington.

In October, a delegation of United States senators and representatives arrived in Hawai'i to investigate the issue of granting statehood to the territory. Wilcox entertained the delegation on Kaua'i. Early the next year, the delegation recommended that statehood be postponed, a severe blow to statehood advocates, who thought the opportunity was ripe and expected most of the members were going to support it. However, the AFL and East Coast sugar refiners had announced they were opposed, as were many Southern congressmen.[45]

The Republicans held their territorial convention in June 1938. Elsie Wilcox was on the platform committee, which drafted a platform calling for statehood, "repeal of anti-labor laws which hinder labor in its right to organize and bargain collectively under federal regulations," reapportionment of the territorial House of Representatives, and creation of a territorial department of labor. Even the Republican party was responding to the voice of labor. The platform also said, "The Republican party records its full confidence in the citizenry of Hawaii, of whatever racial ancestry, and repudiates emphatically the comparatively recent introduction mostly by newcomers, of racial antagonisms, which are foreign to the spirit of Hawaii and un-American in principle."[46]

This last statement may have been in response to anti-Japanese sentiments arising out of the Japanese war in China, which, by 1938, had resulted in large losses of Chinese life and territory. It may also have been aimed at the increasing numbers of American military stationed in Hawai'i because of the situation in East Asia. These people often brought mainland prejudices to Hawai'i and found it difficult to live in a multicultural society where they were not the majority.

That summer, three long-time politicians made surprising announcements. Senator Charles Silva and Representative James Kealoha bolted from the Democratic party and joined the Republicans. Silva had been fighting with David Trask during the previous legislative session and had voted with the Republicans much of the time. Kealoha said the Democrats were too divided, and the Republicans had been helpful to him.[47]

The big surprise was Charles Rice announcing his retirement from political life. He said the "demand of other responsibilities" required it. He did not elaborate. Even though he still held political power, he could not control the legislature the way he had in past years. He was out of favor with the Republicans, and the Democrats were still skeptical of a life-long Republican. He was sixty-two and may have wanted to escape from the pressure of political life in Honolulu.

Although he continued to call himself a Republican, Rice supported David Trask in his contest for election as delegate to Congress. Samuel King decisively beat Trask by a vote of 40,207 to 28,244. The story was different on Kaua'i, where Trask beat King 3,142 to 2,862, perhaps because of Rice's clout. In addition, Lindsay Faye, a "shoo-in" for territorial senator, was beaten by Democrat J. B. Fernandes 3,204 to 2,957.[48]

In 1937, Jack Hall, a prominent union leader in Honolulu, had gone to Kaua'i to help organize the plantations and the waterfront. The ILWU (International Longshoremen's and Warehousemen's Union) claimed three thousand workers on the waterfront and plantations on Kaua'i. An eighty-day waterfront strike ended in compromise.[49] Hall and a few others tried to interest plantation workers in union ideals, but most of them either did not care or feared that attendance at union meetings, much less joining the union, would cost them their jobs. However, Hall was instrumental in Fernandes' win. Hall organized the Kauai Progressive League to elect candidates supportive of labor, and Fernandes represented the League's first victory.[50] During this time, Hall and Rice became friends, a further indication of Rice's estrangement from the establishment.

Labor historian Edward Beechert chronicled considerable union activity in 1937. A strike at Pu'unēnē on Maui ended in defeat for the union, but for the first time, a company agreed to meet with the union to discuss future disputes. The ILWU was formally organized that year.[51] Perhaps most important, the National Labor Relations Board (NLRB) held its first hearing in Hawai'i. In 1935, the Hilo Longshoremen's Association had been created, and the *Voice of Labor,* a labor newspaper, was started.[52] Labor had come a long way since 1930, when "labor organizations in the Hawaiian Islands [were] few in number, small in membership, and, with the exception of the barbers' union, [had] no agreements with the employers."[53] In the late 1930s, labor started organizing by industry and making a direct appeal to class issues rather than race.

The 1939 Legislature: Labor's Presence Felt

The 1939 legislative session saw a Senate more fractured than ever—impossible though that may have seemed—plus a division between the Senate and House so bitter it almost scuttled all major legislation and resulted in the defeat of some key bills. There were eleven Republicans, one Nonpartisan, and only three Democrats.

Members of the 1939 Senate, twentieth legislature, of the Territory of Hawaii. *Standing, left to right:* John B. Fernandes, William H. Hill, Harry H. Holt, Clarence A. Crozier, William H. Heen, David K. Trask, James Kealoha, and Francis H. Ii Brown. *Seated, left to right:* Charles H. Silva, Joseph R. Farrington, Sarah Todd Cunningham, George P. Cooke (president), Eugene H. Beebe (vice-president), Elsie H. Wilcox, and Francis K. Sylva.

Madam President Pro-Tem

March 23, 1939, photograph in the *Honolulu Advertiser.* "Birthday—The territorial senate observed the birthday anniversary yesterday of Senator Elsie H. Wilcox of Kauai in three ways, by resolution, with a basket of flowers and by having her preside in the absence of Senate President George P. Cooke over the afternoon meeting. Several senators forgot and addressed her as Mr. President but she knew her parliamentary law and held the reins tightly during two arguments on the floor."

Elsie Wilcox again chaired the Education Committee. She was also a member of the powerful Ways and Means Committee and the Public Lands Committee, and she chaired the Select Committee for Kaua'i. On her birthday, she was elected president of the Senate for the day.

Governor Poindexter announced that he wanted a balanced biennium budget, taxes on liquor and cigarettes, automatic salary increases for territorial employees, and reapportionment of the territorial House. He was against the proposal to increase the gross income tax, because he did not want to discourage business.[54] The economy, which had been improving, was sliding downhill again—not steeply, but enough to raise concerns.

The governor of the territory had less power over the legislature than did governors in states because he was appointed by the U.S. president and often had no substantial local constituency. This was particularly true of Poindexter, who came to his position without a long record in territorial politics. The governor was not necessarily viewed as the head of his party, and after he distributed whatever patronage jobs were available, he had little clout to use on seasoned politicians of either party.

As usual, the schools came in for a good deal of attention. The governor wanted to control the Department of Public Instruction budget rather than the Commission for Public Instruction sending the budget directly to the legislature. Wilcox and Joseph Farrington "voiced spirited opposition" to the plan. Wilcox said that the existing arrangement, instituted in 1911 to insulate the schools from politics, "assures the automatic continuation of the schools."[55] The Senate majority argued, however, that the schools should be treated like all the other departments in the government. The House agreed with Wilcox, and the proposal failed there.

Wilcox introduced a bill to provide teachers with credit for the five years they did not receive raises. The *Advertiser* commented that the "economic bloc" was opposed to the proposal. She also introduced a bill to change the way teachers were paid, from a scale based on the level of school where the teacher taught to the teacher's credentials and number of years in the system. This was to apply only to new teachers.[56] Both bills failed in the Senate.

More than in any previous session, the voice of labor was heard in the Senate, despite the fact that the composition of the Senate had changed little in the past six years. This was partly because New Deal legislation such as the NLRA (National Labor Relations Act) and the Social Security Act mandated some territorial actions, and because the growing power of the United Mine Workers and other mainland unions received considerable publicity in Hawai'i. In addition, intermittent strikes in the territory, although not especially successful, had raised the community's level of awareness about labor's grievances and the potential power of the labor movement. This was certainly true of Elsie Wilcox. She supported proposals such as maximum hours legislation for men, which she had opposed earlier.

A key labor issue was the creation of a territorial department of labor. The question was not whether there should be a department but whether it should be combined with welfare and social security into a single board and whether it should be headed by a commission or single individual. Labor was unanimous in its opinion that labor should have a separate board, but the CIO supported a commission and the AFL a single person. A majority of the Senate, including Wilcox, voted for a commission to lead the labor board, reflecting the position taken by the business community as well as the CIO. The legislature created separate departments for social security, welfare, and labor.[57]

Labor also proposed a $.60 per hour minimum wage and a forty-four or forty maximum hour law. It called for the repeal of several laws passed after the 1920 strike, including a criminal syndicalism law; anarchistic publications statute; picketing and protection of labor laws that made it "illegal to interfere, singly or conspiring together, with a person's lawful right to work"; and antiloitering and trespassing laws.[58] The unions also wanted agricultural workers included in labor protection laws. Hawai'i had more laborers excluded from the National Labor Relations Act than any state because of the high percentage of agricultural laborers, a situation labor deplored.[59]

The Senate postponed a decision on most of the labor legislation until the 1941 session.[60] It did, however, call for a federal study of the situation, and Dr. James Shoemaker was sent to Hawai'i by the Labor Department in Washington. Elsie Wilcox was part of a group "representing the women of the territory," which urged that Ethel Erickson, also of the Department of Labor, be sent to study the conditions of women and girls in industry.[61] She came in 1940.

By a vote of 8 to 7, with Wilcox in the majority, the Senate passed a civil service bill that became law. It covered the Honolulu police department and most territorial employees, with a few exceptions at the top of each department. As of July 1, 1940, it was to apply to the Maui and Hawai'i police departments. For reasons not stated in the record, the Kaua'i police department was not covered.[62]

The legislature closed with an all-night session. The gallery was packed, and entertainers played and sang during the many recesses. The *Advertiser* concluded that although there had been severe divisions between the two houses, it was the "most productive in history."[63] The governor signed most of the legislation but pocket vetoed the classification plan because, he said, the territory could not afford the $120,000 necessary to implement it, and the civil service commission, which had just been created, had enough to do. He suggested he would approve the plan in the next biennium.

As the legislature was winding down, Wilcox, in a surprise move, announced she would not seek the Republican National Committeewoman position. Bina Mossman, an O'ahu House of Representatives member, had indicated an interest in it, and Wilcox declared Mossman "has worked long and hard for the Republican Party and I will not permit my name to be put up as an opposition candidate."[64] Although she did not say so, she was preparing to withdraw from elective politics.

6 Defeat and Victory

The 1940 Campaign

Elsie Wilcox did not want to run for a third term in 1940. Clem Gomes announced his entry in the Republican primary, and she waited a long time before finally announcing her candidacy. She wrote her brother, Gaylord, in August, "Since no other candidates have presented themselves for the Senate in opposition to Clem Gomes it has been necessary for me, as incumbent, to run again. This is all I can do in fairness to the Republican Party."[1] The same day she wrote several people in Honolulu, "Whatever the outcome, I shall not have failed the party."[2]

She realized the race would be difficult, and her letters portend defeat. The trip back and forth to Honolulu was a strain, and she was now sixty-one. In addition, the world situation was becoming increasingly threatening. Honolulu papers carried the news of Japanese and German movements into new territories almost monthly, and the possibility of war in the Pacific hung over everyday activities in Hawai'i. She was disheartened about events in Kaua'i, the territory, and the world. Many of the issues she had spent her adult life working on seemed to be turning out wrong.

Having agreed to run, she summoned up her usual determination. She now called herself a "liberal Republican" in her ads, something she had, in fact, always been. She gave many speeches at rallies and on the radio. Her theme was the same she had used in 1932 and 1936—her knowledge of the social welfare, educational, health, and infrastructure needs of Kaua'i. She addressed the education issue in a radio speech:

> The appointment [as chair of the Education Committee] was given me for the reason that about twenty years ago I became Commissioner of Education for the County of Kauai. In that position, I saw things that were holding our children back. Many could not go to High School because of the expense of long distances to be traveled—text books were not furnished free—often they could not afford to buy any for themselves. I saw teachers underpaid and undertrained. And—I saw that while we were teaching our boys and girls to read and write and to recite history, science, geography and the like, we were not teaching them how to make a living for themselves.
>
> And so the study of the correction for these weaknesses became my special interest.... As Chairman I have been able to give my Kauai fellow-members assistance in obtaining beneficial measures for our schools.... And as Chairman I have been able to fulfill the hope which grew in me while I was your school commissioner of being able to do something to improve our school system.[3]

She stressed her seniority and the respect of her colleagues in and out of the Senate. She could be a real help to Kaua'i.

She paid particular attention to women voters. Her thesis was that women had special needs and concerns. In one radio talk, she spelled out her view in detail:

> The things to which I refer concern children; they concern the family budget and how it is affected by taxes; they concern the family income and the job that brings it in,—the wages—working hours,—and working conditions of those who earn a living for *your family*. They also concern other things that closely touch the sympathies of women—the welfare of the aged and the needy, and of crippled, neglected and dependent children.
>
> It doesn't matter whether you are married or single. It doesn't matter whether you have children or not. The fact that *you are a woman* makes all these problems very important to you. [Emphasis in original.]

She went on to talk about her work with children as chair of the Welfare Board. Children were ill because they were not properly fed; crippled children could not get help because their parents could not afford it; children were neglected and ended up in industrial homes.

She urged women to vote and reminded them that they were privileged in a way other women had not been:

> You are the women of today—American citizens in your own right. You have been free to go to school—free to make careers for yourselves—free to own your own property—free to think and vote and act for yourselves. Many of you are daughters and granddaughters of women who never knew what it meant to have the rights you enjoy.[4]

The consistent appeals to women may have been unwise, since 4,309 men and 3,201 women were registered to vote.[5]

She also made a pitch to the new voters of Asian ancestry, reminding them that the United States was one of the few countries in the world with the vote:

> As I go about I observe that our young people, these new voters, are accepting their responsibilities thoughtfully. They are proud of their American citizenship and of their coming of age to exercise their rights. We dedicate to them the new patriotic song, "I am an American" a recording by Dick Robertson and his orchestra, now sweeping America.[6]

On several occasions, she said that simply introducing legislation was not enough; money had to be available to pay for projects, and bills had to pass both houses of the legislature. This was an indirect attack on Gomes, who made somewhat extravagant claims about his legislative record.

She tackled the issue of taxes head-on. She said that most of what government did was well worth the money, but it was other people's money:

> There is such a thing as spending the people's money—your money—too freely. Making ends meet is the job of the woman in the house. When you realize that 35 cents out of every dollar your family earns goes to pay taxes, directly or indirectly, don't you think you should be careful to elect public officials who will spend your money carefully and for the most good?[7]

The threat of war is evident in her campaign. More than in previous years, she supported vocational education—not for plantation work but to prepare local youths for good jobs in the burgeoning defense establishment. Machinists, welders, carpenters, and other craftsmen were all needed, and "It grieves me deeply to see these jobs go unfilled by our own boys of Hawaii because they lack the necessary training." Likewise, there was a need to train girls in nursing, welfare work, and "other occupations suitable to them such as dressmaking." She took great pride in the fact that over the years, more and more teachers were local students, and the territory was importing very few from the mainland.[8]

In 1940, much more than in the other campaigns, she stressed her support of labor, of the right to organize, of the need for a Hawaii Labor Bureau, and workmen's compensation. She said that her early welfare work had made her sympathetic to modern labor legislation. "I became convinced that wage-earners should have the right to organize and bargain collectively to improve their earnings and the conditions under which they work." Even on this issue, she brought in her concern for women. "It is just as important to their women folk as it is to them [the men]. For it is the woman in the house who must make ends meet. And when pay is too low and jobs are too uncertain, the biggest load of worry falls on her." She continued, "I am a firm believer in the right of labor to organize and bargain collectively. And I believe quite as strongly in unemployment insurance, in the regulation of hours and wages, and in the enforcement of fair labor practices."[9]

She also spoke in favor of an improved territorial retirement plan, and better county and police pension systems. She regarded these not as handouts but as earnings by the workers. She urged a "go slow" method with study and consultation, especially since labor leaders themselves were divided. "In my opinion it is better to advance slowly, learn from our mistakes and correct them rather than plunge into legislation which may seriously affect the laborer."[10] To what extent labor believed her statements regarding her support of labor is unclear, but the unions did not support her.

The factors in Honolulu did support her, however. John Waterhouse of Alexander and Baldwin wrote, "I am sure that all the A & B interests on Kauai will back you to the limit. If you have any reason to think that they are not, please let me know."[11] H. A. Walker, president of AmFac wrote, "Please advise me if in any way you feel that we are not doing everything possible for your re-election, and I can assure you I will do my utmost to get our interests on that Island to fully cooperate."[12]

On Kauaʻi also, she tried to persuade management to help get out the vote. She wrote to Mr. Burns at Lihue Plantation that one of her workers "is very anxious that management should express itself to its workers. He feels that nothing has been said and that the worker has a great deal more confidence if he knows that the boss approves of what he is doing and that he is free to go ahead."[13] This was part of a system that the unions and Democratic party fought to end. The plantation boss exercised control over the supposedly free vote of the laborers, either through negative coercion or positive reinforcement. Since the laborers' livelihoods depended to a large extent on the good will of the manager or the *luna* (supervisor), most were reluctant to openly oppose the plantation's position on public issues. Whether the pressure was real or imagined, it was effective because workers thought it existed.

Jack Hall returned to Kaua'i in 1940 to write speeches and organize for Clem Gomes.[14] Although Charles Rice had "retired" from politics, he supported Gomes and put his considerable political strength behind the Gomes campaign. Wilcox was being repaid for her desertion from the Rice camp.

Gomes said he would run a clean campaign. "Miss Wilcox is a lady. I shall show the people of Kauai that I am a gentleman and we will have a campaign as clean as the deep blue ocean."[15] Up until the last few days, by contemporary standards it was a clean campaign.

Gomes attacked Wilcox not so much for what she had done but for what she represented—wealth and power. In various ways, he derided her attempts to express empathy with the poor, the sick, and labor:

> I do not have to proclaim my sympathy for poor children, I know from experience and it is this very experience that has prompted me to give so much of my time in the past 16 years so that the children of this Island may have better educational facilities and at less expense than their parents.... Some candidates for public office are on unfamiliar ground when discussing labor.... Capital is the fruit of labor.[16]

He attacked the tax system, claiming that most of the tax burden fell on those least able to pay. The poll tax, for example, was paid by 80 percent of the people of Kaua'i. The 1.5 percent business tax was simply passed on to customers. He objected to the welfare system because he thought plantations, not the government, should take care of their former employees: "The working people are required by the so called representatives of the people who they send to the legislature to support many of those who have given 30 or 40 years of their lives to make Hawaii what it is today. I believe that those who have taken the best years of these workers lives should be required to care for them." He also objected to the newly passed tobacco and liquor taxes. "To many of the people tobacco is as much a necessity of life as bread. A tax on tobacco is definitely a tax on the working people."

He spoke to the newer voters, who were either agriculture workers themselves or whose parents who were plantation laborers. Agriculture workers, he said, were kicked "from pillar to post" because the national social security and unemployment compensation laws did not cover them. He promised to fight for territorial legislation to protect those not covered by the national laws.

He appealed to the racial concerns of his audiences in an interesting way:

> I have found that those who talk of racial equality are those that practice it the least.... The very reason that it is always talked of to me smacks of racial inequality. We citizens of Hawaii are all Americans and just as proud of our citizenship as they. [He did not like the] patronizing pats on the back.... Many of us descend from people who came 30–40 years ago and built up local industry.[17]

Wilcox and her campaign assistants realized only too well that they were not in a position to communicate with all the voters, especially the newly enfranchised Japanese voters whose experience on some of the plantations had not been good. In previous elections, she had traveled freely around the island. This time there were places where, as a member of a plantation owner's family, she was not welcome. Sanford Zalberg's history of the ILWU points out that relations between labor and management deteriorated dramatically during these years. Although by and large management was able to keep a lid on labor unrest until after World War II, the simmering discontent with racial and economic conditions was rising.

Wilcox had a set of cards about various workers written by someone on her campaign staff to help her in her campaigning. One card, discussing a Japanese rent-car driver, read: "The type of voters who [he] represents and who is [sic] wife can also talk to is the type which we are not contacting too well at the present time."[18] Of another, the card read: "Her husband is an outside carpenter and the type of man that we need to have on our side."

Wilcox left no stone unturned in her search for voters. An article in the *Catholic Herald* that looked like a news story read, in part, "Senator Wilcox's friendship for the Catholic church has extended beyond giving financial aid. She has worked toward the goal of peace and harmony and mutual esteem between the churches and a common ground on which to work toward character building among the young people."[19] This statement was disingenuous to say the least, since Wilcox gave little or nothing to the Catholic Church in any of its manifestations. The words "Political Adv." were written in small print at the bottom of the page.

A group calling itself Wilcox's "women friends and admirers" wrote a letter that was published in both the *Garden Island* and the *Star Bulletin*. It listed her accomplishments and stated that since she would not permit them to publish it, they were doing it on their own. It ended with a flourish: "We the women voters of Kauai, who love and trust you for your sterling qualities which you possess both as a woman and as a legislator, feel that you are not presenting your case before the voters of Kauai in the most favorable light because of your modesty, reticence, and innate courtesy."[20]

Without saying so directly, Wilcox and her supporters had ways of getting across the point that she had helped many people in the community. Her campaign manager was quoted in the *Garden Island:* "In campaigning for Senator Wilcox I have found that people call her 'Our beloved Miss Elsie.' . . . Always, in confiding with me, they place their fingers on their mouth and say, 'Don't let your right hand know what your left hand is doing.' " He went on to say that the Wilcoxes had helped many young people, and stated his confidence that these beneficiaries would give her victory.[21]

Wilcox spent $1,730 on the election, including $373 for musicians, $278 for food, $612 for print ads and radio stations, and $210 for gas and cars. Small items give a picture of the kind of campaign people ran during those years. On October 3, she spent $5.90 at the Hanamaulu Cafe and Chop Sui House for ten lunches.[22] A large number of the campaign workers were from Grove Farm. Evidently, they traveled all over the island talking to family and friends, and Wilcox covered their expenses.

Three weeks before the election, Wilcox knew she was in trouble. She wrote Walker:

> I find that I had no organization and the building up of a group in each community who will work for my election has been my chief task to

date. Progress has been made but there is still much to be done, and the time seems almost too short. It is for this reason that I must depend so much on the help of others. In Kekaha Lindsay Faye is handicapped by being a member of the Central Committee who are supposed to be neutral.... Eleele still remains my biggest problem.... There is little doubt that Lihue with about 1900 votes will decide the election. If the election was held tomorrow I feel that I would lose Lihue badly.... At Kapaa I am glad Albert Horner has resigned from the Central Committee so he can personally canvass his district. He has helped with publicity and shown a very keen interest in my campaign. There remains in this district the plantation element. Can I get their support?... Shrewd political observers say I have a tough uphill fight and give as their reasons: (1) Use by Clem Gomes of the signing of his nomination papers by Lindsay and his [Clem's] claim that his withdrawal in 1938 in Lindsay's favor gave him the right to run today as the Republican Candidate. He says he has been double-crossed. (2) Support of Charlie Rice. (He has done some personal campaigning for Clem, but it is mainly his friends—police—County machine, etc.) (3) C.I.O. support for Clem. Perhaps 600 to 1,000 votes is claimed. (4) Clem's natural popularity and vote-getting ability. He is a strong campaigner, working day and night. I am asking employers of labor to see their men as far as possible personally. The "big boss" usually can ask for a favor and carries more influence. Also he has seldom had to do any disciplining personally thus making him more popular with his men.... I went into this for the good of the Republican Party. If we lose this time the game is up. The control is lost for many years to come.[23]

Part of her problem was lack of a cause to rally voters around when union issues were becoming paramount. In the past, she had run on a platform of education and welfare, but these were eclipsed by the growing power of labor and labor's issues. Kaua'i politics had been "cause-less" and personality centered in the 1930s, but by 1940, that had changed.

The combination of Jack Hall and Charles Rice proved too much for Elsie Wilcox. On the Western end of the island, she lost every district except Makaweli, and her win on the Eastern side, where she was better known and had long-standing family ties, was not enough. Gomes carried the island 3,481 to 2,898.

Wilcox took her defeat calmly. She wrote her media consultant to thank him: "What we lacked was *time* and also political *finesse*. The latter, as events turned out, would have been quite beyond anything my sense of honesty would have allowed, so that is that. Frankly, the CIO and the police were used at the last moment to intimidate many who had promised to vote for me."[24]

Her supporters were considerably less sanguine. One wrote, "You have been made a victim of base ingratitude and lack of appreciation of your honest endeavors, and in addition the vicious vindictiveness of one whose position of that of a life-long neighbor, demanded the highest type of gentlemanliness" [presumably Rice].[25] Another said, "We did everything we could to kill stories that were going around.... It is too bad that people who have received so much Wilcox help should work for a 'dumb-bell' as papa calls him."[26] A third decried her loss and said, "I was sickened by the loose talk and very ashamed of our young West Kauai people."[27] A woman who signed her letter "Toyoko" wrote, "I cried when I heard the results."[28] The Reverend Paul Osumi of the Lihue Japanese Christian Church called it dirty politics. "I was praying for your reelection and did all I could to indirectly influence my people to vote for you."[29]

The theme of the threat of unwelcome change ran through several letters. "The good old days of twenty-five or thirty years ago, when Kauai sent a noteworthy delegation to the Legislature, have now been succeeded by parlous times and mediocrity."[30] Another wrote, "It's almost inconceivable that the majority of voters of Kauai would prefer Clem to you, and this on top of Lindsay's defeat two years ago makes it look as if it is almost out of the question to elect the proper type of people to office."[31]

Several people raised the specter of the CIO:

> The election of Clem Gomes marks the entrance into politics of a labor pressure group that is ominous. While I do not pretend to know the internal politics of Kauai, I suspect that the CIO had a hand in Clem's election, and that bodes no good for the Territory. Clem is a windbag and rabblerouser, just the type to play in with the CIO. He would sell his soul for a vote, and has sold it. If this is a victory for the CIO, it will encourage labor leaders on other islands to go into politics and seek to control legislators. This is a danger signal.... But the fight has just begun, and if your defeat opens the eyes of the big boys to what they are up against, it may not be in vain.[32]

It was in vain. The Faye-Wilcox defeats were the first stage in the decline and fall of the Republican party in Hawai'i, even though Faye was beaten by a Democrat and Wilcox by a Republican. The same forces came together to defeat them—the unions and a disenchanted Charles Rice. World War II slowed the process but also made possible the rise of the Democratic party out of the tumult of the 1930s. The story is well told by Lawrence Fuchs in *Hawaii Pono* and will not be repeated here. Suffice it to say that after the war, returning Americans of Japanese Ancestry (AJA) took advantage of the GI bill, gained good educations, and, in conjunction with the ILWU, reorganized the Democratic party into a liberal machine of change. They ousted most of the politicians, Republicans and Democrats, who had made something of a mess of the situation in the 1930s. The ILWU successfully organized most of the sugar plantations by 1945. Starting in the middle 1950s, the AJA's and the ILWU restructured the political system of the territory and then the state. Just as the New Deal and unions made big city bosses obsolete on the U.S. mainland, so they made paternalism in Hawai'i obsolete.

Little has been written about the 1930s in Hawai'i, although it was a decade of considerable change because of the New Deal programs, the unionizing drives on the plantations and the waterfront, and the beginning mobilization of the AJA's into the political system. The 1930s were a time of race and class consciousness raising. Major changes in the self-perception of the AJA's and others took place. Public welfare programs were beginning to replace private philanthropy, leading to less control by a few wealthy individuals and more impersonal assistance. The depression had reduced the ability of private individuals and organizations to intervene in support of people in need, and New Deal Programs moved into the void. The New Deal protected union organizing, which found fertile ground on some of the plantations and on the docks. Second-generation Asian ancestry children who had gone through the public schools, YMCA-YWCA, and other programs were entering adulthood far better prepared to compete meaningfully in the larger culture and economy than were their parents. The end of the decade was quite unlike the beginning.

That Elsie Wilcox should have been one of the first victims of this "bloodless revolution" is replete with irony. The new Democratic party consisted overwhelmingly of the children of immigrants, primarily of Japanese ancestry. These adults were the children whose education she had championed, first as Commissioner for Education, and then as Senator. They were the children whose families she had helped as both social worker and patron. Their success in some measure was a result of the Americanization process, in which the schools, churches,

YWCA, YMCA, and the Reverend Takie Okamura had participated. Wilcox had been active in all of these Americanizing groups. It is difficult to imagine the parents of the children ever being so successful, even if they could have voted. They came from cultures that were not democratic, that did not encourage challenging parental and societal norms, and that certainly did not permit young people to organize to overthrow the status quo. In a very real sense, Elsie Wilcox's success in realizing her vision for Hawai'i, a vision she had sought to implement since the 1920s, was her undoing in 1940.

Retirement

To call Elsie Wilcox's post-defeat years "retirement" is to stretch the meaning of the word. During and after World War II, she continued to be active in community, church, and business activities, although as her health worsened, about 1950, she slowed down considerably.

World War II created many complications on Kaua'i. Gas and some foods were rationed. Troops were stationed there, and Wilcox worked closely with the officers as head of the Kaua'i branch of the USO (United Service Organizations). One weekend a month, four or five military men stayed at the guest house at Grove Farm as the family's guests. Elsie Wilcox received a special award for meritorious work from the USO, having volunteered over 1,800 hours, more than anyone on Kaua'i.[33] A letter from Robert C. Richardson Jr., Lieutenant General, United States Army, Commanding, indicates the extent of her activities:

> During the periods of intense combat activity in this theater, you gave unstintingly of your time and attention for the welfare of the Army personnel in this area. The tremendous influx of soldiers to the Hawaiian Islands brought with it a morale problem of great complexity but, aided by your interest and well-sustained efforts, we achieved and maintained a high morale level throughout the command.[34]

Governor Stainback appointed her to the Hawaii U.S. National War Fund Committee, and she was elected vice-president of the organization.[35] She also volunteered for the Red Cross.

Immediately following the bombing of Pearl Harbor, many of the leaders of the Japanese community were interned. On Kaua'i, Paul

Osumi—minister of Lihue Christian Church, the Japanese Congregational Church—was taken to the Līhu'e jail. He had been working with the Japanese consulate to end the dual citizenship many young second-generation Japanese adults held with the United States and Japan, and his contacts with the consulate evidently made him suspect. After several months, he was sent to an internment camp on the mainland. In April 1942, Elsie Wilcox organized a group of prominent citizens on Kaua'i to sign a letter to the military governor of Hawai'i requesting Osumi's release. It read, in part:

> We have probably no young Japanese Christian leader in Hawaii whose influence has been more constructive in Americanization than Osumi. People of all races respect his leadership which during these unstable times would be a definite force on the maintenance of law and order. If we as a body of citizens may stand sponsor for him we shall be glad to assume this responsibility.[36]

Among those signing the letter were William and Charles Rice, A. H. Waterhouse, L. A. Faye, and Mabel and Elsie Wilcox. On April 10, Elsie also wrote Norman Schenck at the HEA asking him to have Samuel King, the delegate to Congress, discuss the matter with military officials. She said they feared that Osumi would be sent back to Japan, where he might "there meet a tragic fate.... We are eager to do anything we can for Osumi." Unfortunately, nothing came of the effort, and until the end of the war, Osumi was detained in camps or resting in Denver from pleurisy. Failing to obtain his release, Elsie sent him $500, a large sum in light of the fact that he was being paid $19 a month for his work as a minister in the camp. He later viewed the situation as a blessing in disguise because he was able to help so many people in the camps.[37]

During the war, two great-nieces and a great-nephew lived at Grove Farm three nights a week to attend school in Līhu'e at the English standard school. Gas rationing made it impossible for them to commute from their home in Wailua. One of the nieces recalled the time at Grove Farm with great fondness. In the evening, they played games or did puzzles. The aunts would get out a large jigsaw puzzle that everyone worked on for several evenings. Every Sunday afternoon the aunts had a rest, something they never did during the week, and then walked all around the property to be sure everything was in order. Mabel Wilcox and their cousin Helen Lyman, who lived at

Grove Farm for several years, daily had one or two scotches, and then dinner was served at 6:00 P.M. Elsie occasionally had sherry. Elsie continued to plan the meals every day, although she had long since stopped cooking.[38] It was a well-ordered existence.

In 1938, Elsie Wilcox had been elected the first president of the Adult Education Society, an outgrowth of the Adult Education Committee, which she chaired. It was formed in cooperation with the University of Hawaii, Kauai Chamber of Commerce, Mokihana Club, American Legion, YMCA, YWCA, and the Young Buddhist Association. She continued her work with the group for several years after the war, working to spread literacy among the adult population.

For many years, Wilcox was director of the Bishop Trust Company, vice-president of Grove Farm Company, and trustee and second vice-president of the G. N. Wilcox Memorial Hospital. This was highly unusual, particularly her position with Bishop Trust. The Wilcox family was involved financially in Bishop Trust, but even wealthy women rarely served on boards of financial institutions.

She continued to be active in church business, helping ministers and their families and solving problems in the KEA.[39] She was on the Cancer Board of Kaua'i, was the Kaua'i member on the Commission on Historical Sites, served as president and director of Waioli Mission, and was on the board of the Kaua'i YWCA. She was very active in the Republican party on the island. She had been president of the Lihue Cemetery Association since 1934 and held the position until just before her death.

Kenneth Emory, respected anthropologist at the Bishop Museum, spent considerable time with Elsie Wilcox during these years while he and an assistant were excavating various sites on Kaua'i. In his correspondence, he referred to her as "Dear Elsie," and she to him as "Dear Kenneth."[40] She was also writing regularly to Nell Findley, who had retired to the mainland. Findley addressed her as "Dearest Elsie," and called her "my best of friends."[41]

She also continued to give people in need assistance, although not always the kind they sought. She received quite an angry letter from a man who had been a YMCA leader on Kaua'i in the 1920s and then a principal of a public school on O'ahu. She wrote urging him to forget the past and look to the future. Then she added a further suggestion: "If, after going over all this you find you cannot forget and forgive, or at least make allowances for errors and mistakes, may I suggest that there are competent psychologists who can help one remove such burdens from heart and mind. Perhaps you would consult one, but be sure you get a good one."[42] She also turned down his request for money for a Methodist camp he was running and said that almost all her money was going to Kauaʻi organizations.

Elsie Wilcox spent these years almost entirely at Grove Farm, with her sister, Mabel, Helen Lyman, and author and longtime friend, Ethel Damon. Damon continued to travel, as did Mabel, but Helen and Elsie lived a quite domestic existence, aside from all of Elsie's community activities.

Commenting on those years from a perspective of forty years, William Alexander, who knew the sisters well, said they lived in unusual harmony. They worked together on many projects and had many of the same friends. He and others were struck by how simply they lived. Never having been particularly social, in their later years they were even less so, spending almost all their time in the company of a few other women.[43] Ford Coffman, minister at Lihue Union Church after the war, said the sisters were almost like a husband and wife in the ways they worked together. "Everything they did, they did well," he said of them. He observed that they were perhaps somewhat lonely; their privileges, in addition to affording them opportunities, had became something of a burden, isolating them. Perhaps in part because of this they became even more family centered.[44]

In 1949, Elsie Wilcox was diagnosed with breast cancer and underwent a mastectomy at Queen's Hospital in Honolulu. She received further treatment at Stanford Medical Center in 1953. Even while she was quite ill, she continued to entertain groups, including hosting a lunch for seventy-five for the Women's Board of Missions in November 1953. She died June 30, 1954.

The bulk of her estate went to the Elsie Hart Wilcox Foundation, which she had created in 1938. She left $500 bequests to ten employees and $5,000 bequests to a niece and nephew. Eighty percent of the money in the trust was for Mabel until her death, when it would go to the trust. Her estate was valued at $734,378. Her obituary in the *Garden Island* read, in part, "There are many men and women who owe their education to Miss Wilcox, just as there are many elderly who are living out their years in comfort because of her thoughtfulness."[45]

In accord with her wishes, the family held a small service at Grove Farm, and there was no public funeral. Her gravestone reads, "I am among you as one who serves."

7 *Evaluations*

> *What is constantly new is not the past itself but the way we look back at it.*
>
> SHELLEY

Elsie Wilcox, like most subjects of biography, is best understood if she is placed in the context of her own time and place and studied for what the reader may learn from her life. She was remarkably successful in creating an interesting and productive life, in many ways breaking fairly strong social taboos to do so. How she accomplished this sheds light on the relationship among several variables thought to define and influence an individual's goals and behavior.

Most contemporary scholars use race, class, and gender to set the frame of reference for a subject, with particular emphasis on any one of the three, depending on the larger ideological perspective of the scholar. In Elsie Wilcox's case, it seems certain that she was able to accomplish what she did because of the overriding significance of her race and class, negating the debilitating effects of gender. In particular, her wealth forced men to give her power and deference that as a woman she otherwise would not have received. Likewise, had she been born of Chinese or Japanese parents, it is unlikely in the extreme that she would have been able to achieve what she did.

However, Elsie Wilcox's character was formed by variables that were more complex than just those three. Other Caucasian women in the territory with access to wealth, for example, did not become major players in the political life of the community. Why was Wilcox the exception?

First, Wilcox's values, derived from her grandparents, demanded hard work, high self-expectation, and professionalism. Her behavior in supporting educational and religious charities, her concern for women and children, and her modest life-style all were based on values transmitted from her grandparents through their children to her. While these values were shared by others of her race, class, and gender, they are specific to none of these categories. They resulted in a focusing of her substantial energies on institutions of social welfare and education, areas of great need but of little interest to most men.

Second, she remained single. The importance of marital status as a variable in studying women cannot be overemphasized. Even wealthy married women would have found it hard to travel to Honolulu for meetings of the Commissioners for Education in the 1920s and, in the 1930s, for legislative sessions of several months' duration. Wilcox had freedom to do as she chose because she was unencumbered by a husband and children.

Third, she developed close relationships that cut across race, class, and gender, enabling her to gain access to knowledge and power otherwise denied her. She was socialized for a traditional female role but was forced, probably more by circumstances than her own wishes, into the company of single women for socializing and work, and into the company of professional men for work. She had close male and female friends of many ethnic groups. Some of these were middle-class professionals—nurses, teachers, YWCA-YMCA workers, or ministers. By virtue of her birth, she knew the males and females in the ruling class. Through her work, she had access to a large part of the small number of middle-class professionals.

Fourth, she employed her excellent education and access to wealth to become a skilled insider who used many different institutions to accomplish her goals—the church, the YWCA, YMCA, social welfare groups, the Mokihana Club, the Department of Public Instruction, and the territorial legislature. She was in command of the workings of all those institutions.

A key word to understanding Wilcox is *reform*. She was not a radical—she did not want to reinstate the monarchy, undo the *mahele*, or rid the territory of all Caucasians and Asians. She was not a socialist or a communist. There were people in the islands at the time who held at least some of those views, but neither major political party espoused them. As Mary Beard observed at the turn of the century, in their efforts to ameliorate basic problems, women reformers moved from private charity to public welfare to action, but few supported the overthrow of the economic and political systems.[1]

A problem in writing this biography, as noted in the Introduction, has been that almost everything with which Elsie Wilcox was associated is currently in disrepute with at least some elements of academia and the larger society. The coming of Westerners to Hawai'i and other native cultures has been described in the most dire of terms. Cook, Columbus, and other explorers are accused of crimes ranging from greed to genocide. The missionaries are described as insensitive, cultural imperialists, and worse.[2] Plantation owners and managers in Hawai'i are portrayed as harsh, brutish disciplinarians.[3] The Big Five, the large sugar factors, are criticized for controlling the economic, political, religious, educational, and communications institutions in the kingdom and territory to subjugate the rest of the population and steal the Hawaiians' land. They are accused of overthrowing the Hawaiian monarchy with the help of the United States military.[4] The quest for statehood (eventually achieved after Elsie Wilcox's death) is portrayed as the ultimate colonization of Hawai'i, an event to be undone if possible. The Republican party of territorial Hawai'i is described as the party of privilege and suppression.

The debate about Americanization continues. Some people view it as cultural imperialism, used by the dominant Northern European–ancestry majority to control and homogenize all other peoples. Others argue that it was essential to creating a country out of large groups of very different people.[5] The belief that English should be the language of instruction in the schools is under attack. Compulsory, mass education at the early part of this century is condemned as a middle- or upper-class effort to mold the working class into efficient industrial laborers.[6] Social work is held to be the imposition of middle-class, Northern European–ancestry values on everyone else. There are, of course, other interpretations of the same events but a major theme of much recent research, especially from radical scholars, reflects these views.

Patricia Limerick, in a study of the history of the American West, observed, "Studies in comparative sin are always difficult matters of judgment."[7] We are too close to the events, and passions run too high, at least in Hawai'i, to pass judgment on Elsie Wilcox, her place in history, or her values, beliefs, and causes. She was a woman of her time who transcended some of what many people today view as negative elements in her culture. Even though she benefited from the status quo, she spent much of her life providing outsiders access to the culture. Race and class were critical elements in her thinking, but she often ignored them in her public behavior. She was a progressive in a conservative community who used her advantages to improve that community while keeping its primary elements of capitalism, Christianity, Americanism, and democracy. In many ways, Elsie Wilcox's life is a partial answer to the question of how to solve the problems created by the meeting and clashing of several cultures in a small island chain. Some contemporary readers will not like her answer; others will wish for more people like her in public life today.

Appendix

Members of the Hawai'i State Senate, 1933–1939

The 1933 Senate

DISTRICT	NAME	RESIDENCE
First	James R. Campsie (R)	Pāhala, Hawai'i
	Stephen L. Desha Sr. (R)	Hilo, Hawai'i
	William H. Hill (R)	Hilo, Hawai'i
	Robert Hind (R)	Kailua, Hawai'i
Second	George P. Cooke (R)	Kaunakakai, Moloka'i
	Harry H. Holt (R)	Wailuku, Maui
	Harold W. Rice (R)	Pā'ia, Maui
Third	Francis H. Ii Brown (R)	Honolulu, O'ahu
	Henry Freitas (D)	Honolulu, O'ahu
	William H. Heen (D)	Honolulu, O'ahu
	Lester Petrie (D)	Honolulu, O'ahu
	Joseph L. Sylva (R)	Honolulu, O'ahu
	David K. Trask (D)	Honolulu, O'ahu
Fourth	Charles A. Rice (R)	Līhu'e, Kaua'i
	Elsie H. Wilcox (R)	Līhu'e, Kaua'i

The 1935 Senate

DISTRICT	NAME	RESIDENCE
First	James Campsie (R)	Pāhala, Hawai'i
	William H. Hill (R)	Hilo, Hawai'i
	William J. Kimi (R)	Hilo, Hawai'i
	Ernest A. K. Akina (R) Expelled in March and replaced by:	
	Charles H. Silva (D)	Kapa'au, Hawai'i

Second	H. A. Baldwin (R)	Makawao, Maui
	George P. Cooke (R)	Kaunakakai, Molokaʻi
	Harry H. Holt (R)	Wailuku, Maui
Third	Joseph R. Farrington (R)	Honolulu, Oʻahu
	Henry Freitas (D)	Honolulu, Oʻahu
	William H. Heen (D)	Honolulu, Oʻahu
	Lester Petrie (D)	Honolulu, Oʻahu
	Joseph L. Sylva (R)	Honolulu, Oʻahu
	David K. Trask (D)	Honolulu, Oʻahu
Fourth	Charles A. Rice (R)	Līhuʻe, Kauaʻi
	Elsie H. Wilcox (R)	Līhuʻe, Kauaʻi

The 1937 Senate

DISTRICT	NAME	RESIDENCE
First	James Campsie (R)	Pāhala, Hawaiʻi
	Sarah Todd Cunningham (D)	Hilo, Hawaiʻi
	William J. Kimi (R)	Hilo, Hawaiʻi
	Charles H. Silva (D)	Kapaʻau, Hawaiʻi
Second	H. A. Baldwin (R)	Makawao, Maui
	Clarence A. Crozier (NP)	Wailuku, Maui
	Harry H. Holt (R)	Wailuku, Maui
Third	Eugene H. Beebe (R)	Honolulu, Oʻahu
	Francis H. Ii Brown (R)	Honolulu, Oʻahu
	Joseph R. Farrington (R)	Honolulu, Oʻahu
	William H. Heen (D)	Honolulu, Oʻahu
	Joseph L. Sylva (R)	Honolulu, Oʻahu
	David K. Trask (D)	Kāneʻohe, Oʻahu
Fourth	Charles A. Rice (R)	Līhuʻe, Kauaʻi
	Elsie H. Wilcox (R)	Līhuʻe, Kauaʻi

The 1939 Senate

DISTRICT	NAME	RESIDENCE
First	Sarah Todd Cunningham (R)	Hilo, Hawaiʻi
	William H. Hill (R)	Hilo, Hawaiʻi
	James Kealoha (R)	Hilo, Hawaiʻi
	(Filled seat vacated by death of James Campsie)	
	Charles H. Silva (R)	Kohala, Hawaiʻi
Second	George P. Cooke (R)	Kaunakakai, Molokai
	Clarence A. Crozier (NP)	Wailuku, Maui
	Harry H. Holt (R)	Wailuku, Maui

Third	Eugene H. Beebe (R)	Honolulu, Oʻahu
	Francis H. Ii Brown (R)	Honolulu, Oʻahu
	Joseph R. Farrington (R)	Honolulu, Oʻahu
	William H. Heen (D)	Honolulu, Oʻahu
	Francis K. Sylva (R)	Honolulu, Oʻahu
	(Filled seat vacated by death of Joseph L. Sylva)	
	David K. Trask (D)	Kāneʻohe, Oʻahu
Fourth	John B. Fernandes (D)	Kapaʻa, Kauaʻi
	Elsie H. Wilcox (R)	Līhuʻe, Kauaʻi

Genealogies

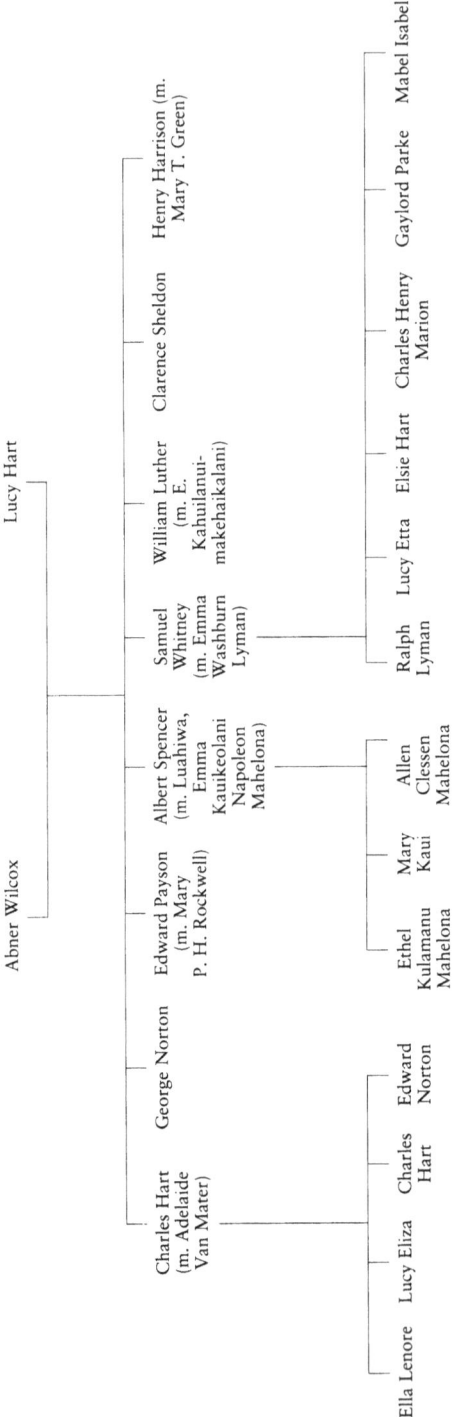

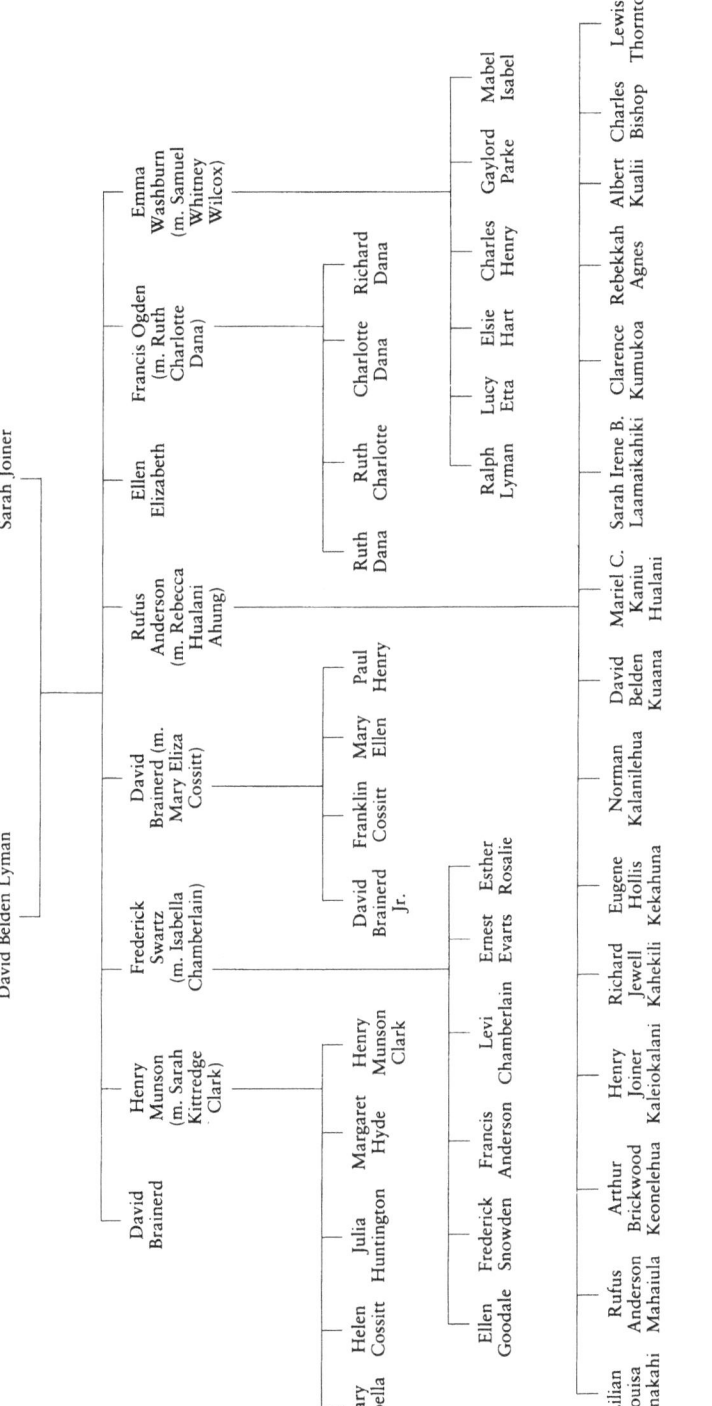

Notes

Introduction

1. Gerda Lerner, *The Majority Finds Its Past: Placing Women in History* (Oxford: Oxford University Press, 1979).
2. Cynthia Fuchs Epstein, *Deceptive Distinctions: Sex, Gender and the Social Order* (New Haven: Yale University Press, 1988); Mary Daly, *Gyn\ Ecology: The Metaethics of Radical Feminism* (Boston: Beacon Press, 1978); Shulamith Firestone, *The Dialect of Sex: The Case for Feminist Revolution* (New York: Bantam Books, 1970); Jessie Bernard, *The Female World* (New York: The Free Press, 1981); Naomi Black, *Social Feminism* (Ithaca: Cornell University Press, 1989).
3. Frederick Jackson Turner, "The Significance of History," in *History, Frontier, and Section: Three Essays by Frederick Jackson Turner* (Albuquerque: University of New Mexico Press, 1993), 46.

Chapter One: In the Beginning

1. *Missionary Album: Portraits and Biographical Sketches of the American Protestant Missionaries in the Hawaiian Islands* (Honolulu: Hawaii Mission Children's Society, 1969), 17.
2. Gavan Daws, *Shoal of Time: A History of the Hawaiian Islands* (Honolulu: University Press of Hawai'i, 1968), 1–60; Ralph S. Kuykendall, Foundation and Transformation, vol. 1 of The Hawaiian Kingdom (Honolulu: University of Hawai'i Press, 1938), 66–70.
3. David E. Stannard, *Before the Horror: The Population of Hawai'i on the Eve of Western Contact* (Honolulu: Social Science Research Institute, 1989); O. A. Bushnell, *The Gifts of Civilization: Germs and Genocide in Hawai'i* (Honolulu: University of Hawai'i Press, 1993).
4. Joseph Tracy, *History of the American Board of Commissioners for Foreign Missions* (New York: M. W. Dodd, 1842), 241.

5. Patricia Grimshaw, *Paths of Duty: American Missionary Wives in Nineteenth-Century Hawaii* (Honolulu: University of Hawai'i Press, 1989), 154–176.

6. Tracy, *History of the American Board*, 225, 243.

7. John A. Andrew III, *Rebuilding the Christian Commonwealth: New England Congregationalists and Foreign Missions, 1800–1830* (Lexington: University Press of Kentucky, 1976), 164–165.

8. Henry M. Lyman, *Hawaiian Yesterdays: Chapters from a Boy's Life in the Islands in the Early Days* (Chicago: A. C. McClurg, 1906), 1.

9. Ethel M. Damon, ed., *Letters from the Life of Abner and Lucy Wilcox, 1836–1869* (Honolulu: privately printed, n.d.), 11.

10. Ibid., 3–4.

11. Philip Greven, *The Protestant Temperament: Patterns of Child-Rearing, Religious Experience, and the Self in Early America* (New York: Alfred Knopf, 1977), 13.

12. Damon, *Letters*, 275.

13. Margaret Greer Martin, ed., *The Lymans of Hilo* (Hilo: Lyman House Memorial Museum), 107.

14. Damon, *Letters*, 274.

15. Greven, *Protestant Temperament*, 35.

16. Damon, *Letters*, 350.

17. Ibid., 319.

18. Ibid., 360–361.

19. Noel Kent, *Islands Under the Influence* (New York: Monthly Review Press, 1983).

20. Elizabeth Buck, *Paradise Remade: The Politics of Culture and History in Hawai'i* (Philadelphia: Temple University Press, 1993), 16–17.

21. Bob Krauss with W. P. Alexander, *Grove Farm Plantation: The Biography of a Hawaiian Sugar Plantation*, 2nd ed. (Palo Alto: Pacific Books, 1965), 67.

22. Linda K. Menton, "Everything that Is Lovely and of Good Report: The Hawaiian Chief's Children's School, 1839–1850," (Ph.D. dissertation, University of Hawai'i, 1982), 358.

23. Lilikala Kame'eleihiwa, *Native Land and Foreign Desires: Ko Hawai'i 'Aina a me Na Koi Pu'umake a ka Po'e Haole* (Honolulu: Bishop Museum Press, 1992).

24. Krauss, *Grove Farm*, 132, 145.

25. Ibid., 171.

26. Ibid., 220.

27. Ibid., 257–263.

28. "The Blount Report," *Executive Documents of the House of Representatives*, for the Third Session of the Fifty-Third Congress, 1894–1895, vol. 1 (Washington, D.C.: Government Printing Office, 1895), 584–601.

29. Ibid.

Chapter Two: The Early Years

1. Elsie Hart Wilcox, "Early Race Relations on Kauai" (Kauaʻi: n.d.).
2. Ibid.
3. Bob Krauss with W. P. Alexander, *Grove Farm Plantation: The Biography of a Hawaiian Sugar Plantation*, 2nd ed. (Palo Alto: Pacific Books, 1965), 305.
4. Elsie Hart Wilcox Scrapbook (Līhuʻe: Grove Farm Plantation Museum) 4P-3-1. (All Wilcox original document citations are from "Register of the Grove Farm Plantation Records and Papers of George N. Wilcox, Samuel W. Wilcox, Emma L. Wilcox, Elsie H. Wilcox and Mabel I. Wilcox," compiled by Margaret R. O'Leary. Līhuʻe: Grove Farm Homestead, 1982).
5. Wilcox, "Early Race Relations on Kauai."
6. Lynn D. Gordon, *Gender and Higher Education in the Progressive Era* (New Haven: Yale University Press, 1990), 2.
7. Helen Lefkowitz Horowitz, *Alma Mater: Design and Experience in Women's Colleges from Their Nineteenth-Century Beginnings to the 1930's* (New York: Alfred Knopf, 1984), 53.
8. Patricia A. Palmieri, "Here Was Fellowship: A Social Portrait of Academic Women at Wellesley College, 1895–1920," *History of Education Quarterly* 23:2 (Summer 1983): 195.
9. Gordon, *Gender and Higher Education*, 3.
10. Palmieri, *Here Was Fellowship*, 195, 204, 207.
11. Horowitz, *Alma Mater*, 169.
12. Palmieri, *Here Was Fellowship*, 205.
13. Elsie Hart Wilcox, Report Card, Wellesley College (Līhuʻe: Grove Farm Plantation Museum), 4P-3-2.
14. Elsie Hart Wilcox, "Day Books" (Līhuʻe: Grove Farm Plantation Museum), 6, 8.
15. Nancy Woloch, *Early American Women: A Documentary History* (Belmont, Calif.: Wadsworth, 1992), 211.
16. Wilcox, "Day Book," 24 July 1902.
17. Krauss, *Grove Farm*, 291.
18. Wilcox, "Day Book," 21 November 1902; 20 October 1902; 16 July 1903.
19. Robyn Muncy, *Creating a Female Dominion in American Reform, 1890–1935* (New York: Oxford University Press, 1991), 5, 11.
20. Allen F. Davis, *Spearheads for Reform: The Social Settlements and the Progressive Movement, 1890–1914* (New York: Oxford University Press, 1967), 37.
21. Wilcox, "Day Book," 15 November 1902.
22. Ibid., 19 June 1903.
23. Wilcox to Handy, 16 October 1930.

24. Jane C. Croly, "Sorosis: Its Origins and History," in Francis Gerry Fairfield, *The Clubs of New York: With an Account of the Origin, Progress, Present Condition and Membership of the Leading Clubs: An Essay on New York Club Life* (New York: Henry Hinton, 1873), 14.

25. Mary Beard, *Women's Work in Municipalities* (New York: Arno Press, 1972), vi.

26. William L. O'Neill, *Everyone Was Brave: A History of Feminism in America* (New York: Quadrangle, 1969), 81–82.

27. Karen J. Blair, *The Clubwoman as Feminist: True Womanhood Redefined, 1868–1914* (New York: Holmes and Meier, 1980), 4.

28. Ibid., 1.

29. Anne Firor Scott, *Natural Allies: Women's Associations in American History* (Urbana: University of Illinois Press, 1991), 177.

30. Alice C. Wedemeyer, *The Story of the Mokihana Club* (USA: privately printed, 1987), 117.

31. Ibid., 12.

32. Ibid., 16.

33. Woloch, *Early American Women*, 470.

34. Barbara Miller Solomon, *In the Company of Educated Women: A History of Women and Higher Education in America* (New Haven: Yale University Press, 1985), 120.

35. Sara M. Evans, *Born for Liberty: A History of Women in America* (New York: The Free Press, 1989), 147.

36. Carolyn G. Heilbrun, *Writing a Woman's Life* (New York: W. W. Norton, 1988), 52.

37. Carl N. Degler, *At Odds: Women and the Family in America from the Revolution to the Present* (Oxford: Oxford University Press, 1980), 152.

38. Wilcox, "Day Book," 7 October 1908.

39. Ibid., 5 April 1910.

40. Ibid., 23 March 1910.

41. Ibid., 22 May 1910.

42. Ibid., 14 August 1910.

43. Eileen H. Tamura, *Americanization, Acculturation, and Ethnic Identity: The Nisei Generation in Hawaii* (Chicago: University of Illinois Press, 1994), xv.

44. Wedemeyer, *Mokihana Club*, 17.

45. Scott, *Natural Allies*, 142.

46. Wedemeyer, *Mokihana Club*, 20.

47. Scott, *Natural Allies*, 165.

48. Wedemeyer, *Mokihana Club*, 23.

49. Ibid.

50. Ibid., 126.

51. Ibid., 128.

52. Ibid., 129.
53. Ibid., 131.
54. Ibid., 138–139.
55. Ibid., 24–25.

Chapter Three: The Good Years

Sections of this chapter first appeared in Judith Gething, "The Educational and Civic Leadership of Elsie Wilcox, 1920–1932," *The Hawaiian Journal of History* 16 (1982): 184–205; and Judith Hughes, "The Demise of the English Standard School System in Hawaii," *The Hawaiian Journal of History* 27 (1993): 65–89. Excerpted here with permission.

1. Bob Krauss with W. P. Alexander, *Grove Farm Plantation: The Biography of a Hawaiian Sugar Plantation,* 2nd ed. (Palo Alto: Pacific Books, 1965), 309, 339.

2. Hundley to MacCaughey, 27 May 1919, Hawaii State Archives (AH), Governor McCarthy, Territorial Depts., Public Instruction in re: Mrs. Burke and Ms. Thompson. (Hereinafter, all AH references are to McCarthy unless otherwise noted.)

3. AH, Public Instruction Commissioners, 20 May 1919.
4. Ibid., 4 June 1919.
5. Ibid., 8 September 1919.
6. Ibid., n.d.
7. Ibid., 9 September 1919.
8. Ibid., 23 December 1919.
9. Ibid., 30 December 1919.
10. *Garden Island,* 12 October 1920; 10 January 1922; 23 December 1924.

11. "Labor Conditions in Hawaii," letter from the Secretary of Labor, Fifth Annual Report of the Commissioner of Labor Statistics, Sen. Doc. No. 432, 64th Cong., 1st Sess., 1916, p. 40.

12. Gordon C. Sato, "Hawaii's Public Schools: A Primary Agency for Behavioral Assimilation, 1920–1940" (M.Ed. thesis, University of Hawai'i, 1973), 32.

13. *Proceedings of the Forty-Ninth Annual Meeting of the HSPA* (Honolulu: Star-Bulletin, 1930), 8.

14. Royal D. Mead, "The Sugar Industry in Hawaii," *San Francisco Chronicle,* 18 July 1910, quoted in "Labor Organization in Hawaii: A Study of Efforts of Labor to Obtain Security through Organization," Richard A. Liebes (M.A. thesis, University of Hawai'i, 1938), 74.

15. Andrew W. Lind, *Hawaii's People* (Honolulu: University Press of Hawai'i, 1967), 28.

16. Ronald Takaki, *A Different Mirror: A History of Multicultural America* (Boston: Little, Brown, 1993), 265.

17. U.S. Department of Interior, U.S. Office of Education, *Survey of Education in Hawaii* (Washington, D.C.: Government Printing Office, 1920), 35, 41, 66, 74, 79, 83, 155, 184, 214. (Hereinafter cited as *1920 Survey.*)

18. Floy T. Gay, "A Study of the Development of the Senior High Schools" (M.A. thesis, University of Hawai'i, 1945), 7–10.

19. *1920 Survey,* 4–5.

20. Ibid., 35.

21. Gay, "A Study of the Development of the Senior High Schools," 120.

22. Ibid., 45.

23. "Minutes," Department of Public Instruction, 3 October 1931, AH.

24. Ibid., 21 August 1928.

25. Ibid., 29 September 1931.

26. Sato, "Hawaii's Public Schools," 42–44.

27. "Minutes," Department of Public Instruction, 9 March 1921.

28. Ibid., 10 March 1921.

29. *Farrington v. Tokushige,* 273 US 284 (1926).

30. *1920 Survey,* 127.

31. *The Friend,* vol. XCI, no. 3 (Honolulu: Hawaiian Evangelical Society, 1922), 61–62.

32. "Minutes," Department of Public Instruction, 23 May 1922.

33. Judith Hughes, "The Demise of the English Standard School System," *The Hawaiian Journal of History* 27 (1993): 77.

34. "Minutes," Department of Public Instruction, 7 September 1920.

35. Bernice Hundley, "Thank You, Miss Elsie Wilcox," *Garden Island,* 21 July 1954.

36. *Honolulu Star-Bulletin,* 19 March 1929.

37. Ibid.

38. Ibid., 12 December 1930.

39. Governor's Advisory Committee on Education, *Survey of Schools and Industry* (Honolulu: Printshop, 1931), 8–9.

40. Edward D. Beechert, *Working in Hawaii: A Labor History* (Honolulu: University of Hawai'i Press, 1985), 244.

41. Horace H. Leavitt to Wilcox, 15 January 1932.

42. Wilcox to Adams, 21 March 1921, Grove Farm Plantation Museum, I-4-C. (All letters hereinafter are at Grove Farm Plantation Museum, in the I-4-C files, unless otherwise noted.)

43. Judith R. Hughes, "Social Service in the Early Territorial Period," in "Perspectives on Health Care and Healing on Kauai" (Honolulu: Hawaii Committee for the Humanities, 1988), 11.

44. Ibid.

45. Beechert, *Working in Hawaii,* 133–134.

46. Takaki, *A Different Mirror,* 246.

47. Barbara Miller Solomon, *In the Company of Educated Women: A History of Women and Higher Education in America* (New Haven: Yale University Press, 1985), 124.
48. Elsie or Mabel Wilcox to Estelle Roe, 14 September 1920.
49. Beechert, *Working in Hawaii*, 193–194.
50. Wilcox to Mrs. C. W. Whipple, 4 September 1926.
51. *Garden Island*, 7 January 1919.
52. Ibid., 16 September 1919; 14 January 1919; 15 September 1919; 11 October 1921.
53. Bergen to Wilcox, 7 January 1924.
54. Baldwin to Wilcox, 13 January 1924.
55. Wilcox note, I-4-C3.
56. Beechert, *Working in Hawaii*, 245.
57. Ibid., 242.
58. *Garden Island*, 12 December 1922.
59. Mary Beard, *Women's Work in Municipalities* (New York: Arno Press, 1972), 61.
60. Layman to Wilcox, 23 May 1930.
61. Charles Fern, interviewed by author, 23 May 1980, Honolulu.
62. Harry Tanaka to Wilcox, 7 December 1930.
63. Yuko Tanaka to Wilcox, 18 December 1930.
64. Wilcox to Priory principal, 13 September 1930.
65. Wilcox to Miss DeBruille, 12 November 1930.
66. Toyoko Doi to Wilcox, undated, 1930.
67. Eileen Tamura, *Americanization, Acculturation, and Ethnic Identity: The Nisei Generation in Hawaii* (Urbana: University of Illinois Press, 1994), 49.
68. Lawrence H. Fuchs, *The American Kaleidoscope: Race, Ethnicity and the Civic Culture* (Hanover: Wesleyn University Press, 1990).
69. *Kauai News*, 30 January 1951.
70. Killam to Wilcox, 11 August 1925.
71. William McCluskey, "Kauai High School," in T. H. Gibson, *Some Landmarks in the Development of Hawaii's Public School System*, 57.
72. Wilcox to Locke, undated, 1925.
73. Wilcox to Channon, 5 February 1921.
74. Wilcox to Schenck, 19 July 1924.
75. Loomis to Wilcox, Thanksgiving 1920.
76. Killam to Wilcox, 2 December 1920.
77. Locke to Wilcox, 4 September 1926.
78. Wilcox to Locke, 14 December 1928.
79. Locke to Wilcox, 8 September 1928.
80. Kubo to Wilcox, 16 February 1929.
81. Schenck to Edith Hansen, 16 September 1926.

82. Wilcox to Schenck, 21 September 1926.
83. Locke to Wilcox, 24 May 1926.
84. Wilcox to Marvin, 30 November 1926.
85. Watada to Wilcox, 16 May 1930.
86. Scott to Wilcox, 30 August 1930.
87. Wilcox to Scott, 13 September 1930.
88. Okamura to Wilcox, 27 October 1919.
89. Suyeki Okamura, interviewed by author, 7 August 1987, Honolulu.
90. Tamura, *Americanization, Acculturation, and Ethnic Identity,* 132.
91. Wilcox to Childs, 13 November 1922.
92. Wilcox to Loomis, 9 October 1926.
93. Wilcox to Y. P. Yen, 11 April 1931.
94. Paul F. Hooper, *Elusive Destiny: The Internationalist Movement in Modern Hawaii* (Honolulu: University Press of Hawai'i, 1980), 80, 112.
95. Ford to Wilcox, 19 September 1928.
96. Wilcox to Dr. Philip Allen Schwartz, 12 November 1929; 1 November 1929.
97. Wilcox to Bourne, 8 January 1924.
98. Coe to Wilcox, 18 January 1924.
99. For a good survey of recent literature on the subject, see chapter 2 of Margit Misangyi Watts, *High Tea at Halekulani: Feminist Theory and American Clubwomen* (Brooklyn, N.Y.: Carlson Publishing, 1993).

Chapter Four: The Plunge into Politics

1. Wilcox to Eddie, undated, 1931. (All letters hereinafter are at Grove Farm Plantation Museum, in the I-4-C files, unless otherwise noted.)
2. Wilcox to Eddie, 4 August 1931.
3. Eddie to Wilcox, 21 August 1931.
4. Eddie to Wilcox, 4 March 1933.
5. Wilcox to Mr. William Kwai Fong Yap, 18 July 1933.
6. Wilcox to Frye, 26 September 1933.
7. Wilcox to Rowlinson, 17 January 1933.
8. Wilcox to John Erdman, treasurer, the Board of Evangelical Association, 12 December 1932.
9. Grove Farm Plantation Museum, I-4-C-10, p. 2.
10. Lawrence Walworth to Wilcox, 14 May 1930.
11. Wilcox to Chang, undated, 1931.
12. Grove Farm Plantation Museum, I-4-C-10, 1931, pp. 8, 12, 14.
13. Lillian Kinney to Wilcox, 2 April 1932.
14. Ray Wilbur to Wilcox, 1 April 1931.
15. Marian Wilcox to Cyrle Damon, 23 November 1932.
16. Grove Farm Plantation Museum, I-4-C-10, 1931, p. 5.

17. Wilcox to Judd, 15 February 1932.
18. Wilcox to Mr. and Mrs. Turner in China, 28 July 1932.
19. *Advertiser,* 14 April 1931.
20. *Star-Bulletin,* 1 August 1932.
21. *Garden Island,* 7 May 1931.
22. *Star-Bulletin,* 1 August 1932.
23. Fernandez to Wilcox, 11 May 1931.
24. Wilcox to Fernandez, 20 July 1932.
25. *Garden Island,* 11 August 1931.
26. *Star-Bulletin,* 1 August 1932.
27. Leavitt to Wilcox, 22 July 1932.
28. Wilcox to Leavitt, 28 July 1932.
29. Juliette Rice Wichman, interviewed by author, Līhuʻe, Kauaʻi, 15 January 1986.
30. *Garden Island,* 27 September 1932.
31. Ibid., 11 August 1931.
32. Nancy Goodale, interviewed by author, Līhuʻe, Kauaʻi, 11 November 1988.
33. *Star-Bulletin,* 1 August 1932.
34. *Garden Island,* 26 July 1932.
35. Ibid., 5 June 1934.
36. Goodale interview.
37. *Garden Island,* 27 September 1932.
38. Ibid., 20 September 1932.
39. "Official Tabulation," no publication information.
40. *Advertiser,* 17 August 1932.
41. Ibid., 15 November 1932.
42. Donald D. Johnson, *The City and County of Honolulu: A Governmental Chronicle* (Honolulu: University of Hawaiʻi Press, 1991), 128–129.
43. *Advertiser,* 9 November 1932.
44. Cady to Wilcox, 4 October 1932.
45. Governor Judd, Territorial Departments, Department of Public Instruction, 3 August 1932, Hawaii State Archives (AH); Aki to Judd, 26 July 1932.
46. Bob Krauss with W. P. Alexander, *Grove Farm Plantation: The Biography of a Hawaiian Sugar Plantation,* 2nd ed. (Palo Alto: Pacific Books, 1965), 322.
47. Charles E. Peterson, "The Iolani Palaces and Barracks," *Journal of the Society of Architectural Historians* XXII, no. 2, May 1963.
48. *Senate Journal,* 14th Legislature, 15 February 1933, pp. 31–32.
49. *Advertiser,* 9 December 1932.
50. Grove Farm Plantation Museum, I-C-4, 31 October 1931.
51. *Advertiser,* 22 December 1932; 19 November 1932.

52. Edward D. Beechert, *Working in Hawaii: A Labor History* (Honolulu: University of Hawaiʻi Press, 1985), 253.
53. *Advertiser,* 30 January 1934; 24 November 1932; 22 December 1932.
54. Ibid., 12 April 1933; 14 July 1933; 28 July 1933; 3 August 1933; 30 August 1933; 1 September 1933; 4 September 1933.
55. Ibid., 24 February 1933; 22 March 1933; 2 June 1933; 18 April 1933; 9 May 1933.
56. Ibid., 8 December 1932.
57. Act 189, Act 188, 1933 Session Laws, 17th Legislature.
58. *Advertiser,* 20 June 1933.
59. Ibid., 2 May 1933.
60. Ibid., 26 October 1932.
61. Ibid., 12 October 1932.
62. Ibid., 6 April 1933.
63. Ibid., 27 March 1933; 8 April 1933.
64. Ibid., 19 May 1933.
65. Act 189, Act 188.
66. *Advertiser,* 9 November 1933.
67. Act 192.
68. *Advertiser,* 25 March 1933; 3 June 1933; 18 April 1933.
69. William Henry Chafe, *The American Woman: Her Changing Social, Economic and Political Roles, 1920–1970* (New York: Oxford University Press, 1972) 108; Susan Ware, *Holding Their Own: American Women in the 1930's* (Boston: Twayne, 1980), 105.
70. *Advertiser,* 21 March 1933.
71. Judd, AH. Governor's Commission on Emergency Relief Unemployment Relief of Hawaii.
72. *Advertiser,* 28 February 1933.
73. Ibid., 8 March 1933.
74. Hopkins to Col. W. F. Dillingham, 3 August 1933; Judd, Emergency Relief: Governor's Commission on Unemployment Relief of Hawaii, June–August 1933, AH.
75. 5 September 1933, AH.
76. *Advertiser,* 7 February 1933; 19 February 1933.
77. *Senate Journal* 203, p. 193.
78. *Advertiser,* 21 March 1933.
79. Ibid., 9 June 1933.
80. 376 U.S. 1 (1964).
81. Joint Resolution No. 2.
82. *Advertiser,* 30 May 1933.
83. Ibid., 3 June 1933.
84. Act 209.
85. *Advertiser,* 2 June 1933.

86. "Senator Elsie H. Wilcox, eight years of social progress, a life of public service," in 1940 campaign box at Grove Farm, PO-1.

87. *Advertiser,* 19 January 1934; 11 September 1933; 18 September 1933; 28 September 1933.

88. Ibid., 20 October 1933; 26 October 1933; 18 November 1933; 6 November 1933; 29 November 1933; 28 November 1933; 6 December 1933.

89. Ibid., 14 December 1933.

90. Ibid., 12 January 1934.

91. Ibid., 1 December 1933; 6 January 1934; Act 40 Special Session, 1933.

92. Ibid., 11 January 1934; 13 January 1934.

93. Ibid., 16 December 1933; 17 December 1933; 21 December 1933.

94. Ibid., 1 February 1934.

95. James Buchanan Lane, "The Poindexter Administration: Hawaii in Transition" (M.A. thesis, University of Hawai'i, 1966), 20–21.

96. *Advertiser,* 10 July 1934.

97. Ibid., 11 July 1934; 24 August 1934.

98. *Garden Island,* 5 June 1934.

99. *Advertiser,* 28 October 1934; 5 February 1935; 16 December 1934; 26 October 1934; 7 December 1934; 12 September 1934.

100. Johnson, *City and County of Honolulu,* 133.

101. Lawrence H. Fuchs, *Hawaii Pono: A Social History* (San Diego: Harcourt, Brace, Jovanovich, 1961), 135.

102. *Advertiser,* 1 September 1934; 30 September 1934.

103. Ibid., 16 February 1935; 6 January 1935.

104. Ibid., 7 March 1935.

105. Ibid., 16 January 1935; 15 November 1934; 11 January 1935.

Chapter Five: Lady Politician

1. *Advertiser,* 21 February 1935.

2. *Garden Island,* 26 February 1935.

3. *Advertiser,* 12 March 1935; 19 March 1935.

4. Ibid., 6 March 1935.

5. Ibid., 9 April 1935.

6. Ibid., 16 April 1935; 14 April 1935.

7. Act 40.

8. Senate Concurrent Resolution 33.

9. *Advertiser,* 25 April 1935.

10. Ibid., 12 May 1935; 14 May 1935.

11. Act 76.

12. "Senator Elsie H. Wilcox, eight years of social progress, a life of public service," in 1940 campaign box at Grove Farm, PO-1.

13. *Advertiser,* 21 June 1935.

14. Ibid., 1 January 1936; 29 February 1936; 3 June 1936; 24 November 1936.
15. Ibid., 25 November 1935.
16. Ibid., 8 March 1936; 1 April 1936; 29 April 1936; 30 April 1936; 7 May 1936; 16 September 1936; 8 May 1936; 16 July 1936.
17. *Garden Island,* 7 July 1936.
18. Elsie Wilcox, "Present Trends in Social Work," *The Friend* (August 1936): 145.
19. Judith R. Hughes, "Social Service in the Early Territorial Period," in "Perspectives on Health Care and Healing on Kauai" (Honolulu: Hawaii Committee for the Humanities, 1988).
20. *Garden Island,* 7 July 1936.
21. Eddie to Wilcox, 4 March 1933.
22. Wilcox to O. F. Shepard, principal, Punahou School, n.d.
23. *Advertiser,* 20 March 1936.
24. Ibid., 29 September 1936.
25. Ibid., 1 October 1936.
26. Wilcox to Mr. J. W. Garrett, 28 January 1936.
27. *Advertiser,* 4 October 1936.
28. Ibid., 14 November 1936.
29. Wilcox to Ellen Light Smythe, 11 December 1936.
30. Act 94, Act 182, Act 242, 1937 Legislative Session.
31. *Advertiser,* 17 April 1937; 21 April 1937.
32. Act 155; Act 190.
33. *Star-Bulletin,* 26 February 1937.
34. *Advertiser,* 4 March 1937; 8 April 1937.
35. Senate Concurrent Resolution 3.
36. *Advertiser,* 11 March 1937.
37. Ibid., 13 March 1937; 3 April 1937.
38. Undated 1937 speech.
39. Donald D. Johnson, *The City and County of Honolulu: A Governmental Chronicle* (Honolulu: University of Hawai'i Press, 1991), 80.
40. *Advertiser,* 8 May 1937.
41. Ibid., 29 April 1937.
42. Ibid., 29 July 1937; 11 May 1937; 19 May 1937; 20 May 1937.
43. "Senator Elsie H. Wilcox, eight years of social progress, a life of public service," in 1940 campaign box at Grove Farm, PO-1.
44. *Advertiser,* 24 July 1937.
45. Ibid., 6 October 1937; 15 January 1938.
46. Ibid., 28 June 1938.
47. Ibid., 9 June 1938; 17 June 1938.
48. Ibid., 9 November 1938; 7 November 1938.

49. Sanford Zalberg, *A Spark Is Struck: Jack Hall and the ILWU in Hawaii* (Honolulu: University Press of Hawai'i, 1979), 28.
50. Ibid.
51. Edward D. Beechert, *Working in Hawaii: A Labor History* (Honolulu: University of Hawai'i Press, 1985), 229–230.
52. Zalberg, *A Spark Is Struck*, 8–9.
53. Beechert, *Working in Hawaii*, 248.
54. *Advertiser*, 16 February 1939.
55. Ibid., 6 March 1939; 9 March 1939.
56. Ibid., 6 March 1939.
57. Ibid., 27 March 1939; 11 April 1939.
58. Beechert, *Working in Hawaii*, 214–215.
59. *Advertiser*, 30 March 1939.
60. Ibid., 12 April 1939.
61. Wilcox Radio Talk, 18 September 1940, Grove Farm, PO-1.
62. Act 187.
63. *Advertiser*, 1 May 1939.
64. *Star-Bulletin*, 20 April 1940.

Chapter Six: Defeat and Victory

1. Elsie Wilcox to Gaylord Wilcox, 27 August 1940.
2. Wilcox to Walker, Faye, Burns, Horner, Shackelton, and Gaylord Wilcox, 27 August 1940.
3. Typed speech in Grove Farm 1940 election box, dated Wednesday, 6:13 P.M., PO-1.
4. Ibid., Wilcox speech, Monday, 5:58 P.M., and Thursday, 5:45 P.M.
5. "Registered Voters 1940 Primary Election, Sixth Representative District, County of Kauai," in election box at Grove Farm, PO-1.
6. 1940 election box, transcript of program.
7. "Radio Talk," 25 September 1940. Grove Farm, PO-1.
8. *Star-Bulletin*, 32 September 1940.
9. "Radio Talk," 25 September 1940.
10. Ibid.
11. Waterhouse to Wilcox, 28 August 1940.
12. Walker to Wilcox, 28 August 1940.
13. Wilcox to Ses Burns, 27 September 1940.
14. Sanford Zalberg, *A Spark Is Struck: Jack Hall and the ILWU in Hawaii* (Honolulu: University Press of Hawai'i, 1979), 43.
15. *Star-Bulletin*, 7 September 1940.
16. Typed speech, 19 September 1940.
17. Typed Speech, 26 September 1940.

18. 1940 election box, Grove Farm, PO-1.
19. *Catholic Herald,* 27 September 1940.
20. *Garden Island,* 1 October 1940; *Star-Bulletin,* 30 September 1940.
21. *Garden Island,* 26 September 1940.
22. 1940 election box.
23. Wilcox to Walker.
24. Wilcox to D. W. Cummings, 8 October 1940.
25. Walter Witte, AmFac, to Wilcox, 7 October 1940.
26. Dora S. Contrades to Wilcox, 10 October 1940.
27. Francis Pugh to Wilcox, 9 October 1940.
28. Toyoko to Wilcox, 8 October 1940.
29. Osumi to Wilcox, 7 October 1940.
30. Henry P. Judd to Wilcox, 11 October 1940.
31. R. M. Allen to Wilcox, 9 October 1940.
32. W. H. George to Wilcox, 7 October 1940. *Advertiser,* 18 September 1940.
33. Election box at Grove Farm, PO-1.
34. Richardson to Wilcox, 20 December 1944.
35. *Garden Island,* 10 August 1943.
36. Wilcox, et. al., to Emmons, 7 April 1942.
37. Paul Osumi, interviewed by author, 10 February 1987, Honolulu.
38. Interview with Nancy Goodale.
39. Ralph W. Bayless, district secretary, American Bible Society, to Elsie and Mabel Wilcox, 21 March 1952.
40. Emory to Wilcox, 19 May 1952; Wilcox to Emory, 16 July 1952.
41. Findley to Wilcox, 25 November 1952.
42. Wilcox to Lawrence A. Walworth, 4 October 1952.
43. William Alexander, interviewed by author, Honolulu, 9 May 1980.
44. Ford Coffman, interviewed by author, Honolulu, 21 May 1980.
45. *Garden Island,* 27 July 1954.

Chapter Seven: Evaluations

1. Mary Beard, *Woman's Work in Municipalities* (New York: Arno, 1972), 221.
2. David E. Stannard, *American Holocaust: Columbus and the Conquest of the New World* (New York: Oxford, 1992); Forrest G. Wood, *The Arrogance of Faith: Christianity and Race in America from the Colonial Era to the Twentieth Century* (New York: Alfred A Knopf, 1990).
3. Gary Y. Okihiro, *Cane Fires: The Anti-Japanese Movement in Hawaii, 1865–1945* (Philadelphia: Temple University Press, 1991).
4. Laurence H. Fuchs, *Hawaii Pono: A Social History,* part 2 (San Diego: Harcourt Brace Jovanovich, 1961).

5. Laurence H. Fuchs, *The American Kaleidoscope: Race, Ethnicity, and the Civic Culture* (Hanover: University Press of New England, 1990); Michael Novak, *The Rise of the Unmeltable Ethnics: Politics and Culture in the Seventies* (New York: Macmillan, 1972); Werner Sollors, *Beyond Ethnicity: Consent and Descent in American Culture* (New York: Oxford University Press, 1986); Stephen Steinberg, *The Ethnic Myth: Race, Ethnicity, and Class in America* (New York: Atheneum, 1981); Ronald T. Takaki, *Iron Cages: Race and Culture in Nineteenth-Century America* (New York: Alfred A. Knopf, 1979).

6. Paul C. Violas, *The Training of the Urban Working Class: A History of Twentieth Century American Education* (Chicago: Rand McNally, 1978); Clarence J. Karier, "Business Values and the Educational State," in Clarence J. Karier, et al., *Roots of Crisis: American Education in the Twentieth Century* (Chicago: Rand McNally, 1973).

7. Patricia N. Limerick, *The Legacy of Conquest: The Unbroken Past of the American West* (New York: W. W. Norton, 1987), 257.

Bibliography

Alexander, William. Interview by author. Honolulu, Hawai'i, 9 May 1980.
Andrew, John A., III. *Rebuilding the Christian Commonwealth: New England Congregationalists and Foreign Missions, 1800–1830*. Lexington: University Press of Kentucky, 1976.
Beard, Mary. *Women's Work in Municipalities*. New York: Arno Press, 1972.
Beechert, Edward D. *Working in Hawaii: A Labor History*. Honolulu: University of Hawai'i Press, 1985.
Bernard, Jessie. *The Female World*. New York: The Free Press, 1981.
Black, Naomi. *Social Feminism*. Ithaca: Cornell University Press, 1989.
Blair, Karen J. *The Clubwoman as Feminist: True Womanhood Redefined 1868–1914*. New York: Holmes and Meier, 1980.
Buck, Elizabeth. *Paradise Remade: The Politics of Culture and History in Hawai'i*. Philadelphia: Temple University Press, 1993.
Bushnell, O. A. *The Gifts of Civilization: Germs and Genocide in Hawai'i*. Honolulu: University of Hawai'i Press, 1993.
Catholic Herald. 27 Sept. 1940.
Chafe, William Henry. *The American Woman: Her Changing Social, Economic and Political Roles, 1920–1970*. New York: Oxford University Press, 1972.
Coffman, Ford. Interview by author. Honolulu, Hawai'i, 21 May 1980.
Croly, Jane C. "Sorosis: Its Origins and History." In *The Clubs of New York: With an Account of the Origin, Progress, Present Condition and Membership of the Leading Clubs; an Essay on New York Club Life*, edited by Francis Gerry Fairfield. New York: Henry Hinton, 1873.
Daly, Mary. *Gyn\Ecology: The Metaethics of Radical Feminism*. Boston: Beacon Press, 1978.
Damon, Ethel M., ed. *Letters from the Life of Abner and Lucy Wilcox, 1836–1869*. Privately printed. Honolulu, date unknown.
Davis, Allen F. *Spearheads for Reform: The Social Settlements and the Pro-

gressive Movement 1890–1914. New York: Oxford University Press, 1967.
Daws, Gavan. *Shoal of Time: A History of the Hawaiian Islands*. Honolulu: University Press of Hawai'i, 1968.
Degler, Carl N. *At Odds: Women and the Family in America from the Revolution to the Present*. Oxford: Oxford University Press, 1980.
Epstein, Cynthia Fuchs. *Deceptive Distinctions: Sex, Gender, and the Social Order*. New Haven: Yale University Press, 1988.
Evans, Sara M. *Born for Liberty: A History of Women in America*. New York: The Free Press, 1989.
Farrington v. Tokushige. 273 US 284 (1926).
Fern, Charles. Interview by author. Honolulu, Hawai'i, 23 May 1980.
Firestone, Shulamith. *The Dialect of Sex: The Case for Feminist Revolution*. New York: Bantam Books, 1970.
The Friend. 1843–1954.
Fuchs, Lawrence H. *The American Kaleidoscope: Race, Ethnicity, and the Civic Culture*. Hanover: Wesleyan University Press, 1990.
———. *Hawaii Pono: A Social History*. San Diego: Harcourt, Brace, Jovanovich, 1961.
Gay, Floy T. "A Study of the Development of the Senior High School." Master's thesis, University of Hawai'i, 1945.
Goodale, Nancy. Interview by author. Līhu'e, Kaua'i, 11 Nov. 1988.
Gordon, Lynn D. *Gender and Higher Education in the Progressive Era*. New Haven: Yale University Press, 1990.
Governor's Advisory Committee on Education. *Survey of Schools and Industry*. Honolulu: Printshop Co., 1931.
Greven, Philip. *The Protestant Temperament: Patterns of Child-Rearing, Religious Experience, and the Self in Early America*. New York: Alfred A. Knopf, 1977.
Grimshaw, Patricia. *Paths of Duty: American Missionary Wives in Nineteenth-Century Hawaii*. Honolulu: University of Hawai'i Press, 1989.
Hawaii Mission Children's Society. *Missionary Album: Portraits and Biographical Sketches of the American Protestant Missionaries in the Hawaiian Islands*. Honolulu: 1969.
Heilbrun, Carolyn G. *Writing a Woman's Life*. New York: W. W. Norton, 1988.
Honolulu Advertiser. 1931–1940.
Honolulu Star Bulletin. 1932–1940.
Hooper, Paul F. *Elusive Destiny: The Internationalist Movement in Modern Hawaii*. Honolulu: University Press of Hawai'i, 1980.
Horowitz, Helen Lefkowitz. *Alma Mater: Design and Experience in Women's Colleges from Their Nineteenth-Century Beginnings to the 1930's*. New York: Alfred A. Knopf, 1984.

Hughes, Judith. "The Demise of the English Standard School System." *The Hawaiian Journal of History* 27 (1993): 77.

———. "Social Service in the Early Territorial Period." In *Perspectives on Health Care and Healing on Kauai*. Honolulu: Hawaii Committee for the Humanities, 1988.

Hundley, A. Letters to Governor McCarthy and Public Instruction Commissioners. 1919. Hawai'i State Archives, Honolulu.

Hundley, Bernice. "Thank You, Miss Elsie Wilcox." *Garden Island* (21 July 1954).

Johnson, Donald. D. *The City and County of Honolulu: A Governmental Chronicle*. Honolulu: University of Hawai'i Press, 1991.

Judd, Lawrence M. Governor of Territory of Hawai'i. Territorial Departments. Department of Public Instruction. 26 July 1932; 3 Aug. 1932. Hawai'i State Archives, Honolulu.

———. Governor's Commission on Emergency Relief Unemployment Relief of Hawai'i. Date unknown. Hawai'i State Archives, Honolulu.

Kame'eleihiwa, Lilikala. *Native Land and Foreign Desires: Ko Hawai'i 'Aina a me Na Koi Pu'umake a ka Po'e Haole*. Honolulu: Bishop Museum Press, 1992.

Karier, Clarence J. "Business Values and the Educational State." In *Roots of Crisis: American Education in the Twentieth Century*, edited by Clarence J. Karier and Paul C. Violas. Chicago: Rand McNally, 1973.

Kauai Garden Island. 1919–1954.

Kauai News. 30 January 1951.

Kent, Noel. *Islands Under the Influence*. New York: Monthly Review Press, 1983.

Krauss, Bob, and W. P. Alexander. *Grove Farm Plantation: The Biography of a Hawaiian Sugar Plantation*. 2d ed. Palo Alto: Pacific Books, 1965.

Kuykendall, Ralph S. *The Hawaiian Kingdom*. Vol. 1. *Foundation and Transformation*. Honolulu: University of Hawai'i Press, 1938.

Lane, James Buchanan. "The Poindexter Administration: Hawaii in Transition." Master's thesis, University of Hawai'i, 1966.

Lerner, Gerda. *The Majority Finds Its Past: Placing Women in History*. Oxford: Oxford University Press, 1979.

Liebes, Richard A. "Labor Organization in Hawaii: A Study of Effort of Labor to Obtain Security through Organization." Master's thesis, University of Hawai'i, 1938.

Limerick, Patricia N. *The Legacy of Conquest: The Unbroken Past of the American West*. New York: Norton, 1987.

Lind, Andrew W. *Hawaii's People*. Honolulu: University Press of Hawai'i, 1967.

Lyman, Henry M. *Hawaiian Yesterdays: Chapters from a Boy's Life in the Islands in the Early Days*. Chicago: A. C. McClurg, 1906.

Martin, Margaret Greer, ed. *The Lymans of Hilo*. Hilo: Lyman House Memorial Museum, date unknown.
McCluskey, William. "Kauai High School." In *Some Landmarks in the Development of Hawaii's Public School System*, edited by T. H. Gibson. Publication information unavailable.
Mead, Royal D. "The Sugar Industry in Hawaii." *San Francisco Chronicle* (18 July 1910).
Menton, Linda K. "Everything That Is Lovely and of Good Report: The Hawaiian Chief's Children's School, 1839–1850." Ph.D. diss., University of Hawai'i, 1982.
Muncy, Robyn. *Creating a Female Dominion in American Reform, 1890–1935*. New York: Oxford University Press, 1991.
Novak, Michael. *The Rise of the Unmeltable Ethnics: Politics and Culture in the Seventies*. New York: Macmillian, 1972.
"Official Tabulation." No publication information.
Okamura, Suyeki. Interview by author. Honolulu, Hawai'i, 7 Aug. 1987
Okihiro, Gary Y. *Cane Fires: The Anti-Japanese Movement in Hawaii, 1865–1945*. Philadelphia: Temple University Press, 1991.
O'Leary, Margaret R., ed. "Register of the Grove Farm Plantation Records and Papers of George N. Wilcox, Samuel W. Wilcox, Emma L. Wilcox, Elsie H. Wilcox, and Mabel I. Wilcox." Grove Farm Homestead, Līhu'e. 1982.
O'Neill, William L. *Everyone Was Brave: A History of Feminism in America*. New York: Quadrangle, 1969.
Osumi, Paul. Interview by author. Honolulu, Hawai'i, 10 Feb. 1987.
Palmieri, Patricia A. "Here Was Fellowship: A Social Portrait of Academic Women at Wellesley College, 1895–1920." *History of Education Quarterly* 23, no. 2 (Summer 1983): 195.
Peterson, Charles E. "The Iolani Palaces and Barracks." *Journal of the Society of Architectural Historians* 22, no. 2 (May 1963): 2.
Proceedings of the Forty-Ninth Annual Meeting of the HSPA. Honolulu: Star Bulletin, 1930.
Sato, Gordon C. "Hawaii's Public Schools: A Primary Agency for Behavioral Assimilation, 1920–1940." Master's thesis, University of Hawai'i, 1973.
Scott, Anne Firor. *Natural Allies: Women's Associations in American History*. Urbana: University of Illinois Press, 1991.
"Senator Elsie H. Wilcox, eight years of social progress, a life of public service." In 1940 campaign box at Grove Farm, Līhu'e. PO-1.
Sollers, Werner. *Beyond Ethnicity: Consent and Descent in American Culture*. New York: Oxford University Press, 1986.
Solomon, Barbara Miller. *In the Company of Educated Women: A History of Women and Higher Education in America*. New Haven: Yale University Press, 1985.

Stannard, David E. *American Holocaust: Columbus and the Conquest of the New World*. New York: Oxford University Press, 1992.

———. *Before the Horror: The Population of Hawai'i on the Eve of Western Contact*. Honolulu: Social Science Research Institute, 1989.

State of Hawai'i. Department of Public Instruction. "Minutes." Hawai'i State Archives, Honolulu. 7 Sept. 1920, 9 March 1921, 23 May 1922, 19 March 1929, 3 October 1931, 10 March 1921.

Steinberg, Stephen. *The Ethnic Myth: Race, Ethnicity, and Class in America*. New York: Atheneum, 1981.

Takaki, Ronald. *A Different Mirror: A History of Multicultural America*. Boston: Little, Brown, 1993.

———. *Iron Cages: Race and Culture in Nineteenth-Century America*. New York: Alfred A. Knopf, 1979.

Tamura, Eileen. *Americanization, Acculturation, and Ethnic Identity: The Nisei Generation in Hawaii*. Chicago: University of Illinois Press, 1994.

Tracy, Joseph. *History of the American Board of Commissioners for Foreign Missions*. New York: M. W. Dodd, 1842.

Turner, Frederick Jackson. "The Significance of History." In *History, Frontier, and Section: Three Essays by Frederick Jackson Turner*. Albuquerque: University of New Mexico Press, 1993.

U.S. Congress. "The Blount Report." In *Executive Documents of the House of Representatives*. 53rd Cong., 3rd sess., (1894–1895), v.1. Washington, D.C.: Government Printing Office, 1895.

U.S. Department of the Interior. U.S. Office of Education. *Survey of Education in Hawaii*. Washington, D.C.: Government Printing Office, 1920.

U.S. Secretary of Labor. "Labor Conditions in Hawaii." Letter in *Fifth Annual Report of the Commissioner of Labor Statistics*. 64th Cong., 1st sess. S. Doc. 432. 1916. Washington D.C.: Government Printing Office.

Violas, Paul C. *The Training of the Urban Working Class: A History of Twentieth Century American Education*. Chicago: Rand McNally, 1978.

Ware, Susan. *Holding Their Own: American Women in the 1930's*. Boston: Twayne, 1980.

Watts, Margit Misangyi. *High Tea at Halekulani: Feminist Theory and American Clubwomen*. Brooklyn: Carlson Publishing, 1993.

Wedemeyer, Alice C. *The Story of the Mokihana Club*. Privately published, 1987.

Wichman, Juliette Rice. Interview by author. Līhu'e, Kaua'i, 15 Jan. 1986.

Wilcox, Elsie Hart. "Present Trends in Social Work." *The Friend* (August 1936): 45.

———. "Day Books." Unpublished and undated manuscript. Grove Farm Plantation Museum, Līhu'e.

———. "Early Race Relations on Kauai." Unpublished and undated manuscript. Kaua'i.

———. "Scrapbook." 4P-3-1. Grove Farm Plantation Museum, Kaua'i.
———. Wellesley College Report Card. 4P-3-2. Grove Farm Plantation Museum, Kaua'i.
Woloch, Nancy. *Early American Women: A Documentary History.* Belmont, CA: Wadsworth, 1992.
Wood, Forrest G. *The Arrogance of Faith: Christianity and Race in America from the Colonial Era to the Twentieth Century.* New York: Alfred A. Knopf, 1990.
Zalberg, Sanford. *A Spark Is Struck: Jack Hall and the ILWU in Hawaii.* Honolulu: University Press of Hawai'i, 1979.

Index

acculturation. *See* Americanization
Adams, Romanzo, 70, 75, 91
Addams, Jane, 37, 46, 92, 95
Agard, D., 105–106, 122
Aki, Henry, 102–105, 130–132
Alexander and Baldwin, 103, 123, 146
ali'i, 3, 12
American Board of Commissioners for Foreign Missions (ABCFM), 2–3, 5, 9–11, 40, 96; Elsie Wilcox elected to, 130–131. *See also* Hawaiian Evangelical Association; missionaries
American Factors (AmFac), 57, 103, 124
Americanization, 93, 95, 128, 152–154; businessmen's support of, 61, 85–86; criticism of, 91, 159; demise of, 91; goals, 81–83; New Americans' conventions, 90; Takie Okamura, 89–91, 153; YMCA, 82–89; YWCA, 83–88
Americans of Japanese Ancestry (AJA), 75, 152–153; education of, 21, 65, 78, 89; emperor worship, 65; interned during WWII, 153–154; language papers, 50, 65–66, 89, 117–118; language schools, 65–66, 81; New American's Convention, 90; and NRA, 117–118; post-WW II, 152; voting in 1930s, 122–123, 131, 148, 151–152
Anderson, Rufus, 9
assimilation. *See* Americanization
Atherton, Frank, 84

Baldwin, Ethel S., 74
Baldwin, H. A., 120, 127, 132, 162

Bary, Helen, 136
Beard, Mary, 40, 76, 158
Beecher, Catherine, 30
Beechert, Edward, 69, 71, 137
Bergen, Margaret, 72, 74–75
Big Five, 13, 103, 159
Bilger, Leonora, 133
Blair, Karen, 41
bloodless revolution, 152
Brandt, Claire, 59
Buck, Elizabeth, 11

C. Brewer & Co., 103, 114
capitalism, 60, 160
Carey, Miles, 60–61
Castle, S. N., 111
Catholics, 50, 116, 149
Caucasians: children, 99; and economy, 12–13, 82, 118, 123; and politics, 14–15, 49; teachers, 51; women, 30, 43–44, 157
Chamber of Commerce, 59, 68, 155
Channon, Grace, 84
charity: Associated Charities, 72, 80; Child and Family Services, 72; Child Welfare Board, 106, 120, 129–130; Elsie Wilcox, 77–81, 114, 158; G. N. Wilcox, 15–16; in great depression, 96–98, 114. *See also* philanthropy
child nutrition, 72, 74, 76
China: *Chinese Recorder,* 97; Elsie Wilcox's support of missionaries, 91–92, 98; Elsie Wilcox's visit, 45; Mass Education Movement, 91
Chinese in Hawai'i: businesses, 118; churches, 93, 97; Elsie Wilcox

189

and, 80; at Grove Farm, 18, 23, 24, 31; language schools, 65; in population, 61; voters, 123
churches: Central Union, 69, 93, 102; Episcopalian, 37, 50, 94, 97; First Chinese, 97; Kawaiahao, 34; Lihue Union, 37–38, 42, 92, 97, 156; Makiki Christian, 89–90, 97; Methodist, 93–94, 97, 156. *See also* Congregational Church
CIO, 122, 141, 152
civil service, 126–127, 134, 135
class: as category in biography, 158
Cleveland, President Grover, 15
Coan, Fidelia Church and Titus, 5
Coffman, Ford, 156
Coman, Katherine, 27–28, 49
Commissioners for Education: Elsie Wilcox, 58–70, 152; English standard schools, 66–68; and foreign language schools, 65–66; responsibilities, 58; and vocational education, 62–64
Congregational Church, 1–2, 6, 49, 94, 154. *See also* American Board of Commissioners for Foreign Missions; Hawaiian Evangelical Association; Kauai Evangelical Association
Congress, U.S., 15, 39, 41, 116; delegate to, 105, 109, 122, 137; women's vote, 133. *See also* New Deal
conversion to Christianity: Abner Wilcox, 6; Hawaiians, 2–3; *Protestant Temperament*, 6; Wilcox boys, 8
Cook, James, 2
Cooke, George, 118, 125
Cooke, Richard A., 61, 69, 75, 114–115, 120
Crawford, Will, 68, 112, 119
Croly, Jane, 40
Crozier, Clarence, 129, 132–135, 138
Crozier, William, 117, 129, 132
cult of domesticity, 30
Cunningham, Sarah Todd, 132, 138

Davies, Theo, 13
Degler, Carl, 44
democracy, 57, 60–62, 65, 160
Democratic party: "bloodless revolution," 152; on Kauaʻi, 105, 122, 137; in 1920s, 50; during 1932 election, 122–123; 1936 election, 128–129; platforms, 105, 121
demographics: changes in 1900s, 61; implication for politics, 152
Department of Public Instruction, 50, 58–59, 119, 140; budget, 62, 69, 112–113, 115, 118, 127, 140; 1920 Survey, 62–63, 66, 69, 112. *See also* Commissioners for Education; Prosser Report; Superintendent of Public Instruction
depression, the great: impact on charities, 96–98, 114; impact on education, 111–113; impact on Hawaiʻi, 108–109, 114–121, 152; recovery from, 124, 127, 135, 152
Dewey, John, 68
diversified farming, 63, 121
Doi, Isami, 80–81

economics: capitalism, 60, 160; laissez-faire, 109–110, 124
educational issues: class size, 112–113; English standard schools, 66–68, 154; foreign language schools, 65–66, 81; funding, 113, 127; high school tuition, 112, 123; kindergartens, 62, 71, 133; mandatory attendance, 64; 1929 Survey, 63; Prosser Report, 69–70; Smith-Hughes Act, 63; teachers' salaries, 111–113, 121, 127, 131, 140; vocational education, 62–64, 69, 127, 135, 145
Elsie Hart Wilcox Foundation, 156
Emerson, W. R. P., 76
Emory, Kenneth, 155
emperor worship, 65
English standard schools, 66–68, 154
Erickson, Ethel, 141
Europe: Elsie Wilcox travels in, 30, 47–49; Mabel Wilcox as nurse in war, 56; war in, 55–56, 153–154
Evangelicals, 6, 8. *See also* Abner Wilcox

factors, 102, 108, 123, 146, 159
Farrington, Joseph, 126, 132, 135, 138, 140
Faye, Lindsay, 137, 150–151, 154
feminists, 41
Fernandes, John B., 101, 137–138

Fernhurst, 85
Filipinos: Elsie Wilcox and, 25, 87–88, 91; at Grove Farm, 73; on Kaua'i, 94; on plantations, 105, 120; in population, 61; YMCA, 85; YWCA, 87–88. *See also* labor
Findley, Nell, 91, 116, 130, 155; and child welfare, 80, 114, 129
foreign language schools, 65, 66, 81
Fuchs, Lawrence, 123, 152

Gay, Floy, 63
gender issues: as category in biography, xi, 158. *See also* women's issues
German culture: and Elsie Wilcox, 42, 48–49, 55, 143; at Lihu'e, 13
Gibson, Walter Murry, 50
Gomes, Clem: legislative bills, 127; 1932 campaign, 101–103, 105; 1940 campaign, 143, 145, 150–151
Gordon, Lynn, 27
government, territorial: budgets, 109–111, 113, 118–119, 140; civil service, 126, 134–135; education committee, 125–126, 133, 140; Elsie Wilcox and, election to, 70, 100–105, 1933 session, 107–124, 1935 session, 125–129, 1937 session, 132–135, 1939 session, 138–142; and governor, 108, 118, 123, 127, 135, 140, 142; Hawaiian Homesteads, 116, 126; House of Representatives, 101–102, 105, 142; public lands committee, 108, 140; reapportionment, 116, 121, 126, 133, 136, 140; retirees, 113; retirement fund, 113, 118, 161–163; sterilization, 116; unemployment assistance, 113–115, 117, 146, 148; ways and means committee, 125, 130, 132, 140. *See also* taxes; welfare issues; welfare organizations; women's issues
government, United States: annexation of Hawai'i, 14–15, 49; Federal Emergency Relief Administration (FERA), 115, 124, 132; money to Hawai'i during depression, 110–111, 117; National Recovery Act, 117–118, 123, 128–129; overthrow of monarchy, 14–15;

Reconstruction Finance Corporation, 110; Social Security, 129–130, 136, 141, 148
governor: Judd, 106, 108–109, 114, 117–118; McCarthy, 58–59; Poindexter, 109, 111, 121, 123, 127–129, 133, 135, 140, 142; powers of, 140; Stainback, 153, 159
grandparents: influence on Elsie Wilcox, 2, 11, 12, 14, 95, 120, 157, 158; Lymans, 1, 4; Wilcoxes, 1, 5
Greven, Philip, 6, 8
Grove Farm: agriculture, 19, 21; early years, 12–14, 17, 22, 32–35; Elsie Wilcox's final years at, 153–156; life at, 14, 17–25, 30–39, 46; managers, 50–51, 57, 106; politics, 14, 149; preservation of, 99; Puhi Camp 73, 94; social work, 72–73; work force, 13, 18, 24, 46; WW II, 149, 154

Hall, Jack, 137, 147, 150
Hanalei, 5, 13, 16, 99, 131
Hansen, Edith, 87, 88
haole: See Caucasians
Hawai'i, kingdom: *mahele,* 13, 158; overthrow of monarchy, 14, 15
Hawaii Hochi, 118
Hawaiian Evangelical Association (HEA): Elsie Wilcox and, 39–40, 85, 87, 93, 98; power of, 49–50; Rev. Osumi, 154. *See also* Congregational Church
Hawaiian homesteads, 116, 126
Hawaiian language, 3, 38, 71, 93, 108
Hawaiian monarchy, 13–15, 34, 39, 158–159
Hawaiian Pineapple Co., 108
Hawaiian Sugar Planters Association (HSPA), 61, 75, 109, 121, 122, 128
Hawaiians, 11; child welfare, 120; education, 21, 67; Elsie Wilcox and, 18, 24, 39, 94; and intermarriage, 13, 34, 43, 44, 55; land issues, 13, 126, 159; and missionaries, 2–4, 70; voters, 122
Hazard, Caroline, 27
Heen, William, 119, 122, 132, 135
Heilbrun, Carolyn, 43
high school: *See* educational issues

Hilo Boarding school, 4
Hind, Robert, 106, 107
historic preservation: Commission on Historical Sites, 155; Grove Farm, 99–100; Lyman House, 99; Wilcox sisters and Waioli, 99, 155
hoʻiki, 38
holidays, 51; birthdays, 34, 78, 80, 139, 140; Chinese New Year, 24, 31; Christmas, 22–23, 31, 38, 55, 78, 80, 83; Japanese emperor's birthday, 31; New Year's eve, 36
Holt, Harry, 125, 132
Hopkins, Harry, 115
Horowitz, Helen, 28
hospitals: Children's, 53; G. N. Wilcox Memorial, 156; Kuakini, 90; Mahelona, 117
house of representatives, territorial: *See* government, territorial
Houston, Victor, 105
Hundley, Bernice, 58

Ickes, Harold and Democrats in Hawaiʻi, 109, 126
immigrants: Americanization of, 81–83; demographic changes, 61; parents' goals for children, 61–62; on plantations, 71–73
Independent Labor Party, 129
Institute of Pacific Relations (IPR), 91
International Longshoremen's and Warehousemen's Union (ILWU), 137, 148, 152
Internationalism, Institute of Pacific Relations, 91; National Council for the Prevention of War, 92, 98; Pan Pacific Union, 92, 98
Iʻolani Palace, 107
Isenberg, Paul, 14, 55

Japan: Elsie Wilcox travels in, 45; and YMCA, 86
Japanese Counsel, 65
Japanese in Hawaiʻi: businesses, 124; demographics, 61; diet, 76; Elsie Wilcox and, 46, 80; at Grove Farm, 18, 23–34, 73; language, 93, 103; plantation workers, 47, 71, 89; values, 65. *See also* Americanization; Americans of Japanese Ancestry; Okamura, Takie

Johnson, Donald, 105, 123, 134
Jones-Costigan Act, 122
Judd, Governor Lawrence, 106, 108–109, 114, 117–118

Kalākaua, King David, 14
Kalanianaʻole, Prince Jonah Kūhio, 39
Kamehameha Schools, 78–79
Kapaʻa, 58–59
kapu, 2–3
Kauai Evangelical Association, 93, 155
Kauaʻi Historical Society, 40
Kauai Progressive League, 137
Kealoha, John, 103, 137
Keʻelikolani, Princess Ruth, 14
Keliinoi, Rosalie, 103
Killam, Lloyd, 82
kindergartens, 62, 71, 133
King, Samuel Wilder, 125, 137, 154
Knudsen, Eric A., 58–59
Koreans in Hawaiʻi, 25, 61, 65, 93

labor: anti-labor laws, 136, 141; collective bargaining, 137, 141; Jack Hall on Kauaʻi, 137, 147, 150; maximum hours, 120, 134, 141; minimum wage, 76, 117–118, 120, 127, 134, 141; single wage scale, 117–118; strikes, 47, 49, 82, 95, 137, 141; unions, 71, 95, 141, 146; voters, 147, 150, 152; workmen's compensation, 127, 146. *See also* International Longshoremen's and Warehousemen's Union (ILWU)
Landon, Alfred, 130
Lane, James, 121
Liholiho, 2
Lihue: Cemetery Association, 155; hall, 40; plantation, 12–14, 42, 54, 146; town, 59, 94, 150; Union church, 37–38, 42, 92, 97, 156
Liliʻuokalani, Queen, 14–15
Limerick, Patricia, 159
Locke, Neil, 84, 86, 88
Loomis, Charles, 85, 91
Lowrey, Sherwood, 123
Lydgate, Rev. John, 42
Lyman, David, 1, 4
Lyman, Emma, 4, 12–13, 17–18, 25, 37
Lyman, Sarah Joiner, 1, 4

Mahelona, Emma, 39
Mahelona, Ethel, 39, 45
Marcallino, A. Q., 102–103, 105
McCandless, Lincoln, 105, 109, 122–123, 128
McCarthy, Governor Charles, 59
Mead, Royal, 61
Metzger, Delbert, 109
Mid-Pacific Institute, 16
minimum wage: *See* labor
ministers, 102, 156; and Americanization, 89; and education, 69; Elsie Wilcox's financial support of, 46, 80–81, 93–94, 97, 155; Hawaiian, 108; Japanese 89, 93, 151, 153–154; problems on Kaua'i, 87, 93, 98
missionaries, 1–11, 22; criticism of, 159; evangelicals, 6, 8; foreign, 45, 65, 91, 97–98; and social work, 70–71. *See also* American Board of Commissioners for Foreign Missions
Moir, John T., Jr., 101, 103, 106
Mokihana Club, 59, 158; beautification, 51; Elsie Wilcox as president, 40, 52–53; fundraising, 42, 53; good film movement, 54–55; municipal housekeeping, 51–52; public health nurse, 53–54; school milk program, 76; self-improvement activities, 40–42; social work, 72, 83
Mossman, Bina, 142
Muncy, Robin, 37
municipal housekeeping: *See* Mokihana Club

New Deal: Agricultural Adjustment Act, 129; Civil Works Administration, 120; Federal Emergency Relief Administration, 115; impact on Hawai'i, 110–111, 122, 128, 141, 152; National Labor Relations Act, 141; National Recovery Act, 117, 123, 129; Reconstruction Finance Corporation, 110; Social Security Act, 129–130, 141
Nippu Jiji, 118
normal school, 62, 78, 89

Okamura, Takie: criticism of, 89, 91; and Japanese Hospital, 90; Makiki Christian Church, 89–90, 97. *See also* Americanization
old age pensions, 105, 113, 129–130, 135
old maids, 42, 44
orphans, 78–79
Osumi, Paul, 151, 154
Ouye, Tom, 105

Palmieri, Patricia, 27–28
Pan Pacific Union, 92, 98
Papalinahoa, 19, 32–33, 38, 51
paternalism, 71, 152
perimutuel betting, 120
Petrie, Lester, 126
philanthropy: Elsie Wilcox, 77, 80, 90, 97–98, 106, 130, 152;
G. N. Wilcox, 15, 51, 54; problems with private, 76, 114, 129, 152
plantations: criticism of, 75, 159; early, 11–15; educational issues, 60–64, 111–112; life on, 71–73, 76, 89, 147; nurse/social work, 53–54, 75; owners/managers, 12–13, 15, 21, 47, 49, 76, 159; and politics, 11, 15, 49–50, 102–103, 108, 110, 122–123, 150; voters, 131, 146–148; wages, 75, 120. *See also* Americanization; Grove Farm; labor
Poindexter, Joseph: appointed governor, 121; campaign for governor, 109; criticized by Republicans, 129; Honolulu Taxpayers Association, 111; 1939 agenda, 140
police, 75, 134–135, 141–142, 146, 150–151
populists, 49, 102
Portuguese, 24, 65, 67, 103
pregnant girls, 72, 76, 79
progressives, 27, 49, 57, 60, 138, 160
prohibition: *See* temperance
Prosser, Charles, 69
Prosser Report, 69–70
provisional government, 15
public health: Elsie Wilcox and, 72; Mabel Wilcox and, 88, 100; and Mokihana Club, 51, 53–54
public schools: *See* educational issues
Punahou School, 9–10, 16, 21, 25, 65, 130

race: as category in biography, 157–158, 160; and churches, 93–94; discrimination, 21, 136; Elsie Wilcox and, 18, 24–25, 39; labor and, 82, 138, 152; marriage and, 43–44; relations, 43–44, 46, 152; and voting, 61, 122–123, 131, 136, 148, 152
reapportionment, 116, 121, 126, 133, 136, 140
Red Cross, 56, 153
Republic of Hawai'i, 15
Republican party: criticism of, 109–110, 123, 129, 159; decline of in Hawai'i, 151–152; and Democratic party in Hawai'i, 50, 110–111, 121, 125, 137; Elsie Wilcox and, 109, 116–117, 121, 126, 136, 142–143, 150–152, 155; on Kaua'i, 101–105, 121; national convention, 128, 130; platform, 105, 121, 128, 136; and race issues, 122–123; and reapportionment, 116; and Wilcox family, 39
Restarick, Joseph, 94
revolution: of 1893, 14–15; bloodless, 152
Rice, Charles: criticism of, 101–103; and Elsie Wilcox, 58–59, 100–106, 116–117, 126–127, 150; 1933 session, 111, 114, 116–118, 124; 1935 election and session, 125–127; 1937 election and session, 131–135; as political leader, 100–103, 116, 132, 137; retirement, 137, 147, 150–154
Rice, Daisy, 31–33, 36–38, 44, 50–51
Rice, family and Wilcox family, 42, 55, 103; Daisy Rice and Wilcoxes, 31–33, 36–39; early missionary families, 7, 12; young Wilcox and Rice children, 19, 21
Rice, William, 12, 32

schools: Kamehameha, 78, 79; McKinley High School, 60, 88; Mid-Pacific Institute, 16; The Priory, 78, 79. *See also* Punahou School
Schenck, Norman, 85, 87, 154
single women, 44, 47, 51, 72, 95, 158. *See also* women's issues
Slogett, Digby, 33, 35

Smith-Hughes Act, 63
social critics: muckrakers, 49; progressives, 27, 49, 57, 60, 138, 160
social workers: Conference on Social Workers, 91, 129; criticism of, 159; early, 70–73; Elsie Wilcox, 56, 70–77, 82, 100, 103, 109, 152; White House Conference on Child Health and Protection, 98. *See also* Mokihana Club; welfare issues; welfare organizations
soup kitchens, 114
Spreckels, Claus, 13
Stainback, Governor Ingram, 153
statehood, 121, 128, 133, 136, 159
sterilization, 116
strikes, 47, 49, 82, 95, 141. *See also* labor
sugar: Jones-Costigan Act, 122. *See also* plantations
Sunday school, 37–38, 92–93, 95
Superintendent of Public Instruction, 58, 64, 68, 112, 119
supervisors: county, 120, 127, 135; plantation (lunas), 46, 122, 147, 159
Susanna Wesley Home, 72, 77, 79, 98
Sylva, Joseph, 125–126, 132

Takaki, Ronald, 71
Tamura, Eileen, 50, 81, 91
taxes: Honolulu Taxpayers Association, 111, 114; income, 105, 108, 111, 121, 123–124; 1933 legislative session, 108–111, 117–119; 1935 session, 123–124, 128; 1938 campaign issues, 140, 144–145, 147–148; poll, 108, 111, 147; property, 108–109, 111, 118, 123
teachers: college, 117; cottages, 111; salaries, 111–113, 121, 127, 131, 140
temperance, 98, 119
Territory of Hawai'i: *See* government, territorial
transportation, early, 21, 32; and education, 62; first automobiles on Kaua'i, 46, 53
Trask, David: 1933 legislative session, 116, 119, 120; 1935 session, 125, 132–134; campaign for Congress, 137
Tuberculosis Association, 72
Turner, Frederick Jackson, xii

unemployment: in cities, 115; during depression, 96, 105, 113; and plantations, 71, 109; unemployment assistance, 113–115, 117, 120, 146, 148
Unemployment Work Relief Commission, 115
University of Hawai'i, 61, 70, 78, 112, 133, 155

values: American, 81, 90, 95; capitalistic, xii, 49, 60; Christian, xii, 16, 17, 90, 95; democratic, 60–61, 110; Elsie Wilcox's personal, 1, 11, 12, 30, 117, 119, 120, 157–159; Japanese, 65
vocational education, 62–64, 69, 127, 135, 145
Voice of Labor, 138
voters: by race, 122–123, 131, 145, 148, 151–152; women, 105, 144, 149

Waialua, 5, 33
Waioli: mission, 5, 7, 16, 21, 155; preservation of, 99
Walker, H. A., 146, 149
Waterhouse, A. H., 59, 154
Waterhouse, John, 123, 146
Waterhouse, Marian, 45
welfare issues, 76, 152; child welfare, 50, 51, 68, 100, 103, 107, 127, 133; Elsie Wilcox's concerns, 49, 80, 95, 143, 146, 150, 158; on Kaua'i, 73, 83, 97, 106, 129, 144; legislative issues, 127, 133, 141; level of support, 115, 120; mothers' pension, 74; old age pensions, 105, 113, 120, 129–130, 135; soup kitchens, 114
welfare organizations: Associated Charities, 72, 80; Child and Family Services, 72; Conference of Social Workers, 91, 129; early Child Welfare Board, 106, 120, 121, 128, 130, 145; good film movement, 54; National Conference of Social Work, 129; Red Cross, 56, 153; Salvation Army, 16, 76, 77, 94, 97, 98; Social Services Association, 73; Susanna Wesley Home, 72, 77, 79, 98; Tuberculosis Association, 72; White House Conference on Child Health and Protection, 98
Wellesley: and Elsie's college education, 25, 29; Elsie's life after Wellesley, 33, 36–37, 41, 44, 47, 49; at turn of century, 27–28, 43
white collar jobs, 64
Wichman, Fred, 100–101, 105
Widemann, Hermann, 13
Wilcox, Abner: and ABCFM, 9, 130; childraising, 7–9, 12; financial problems, 10; and holidays, 22; as missionary, 5; as teacher, 3–4
Wilcox, Albert: early life, 5–7, 9, 13; manager of Lihue plantation, 14, 21; after marriage, 34, 39, 43, 45
Wilcox, Charles Hart, 5, 12, 14
Wilcox, Charles Henry: death, 57; early life, 18, 22–23, 33–35, 44; after marriage, 45, 47, 51, 55
Wilcox, Elsie: Americanization supporter, 81–91; appeal to women voters, 105, 131, 144–145; campaigns (1932), 100–105, (1936), 130–132, (1940), 143–153; charity, 77–81, 90, 96–98, 106; commissioner for education, 58–70; death, 156; early life, 17–25, 30–42; economic philosophy, 124, 160; and English standard schools, 68; in Europe, 47–49; and Hawaiians, 18, 37–39; and labor, 141, 148, 150; and marriage, 42–45, 95, 158; opposition to foreign language schools, 66; and Paul Osumi, 151, 153–154; at Punahou, 21–22; on race relations, 24–25, 39, 158; relations with Charles Rice, 100–103, 116–117, 125–126, 147, 150; response to 1920 Survey, 62; response to Prosser report, 69; social security, 129–130, 136; social worker, 70–77, 98–99; support by business, 146–147; support of education in the Senate, 112–113, 115, 133, 140, 144; support of missionaries, 45, 91–92, 96–99; and Takie Okamura, 89–91; on taxes, 109–111, 118, 145; values, 1, 11–12, 30, 60, 117, 119–120, 157–160; and vocational education, 64, 135–136,

145–146; at Wellesley, 25–29; women's issues, 133–134, 141, 144–145; during World War II, 153–155; YMCA, 82–89; YWCA, 83–88
Wilcox, Etta: children, 35, 44–45, 47; Commissioner of Public Instruction, 59, 106; death, 106; early years, 17–19, 21–23; historic preservation, 99; marriage, 31–33
Wilcox, Gaylord: as adult, 44–45, 47, 55, 57, 143; early life, 18, 22, 33, 35
Wilcox, G. N.: buys Grove Farm, 13, 14, 19; early years, 5, 11–12; as employer, 46; first car on Kaua'i, 46; influence on Elsie, 11, 14, 33; life at Grove Farm, 18, 32–35, 50–51, 57, 100; philanthropy, 13–16, 51, 54; in politics, 14–16, 130; and religion, 37; trip to Asia, 45
Wilcox, Henry Harrison, 5, 14
Wilcox, Henry Munson, 4
Wilcox, Lucy Hart, 1, 5
Wilcox, Mabel: Board of Child Welfare, 106; early years, 18–19, 22–23; at Grove Farm, 30–33, 35–37, 39, 42–45, 51; historic preservation, 99; at Johns Hopkins, 25; later years, 100, 103, 154, 156; philanthropy, 77–78; public health nurse, 53, 56, 72, 88; trips abroad, 30, 45, 91, 156; in World War I, 56
Wilcox, Ralph: career, 33, 35, 37, 39; death, 50, 51; early years, 17, 21–22; marriage, 31–32
Wilcox, William Luther, 5, 13, 34, 43
Wilcox Buildings: Mahelona, 117; Mid-Pacific, 16; Punahou, 130; Waioli, 16

Wilson, John, 109, 128
women's issues: jury service, 133–134; marriage 43–44; mother's pension, 74; retrenchment in depression, 113; vote, 144–145, 149; working wives, 113. *See also* YWCA
women's organizations: clubs, history of, 40–42; General Federation of Women's Clubs, 81; Sorosis, 40; and women's legislation, 134. *See also* Mokihana Club; YWCA
World War I, 27, 55–56, 73, 115
World War II: between wars, 55; and business, 108; effects on vocational education, 145; and Japanese, 66, 136, 153–154; and Kaua'i, 153–155; National War Fund Committee, 153; USO, 153; and voters, 122, 148, 152
Wright, Fred, 114

Yale, 12, 55
YMCA: and Adult Education Committee, 155; Americanization effort, 82–88, 90, 95, 152, 153; and Asia, 46, 86–87, 98; Elsie Wilcox on board of directors, 94; Hawai'i beginnings, 70; and Pan Pacific Conference, 92
Young Buddhist Association, 155
YWCA, 105, 158; Americanization effort, 82–90, 95, 152–153; benefits of women's program, 134; Elsie Wilcox on board of directors, 82–83, 94, 155; Fernhurst, 85; financial support, 82, 98; on Kaua'i, 73, 82, 85, 87–88

Zalberg, Sanford, 148

www.ingramcontent.com/pod-product-compliance
Lightning Source LLC
Chambersburg PA
CBHW031437160426
43195CB00010BB/760